AMELIA ABRAHAM

Amelia Abraham is a journalist and author from London. She has worked as an editor at *VICE*, *Refinery29* and *Dazed*, and writes for the *Guardian*, British *Vogue* and many other publications. Her first book, *Queer Intentions: A (Personal) Journey Through LGBTQ+ Culture*, is a roving, first-person exploration of the mainstreaming of queer culture across the West.

Follow Amelia on Twitter @MillyAbraham
And on Instagram @amelia_abraham

T0059851

WE CAN DO BETTER THAN THIS

35 Voices on the Future of LGBTQ+ Rights

Edited by Amelia Abraham

VINTAGE

3 5 7 9 10 8 6 4 2

Vintage is part of the Penguin Random House group of companies
whose addresses can be found at global.penguinrandomhouse.com

Penguin
Random House
UK

This paperback edition published in 2022 by Vintage
First published in Great Britain in 2021 by Vintage

penguin.co.uk/vintage

Penguin Random House does not have any control over, or any responsibility
for, any author or third-party websites referred to in or on this book.

A CIP catalogue record for this book is available from the British Library

ISBN 9781529113310

Printed and bound in Great Britain by Clays Ltd, Elcograf S.p.A.

The authorised representative in the EEA is Penguin Random House Ireland,
Morrison Chambers, 32 Nassau Street, Dublin D02 YH68

Penguin Random House is committed to a sustainable future for
our business, our readers and our planet. This book is made from
Forest Stewardship Council® certified paper.

MIX
Paper from
responsible sources
FSC
www.fsc.org FSC® C018179

This book contains accounts that may make for difficult reading. The issues covered include hate crimes, mental health, medical treatment, sex and relationships, and substance abuse. We have listed organisations on page 335 that provide support, advice and information. We hope this note helps you navigate the book.

Every effort has been made to ensure that the information contained in this book is correct, but it should not in any way be substituted for professional or medical advice.

A Note from the Editor

LGBTQ+ has been used throughout this book as a short-hand for lesbian, gay, bisexual, transgender, queer and other identity categories like intersex and asexual. When speaking about a specific subsection of the LGBTQ+ community, writers have referred to that group directly. 'Queer' is mostly used as an umbrella term for the various identities that fall under the LGBTQ+ banner, but of course, queer means different things to different people – I hope those meanings become clear in context.

On a couple of occasions within this book, names or other minor details have been changed or omitted to protect privacy. For writers from the US, we have retained American English.

Contents

DATING, LOVE AND FAMILY

HEALTH AND SOCIAL CARE

BEYOND THE BINARY

COMMUNITY AND ORGANISING

Introduction

While researching contributors for this book, I found myself watching a YouTube video of Pabllo Vittar, a gender-fluid drag green from a small town in northern Brazil, making her debut performance on a Brazilian TV talent show. Standing there on stage, with long brown hair and thick eyelashes, she sings her heart out to Whitney Houston's 'I Have Nothing' and hits every note perfectly, Whitney-esque but with a hint more camp. I was transfixed, and the audience is too. At the end of the performance, they rise to their feet and rapturously applaud her.

In the years since 2014, when the video came out, Pabllo has become one of the biggest pop stars in Brazil. Yet it's also the country with the highest homicide rate of LGBTQ+ people in the world, with hundreds of LGBTQ+ people murdered in hate crimes each year. You may or may not have heard of Pabllo, but her fame demonstrates the disconnect between the top-level visibility and acceptance of some aspects of queer culture – the queer musicians with millions of fans, or the trans models who feature on the cover of magazines, for example – and the way that so many people within the LGBTQ+ community are still treated at street level or behind closed doors.

When we look at queer 'progress' we see Pride celebrations, same-sex kisses in music videos and films, or LGBTQ+ people winning awards. We see queer happiness, queer love and queer success stories – and we should: those things are vital and intrinsic parts of our lives. But what we see and hear about *less* is what it's like to be queer in parts of the world without LGBTQ+ rights on paper and with lives under threat. Rarely, too, do we hear about the lasting effects of shame and stigma in places where LGBTQ+ people are supposedly 'accepted'. We might see news stories and Instagram posts, but we do not always hear queer experiences of discrimination first-hand, in a way that is non-essentialising and nuanced. It is rarer still to learn what we can do about all of this, how we actually make it better.

In a bid to counter that, this book brings together a range of different queer voices, from activists to actors, writers to performers, artists to academics, and asks them: If you could change something to make life better for LGBTQ+ people, what would it be? And what are some of your ideas for getting there?

By virtue of having a platform, many of the contributors have found a certain degree of privilege compared to other queer people, but it felt important to ask them to use those platforms to shed a light on what others are still going through. While they may be from disparate backgrounds and disciplines, everyone in this book has something in common: they really, truly care about the wellbeing of LGBTQ+ people, and have spoken loudly into the silences that keep us oppressed. So whether they are writers by career or not, they are experts on the topic of making life better for queer people.

Brazil is a long way from the UK – where I have been editing this collection – but the disconnect between top-level visibility and the actual safety of queer people applies here, too. We have had so many gains over the last fifty years it's difficult to list all of them. Yet, despite major rights like same-sex marriage, studies have shown that two out of three LGBTQ+ people do not feel safe holding hands with a partner in public, whether that's due to the sense of a real, immediate threat of violence, or the spectre of it in our minds.[1] Recent Home Office figures show that reported anti-LGBTQ+ hate crime 'has grown at double the rate of other forms of hate crime for the last two years' and that, between 2019 and 2020, anti-trans hate crime increased by 16%.[2] This climate has a dangerous impact on our mental health and wellbeing. Half of LGBTQ+ people in Britain report having experienced depression in the last year, while bisexual people report particularly high rates of depression and anxiety, and are significantly less likely to come out to their friends and family than gays and lesbians.[3] Terrifyingly, one in four young trans people in the UK have attempted suicide and nine in ten have thought about it.[4] Meanwhile, there is still woefully little research on what life is like for other groups, such as intersex and asexual people.

Since I first put together this collection (it was edited in 2020 and I am now writing in 2022), the US has witnessed the worst year on record for anti-trans hate murders – more than 50 trans people were killed in 2021.[5] The end of Trump's presidency offered a moment of hope, as President Biden rescinded several of the anti-trans laws that were passed between 2016 and 2020. Yet, on a state-level, a barrage of anti-trans laws were put forward in 2021 and so far in 2022, blocking young trans people's access to gender-affirming healthcare and attempting to ban trans people from sport. You can read about both of these topics in more detail later on, as well as other stories that bring some of the harrowing figures above to life. These stories demonstrate the violent state of play for people identifying across the LGBTQ+ spectrum and also in countries beyond the West. This can make for tough reading – but it is, I believe, necessary to talk about the challenges we face in order to address them. Once we get a better understanding of what's going on in the world, we can figure out how to make a difference.

So, discussing some of the issues above, the first section of this book looks at issues around material Safety – both in the UK, and then in Brazil, Bangladesh and Nigeria. The next moves on to Visibility and highlights the queer representation we still do not see. In part three, Dating, Love and Family, we look at ways of overcoming discrimination in dating, as well as what must happen before we achieve *real* marriage and parenting equality.

In the Health and Social Care chapter we examine the most urgent frontiers when it comes to queer people's wellbeing, from education to healthcare – all tackled through a deeply personal lens. In Beyond the Binary we step back and take a more abstract approach to dismantling tired ideas around gender and how we can instead expand freedom of expression. Near the end of the book, as we turn to Community and Organising, we are offered powerful cases for learning about queer history, practical tips for allyship and, finally, visions for the kind of activism that can generate true progress.

In assembling a wide range of queer stories side by side, this book demonstrates the interconnectedness of our experiences across lines of gender and sexuality. It also shows the links between everyday, interpersonal gestures and change on a much broader scale, arguing that improvements start at home and that no effort to make life better for LGBTQ+ people should be viewed as too big or too small. In this sense, all of the essays are solution-led – telling us not just where we can do better, but crucially, *how*. In some cases that's volunteering or campaigning, in other cases it's a shift in attitude or the opening up of a conversation.

Of course, we as queer people have been doing this work for a long time. Yet, we can always go further. The collection is, in part, about inspiring LGBTQ+ communities to demand more – especially for those who are more marginalised or invisible. But it is also about asking for help. In spite of a rich history of fighting for – and winning – our own rights, we cannot make the changes we need to see in the world alone. The 'we' in *We Can Do Better Than This* is therefore everyone who might be reading this book. As an ally, it can be difficult to know where to start, where to direct your attention or your resources. I hope this book provides a roadmap for anyone who wants to make things better for LGBTQ+ people.

Finally, a word on process. At the time of writing, homosexuality is still illegal in sixty-nine countries and punishable by death in six, while being trans is still criminalised in thirteen UN member states. We wanted to shed a light on what is going on in various parts of the world, from Uganda to Russia to South Korea, even if we could not cover everywhere. Similarly, the essays here do not address all of the issues facing queer people today. This is just a snapshot.

I chose the contributors because I've met them along the way and they changed my thinking, or because I knew that they would bring to their essays a sense of the joy and pain that underscores so much of the queer experience. Here I think of madison moore (whose essay appears in this collection) and his book *Fabulous*, which talks about how queer people – and particularly gender-nonconforming queer people and queer people of colour – harness style, creativity and ingenuity to flourish in a world that is often hostile. 'Fabulousness almost always stems from a turning point: the moment we realize that suppressing our full selves by trying to fit in does us more harm than good, that it just isn't working, even if sometimes we are forced to blend in to feel safe,' he writes. Everyone in this book is Fabulous.

Taking stock of the strides we've made towards equality is important, and it's vital to remain positive and hopeful and proud. But at the same time, we cannot turn away from the fact that so many places around the world lack basic rights and safety for LGBTQ+ people. Or from how progress does not always move in a straight line – as evidenced by the rollback of LGBTQ+ laws we see currently being implemented by governments all over the globe, and the devastating effects of the Covid-19 pandemic on exacerbating LGBTQ+ homelessness. I hope *We Can Do Better Than This* treads the line between honesty, optimism and humour, and the anger we are entitled to feel. It is a guide to some of the most concerning problems facing queer people, and yet it looks to a brighter future – to practical solutions for change. I hope that it shows where our movement is really at and helps to shape the next ten years of activism, or even the next twenty. But for now, if stepping into someone else's world for a few minutes increases our empathy, we are already on the path to doing better. So thank you to the people in this book for sharing their experiences and calling us to action. And thanks to you for reading it.

---

1 Olivia Petter, 'Two-thirds of LGBT+ people fear holding hands in public, survey finds', *Independent*, 3 July 2018, https://www.inde pendent.co.uk/life-style/lgbt-holding-hands-public-fear-uk-govern ment-survey-penny-mordaunt-a8428381.html

2 https://galop.org.uk/resource/hate-crime-report-2021/; https://www.gov.uk/government/statistics/hate-crime-england-and-wales-2019-to-2020/hate-crime-england-and-wales-2019-to-2020

3 https://www.stonewall.org.uk/lgbt-britain-health; 'Mental health: Stonewall health briefing (2012)', Stonewall, January 2015, https://www.stonewall.org.uk/resources/mental-health-stonewall-health-briefing-2012

4 https://www.stonewall.org.uk/sites/default/files/trans_stats.pdf

5 Madeleine Carlisle, 'Anti-trans violence and rhetoric reached record highs across America in 2021', *Time*, 30 December 2021, https://time.com/6131444/2021-anti-trans-violence/

SAFETY

'The starting point to change is acknowledging there's a lot more to do.'

Tom Rasmussen is an author, journalist and drag performer. Their first book, *Diary of a Drag Queen*, traces a year in the life of them and their drag persona, Crystal. Their second book, *First Comes Love*, offers a queer take on the institution of weddings and marriage.

Crystal's Make-Up

TOM RASMUSSEN

Crystal hasn't felt the sun on her face for five years. So when the sun was shining last week I decided to take her outside – with a friend in tow, for protection of course – to bask in the mid-April rays. Just how she likes it: not too hot, not too cold.

Some context: Crystal is my drag alter ego. She exists entirely behind closed doors. Sure, these doors might lead to basement clubs, sweaty nightlife venues or Edinburgh Fringe theatres, if not my wig-bestrewn bedroom, but since I was attacked in drag five years ago on the street outside my house, Crystal has existed only in places where she's safe. Even the more femme parts of my everyday self, the ones I used to so eagerly celebrate by wearing a cheap sateen ballgown on the tube or a waist-length wig to get coffee, were carefully tucked away for safekeeping. Seen only by those who understand why they must exist. Hidden, as much as possible, from everyone else, because harassment makes you disappear.

But not today, Satan. Out of the house we stepped, onto a busy London road, my lime-green sequinned one-shoulder gown (looks way nicer than it sounds) casting tiny glimmers of light across the tarmac. My friend surveyed the pavement – peering left and right – for loud men and their louder fragility, until the coast was clear. We strode out, and onto a quiet slip road. I rolled a cigarette, leaned against a brick wall, and felt the sun on my made-up face for the first time in half a decade.

It was a very specific feeling: heat and wax-based make-up all melting into one, like my gender does when I get into drag. And then, after three tokes on this nicotine-y goodness, from nowhere a van pulled up. The passengers looked me up and down – that's okay, she's quite the sight, even though my heart started to pump through my lime-green creation.

'Are they looking at us?' I asked my butch, protective friend, while also trying to appear as though I hadn't noticed them. Before my friend could answer, the back door of the van slid open to reveal four men packed tightly in, all of them screaming homophobic, transphobic slurs at me. I would write them here, but they were both offensive and offensively unimaginative, so there's no need to recreate them on the page.

Now, the old me would have done what I had tried to do in my early twenties and retaliated. Told them to fuck off, or found a way to make myself feel superior by putting down their intelligence or their appearance. But I realised, after a few years of utilising the art of reading so deftly, letting my library of insults wash over my attackers never made it better. I just felt guilt instead of relief.

And so I ignored them. I turned around, ran back across the road, and into an alleyway where no cars can go. My friend followed quickly, and asked if I was okay. To which I replied: 'Fine, honestly, happens every single time.'

Then I remembered: this, or some form of this, actually does happen every single time I'm in drag. Every single time. Without fail. Even the times I'm behind closed doors of my own making there'll be something: a shout from a passing car as you enter the club, a look of sheer disgust when you pop out for a smoke, a fist to the glittering face as I walked from a cab to my front door, followed by that night spent in hospital, in 2016.

It really takes the fun out of drag. And what's perhaps more heartbreaking than these encounters – which my friends and I go through weekly, daily, hourly, when our extravagant sides are out for the world to see – is that this behaviour is normalised. If you're queer, you'll likely know what I'm talking about; you will – at some point in your life – have either experienced physical aggression, been threatened, or at the very least been called something you wouldn't even say as a joke. It's so normal we hardly feel it anymore. And yet we're constantly faced with a choice: the choice of whether to go out into the world as ourselves and stay special, or stay safe.

For me, this choice was first confronted years ago. It's fair to say that in Lancaster, the suburban city in north-west England where I grew up in the nineties and noughties, there weren't many people who would accompany me across the street to ensure my safety the way my friend did. There was nobody online, nobody at home, and nobody on television either (unless you count the gays full of shame on *EastEnders*, or the two boys kissing in Christina Aguilera's 'Beautiful' video). There was just me. My most formative memories flit between twirling in a beautiful black chiffon dress in my bedroom, while refuting the fact I was gay in the schoolyard. My nights were spent weeping with a faux emotional depth a twelve-year-old couldn't possibly have to Celine Dion's masterwork *Let's Talk About Love*, and my days were spent pretending I was into women, even though my GHD-straightened hair and my deep hatred of PE screamed otherwise. This would be my existence for the first two years of high school – not the hair, thankfully I stopped that in Year 10 – but living between two worlds, two versions of myself, until I told the wrong friend and I was outed.

I went to a rough school. That's street speak for a northern state comprehensive where you were exalted if you left with two Cs at GCSE. I sound classist, but I'm not: that was my school, no frills, lots of hilarious moments, and a daily serving of homophobic violence in the form of a rock pelted at my back or a ball of phlegm hocked up and spat in my face. Faggot. Poof. Bumboy. Fudge-packer. Backs to the wall, lads. All turns of phrase I grew up laughing off, because I was too weak to ever really defend myself, and because the education system was too underfunded and overcrowded to offer help. It was all supposedly in the name of banter, anyway: everyone bullied everyone – it was the survival technique we used in order to get through high school.

Naturally, after this homophobic hellscape ended, I felt like my only option was to move somewhere that I would be understood. It didn't matter that I was leaving my family behind for the bright lights of the capital because there the Celine Dion fan (synonym for homo-sexual) inside me wouldn't just be accepted, they would be celebrated.

And in truth, when I arrived in London I felt like I'd come home, despite that sounding like the opening to a terribly clichéd mid-noughties romcom about a runaway girl who hates the town she grew up in. Here, in the big city, I made queer friends who would walk me across the street; I joined whole groups of queers who gather weekly in search of queer euphoria – usually on the dancefloor – and who find it. I found real, tangible joy in queer love – both platonic, romantic and somewhere messily in between. I do drag shows where people applaud me for talking about all the things that got rocks thrown at me at high school, I tell anal jokes and far too frequently at dinner parties recount the time I wanked off a turkey (I was training to be a vet, which went tits up). I adore my community, and my family too, after a decade of complications. I'm nonbinary, a drag queen, fat, northern – and I, like many of my peers here in the cultural centre that is London, have in so many ways been given a space to be myself; to make choices my parents, or other queers in the regions or in other parts of the world, aren't afforded; to explore and celebrate my divergent identity more freely than perhaps anyone like us ever has before.

I'm aware of my privilege – that, had even one thing been different for me (say, I'd stayed in Lancaster), my life would have been much, much harder. Let alone had I been born in one of the many countries where it's illegal – punishable by prison or death – to be gay. In one of the countries where you get hunted on Grindr, or where your rights are revoked if you're trans, or never afforded to you in the first place. I can't begin to understand the complexity of identity in a context where it isn't even allowed to exist. Yet while I live in a city that is – like New York, or Stockholm, or Berlin – supposed to be one of the most accepting for LGBTQ+ people in the world, still so much of my time, and of my friends' time, is spent being forced to compute something as basic as safety.

It is not my choice to do this: please don't think I love spending hours contemplating my gender, my sexuality and how it puts me at risk in the world – it's dull, I've done it for three decades, I've read the books on L, G, B, T, Q, I and A. I've answered the questions hurled at me in the street, online, in society. But possibly 50% of my waking time is spent thinking about how to make myself, my friends and our community safer.

Sure, this focus on safety – and the action it brings about – has led to so much progress for the LGBTQ+ community both past and present. Same-sex marriage, the revocation of Section 28 (which previously banned local authorities from promoting homosexuality in England, Scotland and Wales), queer uprisings like Stonewall, legalisations and decriminalisations all around the world. In places like the UK we have the big stuff, the 'social and legal equality' cis heterosexuals have always had, and we have a great deal of visibility: online, in the media, on panels and in the Pride campaigns of countless brands who just love us for the month of June. We now live in a country where I have access to things so few before me did: sure I can have a fab gay wedding, with a fab gay cake. I can cuddle up on the couch with my pink pound (I wish!) and watch RuPaul spill the tea, the *Queer Eye* queers help you live your most gorj life, and Timothée Chalamet fuck a peach in a movie about coming of age as a gay person. But a hypercapitalist drag contest, getting a do-over on your bungalow, or a peach-job isn't enough to help the most vulnerable in our community. We need more. Because while progress has been made, we still get attacked, we still have a disproportionate amount of homelessness, mental health issues, suicide and abuse within and towards our community. We are still spoken about in Parliament, on the street, in the classroom as if we are a problem and not the gift we are. Try to register your gender-neutral pronouns on a passport, or access healthcare as a poor trans person and you'll be clogged in a system that doesn't want you, for an agonisingly long time.

On a personal level, yes: I am glad I can get married, but it doesn't mean all that much if I can't even walk down the street holding my partner's hand (which we've never done in our five years together). I am glad I can be in drag on the cover of a magazine, but what's the point of that if I can't even stand on the street looking the way I feel?

The starting point to change is acknowledging there's a lot more to do. Rights on paper and increased visibility might make it look like we have all we need, but appearances can be deceiving. So often I speak to people online and after my shows who love drag, love Pride, love everything about us, but have no idea what must be done on the ground to ensure our safety. We need people to recognise that they haven't done their part and to properly engage with how they might bring about change – whether that's for the LGBTQ+ community more broadly, or if you're within that community, a letter in the acronym that you haven't been paying attention to.

What I'm talking about is active, proud, vocal, brilliant allyship whereby people stand up in public, private, online and in real life, and align themselves with our global fight for freedom. On a local scale – to call out the group of men on the train who threatened to piss on me on Christmas Eve Eve 2019, for example – but also on a broader scale. Support queer and trans housing and healthcare services by writing to MPs and opening your purses. Think about how your company is structured to ensure that queer people feel safe and respected, and have access to opportunity. Think about what considering both sides of the trans 'debate' (a 'debate' which is explained later on in Juliet Jacques's essay) really means for trans people (hint: our existence shouldn't be up for 'debate' at all). Give away money, time and thought to causes and situations which you might never find yourself in. And as a community, we must consider people who suffer at the hands of imported colonial homophobic laws around the world, and then follow them, listen to them, fight for them. We must lobby governments for these laws to be removed.

We need sanctions, and we need celebrations: of us, of our culture. We need to be heard and supported, and we need to be given a moment off from protecting ourselves so we can help protect others who need it even more.

I am so pleased that much of LGBTQ+ culture and history has been, and is, about fighting. Being different has made us a community; being oppressed, in some twisted way, has made us stronger, brighter, more powerful. Yet sometimes I want to spend more time fighting for those who have it far worse than I do. Sometimes I want to know what safety actually feels like when I step outside my door, and not just imagine it. Sometimes I really want to feel the sun on Crystal's face. Not every day, not always, but sometimes.

'If I have one wish for the LGBTQ+ community in Bangladesh, and globally, it is the decriminalisation of homosexuality.'

Mazharul Islam (Maz), is an LGBTQ+ activist from Bangladesh who fled his country on 29 April 2016, four days after the murder of his two friends, the activists Xulhaz Mannan and Mahbub Rabbi Tonoy. In Bangladesh, Maz was one of the longest-standing members of the LGBTQ+ group Boys of Bangladesh. Each year Maz protests in front of the Bangladesh High Commission in London asking for the decriminalisation of homosexuality in his home country.

Leaving Bangladesh

MAZHARUL ISLAM

The first time I saw an ocean it was with Xulhaz. I remember that we took a trip together to the Sundarbans Reserve Forest, to see the world's largest mangrove forest. I used to live near his office and often, at lunchtimes, we would hang out and have delicious tehari and khichuri from the famous restaurant Shad Tehari Ghar. Xulhaz was like my family. He was a special soul. If I or anyone else ever needed anything, he would be there for us. I remember, on my birthday, he bought me flowers. Somehow, Xulhaz knew that I love chrysanthemums. I made a painting of those flowers and I gifted it to him on his birthday. He hung that painting on the wall in his apartment. I don't know what happened to it after he was killed.

Boys of Bangladesh started as a closed Yahoo group with the name Boys Only Bangladesh. I joined in 2003, but it had been going since November 2002. You had to know someone who would invite you in, someone who could vouch that you were gay. I met the person who added me in another chat room, and we began talking in private messages, introducing ourselves to one another as gay men. We swapped 'ASL' – age, sex, location. Asked the usual questions: Where do you live? What are you looking for? Are you a top or a bottom?

At that time in Bangladesh, internet access wasn't very good, so we used to go to cyber cafes. I'd hire a computer for 30p per hour, trying to find other gays for a date or for sex. It was scary to talk openly with another gay man, even online, but we took the relevant precautions by hiding details about ourselves.

Early on, Boys of Bangladesh was a place to express our feelings, look out for each other, become a small community. We were twelve or fifteen members when we started, and it wasn't created for the sake of activism, it was just a place to talk. We were united by the feeling that our country people, our families and our colleagues were against us, because – even today – homosexuality is criminalised in Bangladesh. The law that bans it, Section 377, was first implemented by the British Government in 1860 during Britain's colonial rule of the Indian subcontinent, and it has survived ever since. It calls homosexual acts 'unnatural offences' punishable with up to life imprisonment. For this reason, most of us in Boys of Bangladesh had never spoken about our sexualities to other people.

Meeting up with the other members of the group in person for the first time was surreal and it's still clear in my mind. Ten to twelve of us gathered in a park, chosen because it was a public place, busy, open – maybe we could blend in. We pretended to be a group of straight guys hanging out among all the other straight guys there that day. But all of us were nervous, and we used fake names and carried fake IDs, just in case the police came or anyone questioned us. It would have been nice to meet in private I suppose, but we were young students – no one had a house big enough.

Until that afternoon, I had no idea that there were so many other gay men in Bangladesh. I was brought up in a tiny village, within Dhaka's city limits but very rural.

There was no internet access and no electricity. The houses were made of clay and our old duplex was surrounded by fruit trees, paddy fields, guava, pineapple, banana and bamboo gardens, plus cattle and goats. We were farmers by income, and our neighbours bought produce from us. During the rainy season, the entire village would be surrounded by water and the only transport that we had was boats. Communication and roads have since been improved, but back then we would walk to school every day for miles and sometimes, during the floods, our school closed for weeks.

My brother is four years older than me and as a kid, I didn't like to play the typical 'male' games that he did, like football or cricket. I was much more comfortable spending time with girls, and I used to play with my aunt and grandmother's high heels (a cliché, I know). Maybe my family knew about my sexuality, but we never talked about those things. Whether or not anyone else knew, there came a time when I could not deny it myself; from the age of ten, it was clear to me that I was attracted to boys. I started to suffer a lot mentally because I couldn't tell anyone. Society – from my community to the mosque – taught me that homosexuality is a sin, so I was terrified of the people around me – my family members, my neighbours – finding out. When I look back at that time, I think about how much I used to hate myself. I felt so guilty that I would cry in the mosque and beg Allah: 'Please, remove this feeling for me. Please, do something, anything.' But nothing changed.

I knew that homosexuality was against Islam, but I didn't know that it was against the law in Bangladesh until I was eighteen, when I passed my exams, went to college and started using the internet for the first time. Before that, I just thought I was 'different' – in Bangladesh we

have a word for this, *shomokami*. When I discovered the
word 'gay' online I came to understand from reading the
news that it didn't just make you a sinner but a criminal,
too. After I joined Boys of Bangladesh, my understanding
expanded even further: I learned that, in the world outside
of Bangladesh, people like me could live openly, have
relationships, and be happy. It was only through Boys of
Bangladesh that I learned that LGBTQ+ could be a
movement.

After the first meet-up, Boys of Bangladesh started to grow.
I became a moderator for the group and would help to
organise the monthly get-togethers – we would tell people
where to go only a few hours beforehand, and change the
location each time for safety: restaurants, cafes, different
parts of the park. Soon, they were happening more than
once a month. More members joined, and at some point, in
2005 or 2006, we opened up membership so that no referrals or interviews were required. We were becoming a bigger
community and starting to feel strong – like we had enough
members to protect ourselves. We were in our twenties and
were excited by feeling like we were part of something.

We started to organise 'HOP social' ('hanging out
place') at a special spot where we would go on Friday
evenings, Xulhaz and I included. We'd share love stories
and sex stories, make fun of one another or bitch about
the other members. We would plan the next activities too,
like parties, movie screenings and picnics. But affection
had to be minimal – it was a public place. If you liked
someone, you'd exchange numbers, and pick up the conversation later.

The more people that joined Boys of Bangladesh, the
more we moved towards becoming an activist organisation.
In May 2005, we decided to send a letter to the editor of

the *Daily Star* newspaper asking them to publish an article about us and they did; it was about celebrating International Day Against Homophobia, Transphobia and Biphobia. Over the next few years, we organised private film screenings and talks. We made connections with international LGBTQ+ organisations and became part of ILGA Asia – a pan-Asian LGBTQ+ rights network – with our members attending their international conferences. In 2011, Xulhaz started planning *Roopbaan*, Bangladesh's first LGBTQ+ magazine. He launched it in 2014 with a party, which journalists and government employees attended. He told me that he did it because someone had to come forward, be the face of the LGBTQ+ community in Bangladesh and tell people what was happening within it.

I was happy that Boys of Bangladesh and Xulhaz were creating visibility and speaking up more and more for LGBTQ+ rights. It really did feel like we could keep growing as an organisation for ever. But now I would say it was not a good decision for us to go so public, given what happened later. We needed more time. Society was not ready to accept us.

In October 2015, I started to receive threatening messages. I had, by this point, left Boys of Bangladesh as I was focusing on my career and studying again. Still, I had remained close to the organisation and a lot of the people I met there.

The texts came from an anonymous group. They tried to blackmail me, stating that if I didn't give them money, they would come to my office and tell my colleagues that I was gay, as well as handing my information to Islamic terrorists. I don't know how, but the blackmailers seemed to know a lot about me; they knew where my office was, where my house was. They used to follow me and send texts that they could see me arriving at work. I started to panic but I couldn't talk to my family or relatives without coming out to them. I felt trapped and increasingly paranoid.

Luckily, because my company was international, I was able to tell my bosses about what was going on and they told me to make a complaint at the police station. I was apprehensive. I knew I couldn't tell the police *why* I was getting the texts – if they had reason to believe I was homosexual then suddenly I would become the suspect. Yet I had to do something. My employers asked a colleague to come with me to the station, and there I gave the police the number that was messaging me. I told them that someone was asking for money and saying that if I didn't give it to them they might kill me, but I didn't show them the texts where they mentioned that I was gay. I submitted the report and went home. The police said they'd look into it, but they never got back to me. In the meantime, my company sent a car to bring me to and from work every day.

Over the next six months, the threats continued. Eventually, I told my brother, who by then knew about my sexuality. 'I don't know what to do,' I said over the phone. 'I constantly feel like I might die tomorrow.' He lived in London and didn't know how to help. I was exhausted, and running out of places to turn; as homosexuality was an offence, the law effectively made it illegal for me to report a crime that was being committed against me. I was constantly jumpy, and I cried all the time.

On 25 April 2016, I left my office at 5 p.m. and went to the grocery store on my way home. I got a call from a friend.

'Where are you?' he said. 'Immediately go home and lock yourself in.'

He told me that a group of Islamic extremists had attacked Xulhaz. 'We don't know what is happening,' he said.

I hurried back and my flatmate was watching the TV. On it, news broadcasters were reporting the murders: there had been two, Xulhaz, and another friend of mine from Boys of Bangladesh called Mahbub Rabbi Tonoy. They had been killed in the same apartment in a machete attack, said the presenter; one other guy who was there had survived by hiding from the attackers. We were silent, staring at the TV, then we looked at one another and cried for a while, until it occurred to us that we could be in immediate danger. The people who had committed the murders could have been on their way to us. The police could, too, given that we'd recently had brushes with the law due to our links to the LGBTQ+ community.

That night, we left for another friend's house. I packed just a few things. When we got there, it was a sleepless night. In the morning I went to work and all of the newspaper headlines read that two LGBTQ+ people had been killed. Everyone at the office was talking about it, they did not realise that it was people I knew well. My boss told me that I didn't need to come to work again until it was safe to do so. I went back to the same friend's house until the morning of 27 April – two days after the murder – when the US Embassy sent a bulletproof car to bring me to them. There I had a phone call with someone higher up at my company who explained that they could relocate me, so I asked to go to London to be near my brother. Soon I had a plane ticket and a visa for Sri Lanka – it was the best they could do in the shortest amount of time and they would work on London later.

On 29 April, I was taken to the airport along with two others from the LGBTQ+ community. The night before, I had called my parents and asked them to come to a hotel near the airport. They were surprised and confused. I told them I had to go away for a long time for work and that it was urgent. I'm still not sure if they know the truth. We said goodbye, then I went to catch my plane.

I was lucky to get out, but I was leaving my family, my friends, my apartment, my country, everything.

For the first two months in Sri Lanka, I stayed in a hotel and only left to go to work. I closed all of my social media. I had no contact with friends, no idea what was going on back home. Then my office got me a work permit to go to London. When I arrived, the only person I knew there was my brother. I felt isolated and devastated; the working environment was new, the culture was new and the weather was horrible – I had to learn everything from scratch, even how to read traffic lights. I felt lost, but at least I was safe.

A year passed, and as justice had still not been served for Xulhaz and Tonoy, a friend and I decided to stage a protest in Trafalgar Square on the anniversary of their deaths. There were just the two of us – we wrote their names on paper, big and bold, and held it up, as well as printing their story on a one-pager to hand out, and explaining what had happened to passers-by. A year later, in 2017, I met an activist called Dan Glass who introduced me to the Peter Tatchell Foundation, and they helped me to stage the protest again, bigger, and in front of the Bangladesh High Commission. We did it again in 2019, and in 2020 and 2021 we held it virtually and circulated a letter to the Bangladesh government calling for decriminalisation. Now, alongside my job, I am a patron for human rights organisation ReportOUT, an active member of ACT UP London, and a volunteer for Gay Liberation Front UK. I also work with a grassroots LGBTQ+ organisation back in Bangladesh, helping them to set objectives and develop initiatives such as a website and a phone helpline for LGBTQ+ people in need.

In 2019, the Bangladeshi police arrested the suspected terrorists who are believed to have carried out the attack on Xulhaz and Tonoy. It's a consolation and might send out a message to other people in Bangladesh who are thinking of targeting the LGBTQ+ community. But in reality, nothing in the five years since 2016 has improved in terms of LGBTQ+ rights in my country. If anything, things have moved backwards; in May 2017, for example, the year after Xulhaz and Tonoy were murdered, twenty-seven men at a private party were arrested by the police for suspected homosexuality.

If I have one wish for the LGBTQ+ community in Bangladesh, and globally, it is the decriminalisation of homosexuality. Knowing that I am not accepted by my country by law – I simply can't explain how that feels. You try to get used to it, you try to lead your life and forget about it, but at the end of the day, it is in your subconscious all the time. Until the day I left Bangladesh, I pretended; I was never myself, and never expressed my real feelings – except for those rare and short-lived moments with my friends.

Xulhaz and Tonoy's murders snatched everything from us because they created a climate of fear, and when everyone is afraid, who is able to fight for change? This is why we need the support of other countries. We need international networks, and we need to know who to ask for help. With stronger links between the Bangladeshi LGBTQ+ commun-ity and the community across the world, if something were to happen again, we could all collectively raise our voices. By campaigning and petitioning to decriminalise homosexuality everywhere, we could reach a place where violence towards LGBTQ+ people would no longer seem to be legitimised. People like me, who love their families, their jobs and their countries, wouldn't need to flee and abandon everything. Millions of young people are suffering in countries where their existence is illegal, just as I did, and it's clear how we can take that suffering away.

Every time I talk about what happened it makes me lighter and stronger. If I hide the things I went through I'm not going to overcome them – they are painful memories, but they shaped who I am today. After Xulhaz's murder, there weren't many people who could publicly ask for justice for him. That's why I ask for justice. I want to make him proud. I'm trying.

'To reduce the numbers of murders in Brazil we need a new government and a new leader who does not spread messages of hate.'

Pabllo Vittar is a Brazilian drag queen, singer and songwriter. In terms of YouTube views and social media following, Pabllo is the most popular drag queen in the world. At the 19th Annual Latin Grammys, she became the first drag queen ever to win a Grammy.

'Acceptance' in Brazil

PABLLO VITTAR

It was 1 November – my eighteenth birthday – when I went out in drag for the first time. I was going to a Halloween party, so I took the opportunity to get dressed up. I dressed as a mummy wearing only bandages and make-up. I went with four of my friends who were also doing drag for the first time. That was the moment I realised what was missing for me, as an artist and a person. The moment when I decided that I wanted to feel free and confident in my own skin every day, not only on Halloween.

I am lucky in that I never really needed to 'come out' at home. My mother always accepted me and let me be whoever I wanted to be. When I was fifteen years old I tried to tell her I was gay and she replied: 'I know!' I had always been very femme, but around the time of that conversation, I started using make-up, wearing more genderfluid clothing, and going to school with long hair. In my family, I could do everything I wanted, but at school things were different; I would get beaten up and people would call me names. Once, a boy threw hot soup on me. My teachers didn't care or help, to them I was just some little faggot.

These were the kinds of things that happened to gay people in small towns in Brazil ten years ago – particularly in the north-east of Brazil, like Maranhão where I am from. I don't remember seeing many celebrities saying 'I'm

LGBTQ+' or 'I'm queer' at that time, and if there was anyone gay on soap operas or TV shows they were always stereotyped, and portrayed in a caricatured way to be laughed at like clowns. If society mocked, insulted or harmed us LGBTQ+ people, they were just copying what they saw on TV.

Ten years later, things are not much better in Brazil – either in small towns or big ones. In some ways, they are worse. Members of the LGBTQ+ community here are attacked every day, particularly if they are Black or on low incomes. Unfortunately, this makes them the perfect targets for the horrific homophobia and racism that our president – Jair Bolsonaro – publicly supports. When he says things like he'd rather his son died in an accident than be gay, calls us 'fags' or condemns 'gender ideology', he is encouraging more hatred.

Often, I receive messages with testimonies from LGBTQ+ people and especially trans girls, detailing the hate crimes that they experience. In Brazil, we have the highest number of murders of LGBTQ+ people of any country in the world. In 2018, there were 420 murders, and in 2019, killings of 130 trans people.[1] But these are just the ones recorded, the ones we know about. It makes me feel sick. We say that here if you are LGBTQ+, you are not just living, you are surviving.

So when I first put a wig on and went out in drag in Brazil, it was a political act. Now, to be a gay person from Maranhão who goes on stage in drag and sings to huge audiences throughout a country where so many LGBTQ+ people are killed is also a political act. That I can be famous as a femme, genderfluid, gay drag queen in a country with so much homophobia, transphobia and all-round prejudice sometimes feels like a huge discrepancy. Often I wonder: How did this happen, when even my very existence as an LGBTQ+ person in Brazil can be seen as inappropriate?

Knowing all of this, I try to use my music to unify people and encourage respect. I try to make music for everyone, whatever their gender or sexuality. This means that some of the people who enjoy my music do not support LBGTQ+ rights, but I have received many messages saying that I have helped to change someone's mind. When parents tell me that my music helped them to accept their son who acts femme, for example, I reply: 'You only have one of your son/daughter, so be the best mom/dad you can be in this life.'

If I had one wish for Brazil, it would be that hate murders of LGBTQ+ people would stop and that we could see justice for everyone in our community who has been brutally killed. It has been several years since the politician and activist Marielle Franco was killed, after fighting for the LGBTQ+ cause and against racism, and to this day, no one knows what really happened; the authorities do not talk about it anymore, the justice system does not prioritise this case. In 2018, I also lost my friend Matheusa Passarelli, an LGBTQ+ activist who was assassinated just for being who they were. Some of the suspects have now been arrested, but this can't change what has already happened. We ask people to have hope, but what hope is there if we don't have justice or signs of top-down change?

To reduce the numbers of murders in Brazil we need a new government and a new leader who does not spread messages of hate. We are not born haters, but are taught to hate – we must break the cycle, or it will continue on and on for many more generations to come. A better government would also improve wealth distribution, which would benefit the Black and queer communities kept in poverty through discrimination, those who have fewer chances to reach their dreams. And on top of new public policies, we need even more LGBTQ+ people visible on TV, in music and in movies. Visibility is so important; I have seen first-hand, through those messages I receive, how it can change people's ways of thinking.

A good future for LGBTQ+ people here in Brazil will take a very long time. I can't be foolish and say that in ten or even fifty years everyone will be loving and accepting of one another, because that's not going to happen. But we can't quit the fight – it's about who we are. The fact that I can be a drag queen pop star in Brazil makes me feel like things are getting better, gradually. Fourteen- and fifteen-year-olds tell me that today they can go to school with make-up on; people say that because of my music they are able to accept themselves more, and many fans have told me that they now identify as genderfluid. This gives me hope, and makes me feel blessed that I can contribute to better acceptance by spreading the message that we should be able to be whatever or whoever we want. That we won't need to label ourselves to say we are A or B. We can be the whole alphabet.

---

1 'Brazil: 420 violent deaths against LGBTQ in 2018', Telesur, 15 February 2019, https://www.telesurenglish.net/news/Brazil-420-Violent-Deaths-Against-LGBTQ-in-2018-20190215-0008.html; Jamie Wareham, 'Murdered, hanged and lynched: 331 trans people killed this year', *Forbes*, 18 November 2019, https://www.forbes.com/sites/jamiewareham/2019/11/18/murdered-hanged-and-lynched-331-trans-people-killed-this-year/?sh=4654f99c2d48

'Is "Pride" walking down the street holding my partner's hand, even if I don't feel safe to do so?'

Shura (aka Alexandra Lilah Denton) is a half-Russian singer, songwriter and producer from the UK, who now lives in New York. Her 2016 debut album *Nothing's Real* marked her out as an ambassador for anyone who feels like an outsider, while her second album *forevher* tells the story of a long-distance lesbian love story between London and New York. Shura is an outspoken LGBTQ+ voice in pop music, and she also spends quite a lot of time gaming on Twitch.

Kissing in Public

SHURA

The first time that it happened I was sixteen. I had started to go to the gay village in Manchester, under age, with my twin brother, who is also gay. It was an amazing place to have access to as a gay teenager, because it wasn't just one bar or one club, it was an entire street that felt like our safe space and where we met kind, older gay people who took us under their wing. Strangely enough, though, my first memory of unwanted attention around a PDA (public display of affection) was in this safe space. I was holding hands with my girlfriend from school when a man drove past and shouted 'Lesbians!' at us. At the time, I laughed. Partly because my first instinct when something like that happens (something that isn't a physical attack) is to try to make a joke out of it. To try to make it less painful by laughing it off. But I also laughed because I thought it was hilarious that this man, who was in the gay village, had seen two lesbians, and had just decided to say what he saw. I remember turning to my girlfriend and saying: 'Well, I'm glad that he said that because I was really struggling with figuring out my sexuality until he just yelled the word "lesbian" at me!'

The second instance I remember was nastier. I was living in London and around twenty years old. My girlfriend and I had just been out somewhere, were a bit tipsy, and were waiting for the bus home. We kissed. It wasn't a big movie snog or anything (not that it should be necessary to qualify the kind of snog it was), just a small kiss. And I remember hearing a man's voice say: 'Kiss again.' I glanced over; he was an enormous guy. He looked at me and repeated: 'Kiss again.' I said no, turned away and tried to ignore him. But he grabbed my shoulder, pulled me back towards him and said it again, in my face. I didn't know what he was going to do next. At that moment, by some miracle, our bus arrived and my girlfriend and I both ran onto it. What stuck with me is how the whole incident was a horrible mixture of homophobia and fetishisation. The message I received was: 'I think gay people are disgusting' but also 'Women should kiss for my entertainment.'

The third instance was a few years later. I was on an escalator in a Shepherd's Bush shopping centre with my then girlfriend and we had a little kiss. Again, it's not like it was a big movie kiss (why do I feel like I keep having to say that? It shouldn't matter). A man coming down the escalator the other way suddenly commented: 'Don't kiss like that.' What he obviously meant was 'Don't kiss another girl romantically' but the way he phrased it was funny to me. I laughed and replied: 'Okay, how do you want us to kiss?'

Although it's these memories that stand out for me, they're not isolated incidents. Often when I'm with my current partner, people stare, or roll their car window down to get a better look. Their eyes hover over us just that little bit too long. Almost every time I hold hands with her in public, at some point on our journey, we get that look, the 'oh, they're *lesbians*' look. It has this funny effect on me. I know that being a lesbian is a big part of how I present to the world, especially through my music, but I don't constantly think about the fact that I'm gay. I suppose because so many people in my life are gay, sometimes I just forget. But when these things happen, it's like I'm suddenly reminded ... I am reminded that, to some people, something about me is 'different'.

In the summer of 2019 there was an attack on two women on a London bus: Chris, who identified as bisexual, and Melania, who identified as gay. They were on their way home from a date when a group of men accosted them, asked them to kiss, and when the women refused, they were beaten up. Photos of the couple covered in blood made global front-page news. People were shocked: that this could happen in Britain, that it was so violent, and that it could happen to two young, pretty, white, femme women – which might have been part of the reason that these pictures travelled so far in the media, even though similar attacks happen around the world every day, a point that Chris made in an article she wrote for the *Guardian* after the attack.[1]

When I saw the pictures, it was the first time that I'd seen an image of a homophobic hate crime that violent against a woman. It felt like I was looking at a photo of myself and my girlfriend, or what could have happened that night at the bus stop when I was twenty. I have a WhatsApp group with my gay female friends where we discussed the attack in the days that followed. No one in the group had experienced anything quite as severe as Chris and Melania, but every single woman had been in a situation that could have escalated to violence if they hadn't been able to escape. There was a scary moment of realisation that it could have happened to any of us. It makes you think: if this could happen in London, a supposedly progressive place, what the fuck is happening elsewhere? And to gay men, people of colour and trans and nonbinary people? And how often?

The images forced us to confront the reality that things haven't come as far as we think. While I might not have been totally surprised by the images, it was overwhelmingly sad to me that, nearly a decade after I was confronted at a bus stop, these sort of fetishising and terrifying attacks were still happening. We want to believe that, over the last ten years, progress has been made. In some ways it has; we have queer people on TV, gay and bi- and pansexual musicians releasing records, and people can be out in a way that they never could be before. But there can be something dangerous about perceived progress. It can create a sense of complacency. It's very easy for some people to look at the world and say: 'Things are so much better for LGBTQ+ people now.' But the fact is – and as those images proved – just because something is better in certain arenas, it can still be bad, worse even, in others. They were a wake-up call to the fact that, for every person who says 'I'm cool with gay marriage' there is still someone who isn't. A lot of people might support our rights in theory, but they still aren't comfortable seeing us holding hands, kissing or being affectionate in public.

Personally, the attack was also a reminder of why my subconscious – not even conscious – brain is trained to think about how I act in public. I know I'm not alone in doing so. It was a reminder of why we look up and down the tube, train or subway car before doing something as banal as putting our head on our partner's shoulder. Why I feel the need to explain in this article how each time I kissed my girlfriend in public it wasn't a big movie kiss. Why, before we go on holiday somewhere, we have to google 'Is it safe to hold hands in public' about wherever we are going. Why, before kissing somewhere outside of our homes, we have to ask ourselves basic questions like: Is anyone else here? Anyone that I don't know?

LGBTQ+ people make these calculations all the time. We are constantly doing the math. If there is one thing I would change for LGBTQ+ people, it's that we didn't have to think: Is there anyone here who might get stressed out by me just being me? Because that is what we are really talking about. We're not just saying, 'Is it safe to kiss?' or 'Is it safe to hold his or her or their hand?' What we are really wondering is: 'Is it safe to be me?'

Every LGBTQ+ person will face different obstacles related to their sexuality. A gay man's experience will be different to a gay woman's, to a bi person's, to a trans man or woman's, to a queer person of colour's. I feel this acutely having grown up alongside my twin brother who is gay; we had very different experiences as part of coming out and discovering our sexuality. These will depend on who you are and where you are.

While I can't speak for other people, what my experiences as a cis white queer woman have taught me is that gay and bisexual women are dealing with misogyny on top of homophobia. What we experience is not necessarily worse than what anyone else under 'LGBTQ+' experiences, but it is specific in that it is often sexist and objectifying. I don't think you'd ever hear of a homophobic woman coming up to two lesbians and saying, 'Kiss for me', which makes it clear to me that there is a certain dynamic between men and gay women that we need to challenge. It's to do with this ingrained idea that the only reason women exist on this planet is for their bodies to be at the service of men, and that lesbians are therefore threatening to men because we don't adhere to this or 'need them'. I don't believe that all lesbians feel that they don't need men; my life is full of men that I love.

I'm not sure how I can tell people not to fetishise lesbians when I sit around hoping that two women on

Westworld will snog – and yes, a big movie kiss – but I think that part of it starts with this, with not reducing women to their bodies. Sometimes I think about pornography (and if I ended the sentence here that would be quite the statement) but I don't believe that porn is the problem. Yes, to some degree porn furthers the idea of lesbianism as spectacle, as something that exists for another person's pleasure. But porn is just made to satisfy desires or fetishes that *already* exist; women showing attraction to one another has been viewed as fascinating, taboo or entertaining – something to roll your car window down and stare at – since long before Pornhub was around.

The problem of fetishisation persists because we still need more representation – more representation of lesbianism or same-sex affection between women that isn't sexualised or entirely for someone else's pleasure, and representation not just of lesbians who are young, femme and straight-passing, but lesbians who are older, butch, trans and gender-nonconforming. Representation of both overt queerness *and* incidental queerness; gay kisses in music videos, but also lead characters who just *happen* to be gay. Representation of the depth and nuance and frankly sometimes boringness or banality of lesbian same-sex love. Stories where the lesbians don't just have sex then die. Stories with happy endings (I'm looking at you *Blue Is the Warmest Colour*).

In other words, I don't think we have to abolish lesbian porn to send out a message that we are diverse, that we're not an attraction or a performance. Queer cinema, TV and music are important because they offer a safe space where we can improve the visibility of same-sex love when we might not feel comfortable doing so on the streets. Where we can expose people to our lives and experiences without putting ourselves at risk. But it also takes the onus off us as individuals.

Often, when I talk to my queer friends about PDAs, they tell me they not only have to calculate where is safe to be affectionate with their partners, but that part of doing the math is wondering to what extent it is their responsibility to shift the narrative. They ask themselves questions like: If I hide my PDAs, am I giving in to prejudice? Should I be exposing people to my way of loving? Is 'Pride' walking down the street holding my partner's hand, even if I don't feel safe to do so?

While these questions are valid, ultimately I don't think it should be the responsibility of gay people to fix straight people to not be homophobic, in the same way that it's not the responsibility of Black people to educate white people in how not to be racist. That doesn't mean we won't do it, because if you love someone and they express an opinion you think is wrong it can be worthwhile to tell them, or because sometimes it's important to stand up to discrimination. But it shouldn't be the responsibility of the LGBTQ+ community to improve acceptance, it should be everyone's responsibility.

Along with better media representation then, what we need is elected leaders to speak out and make it clear that hate crime and discrimination is unacceptable – and they need to do this all the time, not just as a reaction to a specific event. What we need is straight and cis people to stand up for LGBTQ+ folks if they see something bad happening and it is safe for them to do so. What we need is sex education in schools that is more than a biology lesson in reproduction. That covers consent, safe sex, good sex and how to have it if maybe you don't have a penis, don't want to use it or if there are two involved. That not all sex has to include genitals. That people have sex to have babies but, if we're being honest, most of us most of the time are having it because it's fun.

These things will help, but this isn't an issue that we can solve overnight, and the fear of kissing in public may never fully disappear – even in places where we are materially safe, the worry lingers in our minds. 'How do we solve the problem of homophobia?' might sound like a question, but that doesn't mean it necessarily has an answer – or an answer that works for everyone everywhere. There might always be people who believe, on an extreme level, that we LGBTQ+ people shouldn't exist. There might always be people who don't want to see us kiss in public. Just as people are divided politically, they're divided on LGBTQ+ rights.

So maybe the question isn't 'How do we solve the problem of homophobia?' but is, instead, two questions: 'What are those of us who are not homophobic doing to reduce it?' and 'How can we build a world where LGBTQ+ people can stop doing the math and don't have to ask themselves, "Is it safe to be me?"'

---

1   Christine Hannigan, 'You saw me covered in blood on a bus. But do you get outraged about all homophobia?', *Guardian*, 14 June 2019, https://www.theguardian.com/commentisfree/2019/jun/14/homophobic-attack-bus-outrage-media-white

'Queer people in parts of the world like mine should be entitled to basic experiences like safely chatting on apps and going on dates.'

Vincent Desmond is a writer and essayist living in Lagos, Nigeria. His writing has appeared in British *Vogue*, *Dazed*, *i-D*, *Vice*, *Nylon*, *Reuters*, *Elle*, *Paper* and more. In 2019, he was awarded the TIERs Young Activist Award for his work in media advocacy. In 2020, he was shortlisted for the Nigeria Prize for Difference and Diversity and nominated for the Future Award for Leading Conversation.

Kito Diaries

VINCENT DESMOND

In 2014, the then president of Nigeria, Goodluck Jonathan, attempted to win public approval ahead of the coming elections by appealing to the conservative majority of Nigeria. As a conspiracy theory that the US was attempting to pressure African countries into legalising same-sex marriage gained traction, Goodluck Jonathan passed a bill that not only criminalised same-sex unions and cohabiting, but also introduced a wider change. It decreed that: 'A person who registers, operates or participates in gay clubs, societies and organisation, or directly or indirectly makes public show of same sex amorous relationship in Nigeria commits an offence and is liable on conviction to a term of 10 years imprisonment.' The president was praised by many for 'preserving the African culture'.

This law, entitled the Same Sex Marriage (Prohibition) Act, 2013, led to several attacks against queer people by mobs who claimed they were working for Jonathan.[1] The constitutional rights of queer people living in Nigeria – the right to privacy and the right to form civil associations – were all considered to be null and void by the sweeping homophobic law. Queer people were apparently expected to stop existing, at least publicly. Bars and clubs that previously catered to mostly queer people became targets of almost daily harassments from law enforcement as well as homophobes, which forced these venues to shut down.

People suspected to be queer or engaging in sexual inter-course with others of the same gender were tracked down, beaten up, forced to perform sexual activities in public, ostracised and even killed.[2] In the months and years following this bill being passed into existence, the Nigerian LGBTQ+ community was further rejected from mainstream society and forced to redefine how it existed.

In Nigeria, as in many places around the world, the internet provides a platform and a voice for the country's most oppressed groups. It was largely thanks to the internet that #SexForGrades – a documentary and campaign against lecturers victimising their female students in universities – came to challenge and reshape the Nigerian educational system. Movements like #ArewaMeToo, a version of #MeToo focusing on the oppression and sexual abuse of Arewa women in northern Nigeria, as well as #EndSars, a youth-powered movement fighting police brutality within the country, also have the internet to thank for the traction they gained.

The internet is vital for enabling LGBTQ+ people in Nigeria to continue to interact as a community, too. With the passage of the new law in 2014, queer people were forced to get creative. We created AGAs (anonymous gay accounts) on social media, which served as burner accounts where we could share and reshare LGBTQ+-focused content, as well as interacting with other queer people without our identities being known. Code words like 'TB'/'tibi', which translates to being gay, were created as a way to communicate about queerness. Existing almost solely on the internet was hardly compensation for having no actual human rights and it did not make up for offline queer spaces, but it gave us something close to a safe space. That is until even this relative safety came under threat. As the LGBTQ+ community went digital, so did its oppressors.

In February 2020, news broke that a gay man living in the eastern part of Nigeria had been murdered by someone he had made plans to hook up with via Facebook. The murder and the details surrounding it devastated the Nigerian LGBTQ+ community who expressed themselves on social media with the hashtag #EndHomophobiaInNigeria, which trended for days. The outcry was loud, but the crime was not new: a lot of queer people in Nigeria have dealt with being catfished – drawn into a relationship online by someone with a false identity – by people who intend to blackmail or extort. Even if we have never been targeted, the way that we approach online dating is heavily marred by the possibility of being vulnerable to someone who plans to attack us or maybe even kill us.

I deleted Grindr from my phone in 2018 after I had arranged to meet someone from the app, and a friend told me it might not be safe. They explained that the side of town where this person had suggested to meet was the location of multiple attacks on queer people. I never confirmed if the person I was meant to see was actually a catfishing homophobe or a queer person who was unfortunate enough to share a zipcode with them.

The phenomenon is so prevalent that it has a name within the Nigerian LGBTQ+ community: kito. A kito is a person who masquerades as being queer on social media to create a false sense of security in queer people, predominantly men, and makes plans to meet. They will then either blackmail you to pay huge sums of money to avoid being outed or just out you to people you know, which may result in your being beaten up, or worse. These assaults are not as random as they appear at first glance. While many are by homophobic individuals who see an opportunity to use the internet to lure out victims, others involve an organised network of kitos across a relatively large area. The kitos share information on those they suspect or know to be queer and how best to target them.

In October 2019, I spoke to several people for a story on dating while queer in Nigeria. 'No matter how many precautions I take, I'm always really scared,' Ike*, a developer, told me. 'There's always this fear that the guy walking in that I think is super-cute has been catfishing me and has plans to turn the other people seated in the restaurant into a mob. It got to me at a point and now I only go out with friends of friends. It's limiting but it is safer.'

While kito has been around for quite a few years, it became particularly prevalent after the Same Sex Marriage (Prohibition) Act was signed. The act not only essentially legitimised homophobia in Nigeria, it also meant that queer people cannot report hate crimes because, here, being queer is always the bigger crime. In February 2019, Dolapo Badmus, spokesperson for the Lagos Police, addressed the Nigerian LGBTQ+ community on her personal Instagram account, reminding us of our place in Nigerian society:

> If you are homosexually inclined, Nigeria is not a place for you. There is a law (Same Sex Prohibition Act) here that criminalizes homosexual clubs, associations, and organizations with penalties of up to 14 years in jail. So if you are a homosexual in nature, leave the country or face prosecution.[3]

We may have found a word for it, but Nigeria is far from the only place where the kito phenomenon exists. Although in Egypt homosexuality isn't criminalised, the el-Sisi regime has been using a 1950 anti-prostitution law and a 1961 law against debauchery in tandem to target the queer community.[4] Research carried out by the Egyptian Initiative for Personal Rights (EIPR) found that between October

2013 and March 2017, 232 people were arrested on suspicion of being LGBTQ+, compared with a total of 189 across the thirteen years beforehand.[5] There have been reports of law enforcement using apps like Grindr, Hornet and Growler to identify and track down queer people, before showing printouts of conversations to bring charges.[6]

While catfishing is one of the major ways technology is used to oppress us, it isn't the only way. In Paraguay, a Twitter account was set up to expose LGBTQ+ people living in the country by uploading images and conversations from apps. The account was reported yet it took over six weeks before Twitter finally took it down.[7] This is similar to what happened in Ghana in early 2018, when an anonymous Twitter account posted the names, photos and locations of queer Ghanaians and directed homophobia and violence towards them.

In April 2020 Sofia Talouni, a Moroccan trans woman living in Turkey, went on Instagram Live to encourage attacks on queer men. She told cis heterosexual women – wives, mothers, sisters – to create profiles on gay dating apps, and to use the location feature to identify and out the gay men living in their communities. As same-sex relations in Morocco are punishable with up to three years in prison, and queer people are frequently marginalised and subjected to violence, Sofia's actions have left the Moroccan queer community living in fear. One man took his own life after being outed and many others were rejected by their families. The story made global headlines after activists including Adam Eli (who appears later in this book) pushed for the press to cover the events, and Sofia's Instagram and Facebook accounts were eventually suspended.

Digital spaces have often been paraded as safe for marginalised communities but it's clear now that this is not the case. Social media platforms have not always responded quickly to reports of targeted harassment, forced outing and violence organised through their sites or apps. Dating apps like Grindr, Scruff and Tinder do have certain in-app functions to protect LGBTQ+ users – they notify you when you use them in countries where homosexuality is criminalised and advise you to be careful in these places. In response to arrests in Egypt, Grindr disabled the feature that shows users' exact distance from one another, and the app was also involved in a project whereby users in countries where homosexuality is criminalised were surveyed about their safety.[8] The app has since made improvements, such as requiring a pin for users in these places to open the app.[9] But is this enough?

The creators of social media and dating platforms need to keep working with the LGBTQ+ community as well as groups that champion our rights and safety, and to rethink how this technology can guarantee the protection of users. In places where digital catfishing and crime is more prevalent, we can no longer wait for this change to come. We are killed and attacked way too often to afford the luxury of time.

In Nigeria, queer people are having to protect one another, in lieu of adequate protection with technology and from the police. Older queer people take younger queer people under their wings and have created mentor relationships, teaching their 'protégés' how to screen potential dates to work out whether they are kitos. When I speak to Alex*, a designer, he tells me about how he helps young people and tries to ensure their safety:

I was privileged enough to have been schooled in the US where homosexuality wasn't criminalised. When I came back to Nigeria, I was taken for a fool multiple times because I was an ajebo. [An ajebo is a person who grew up wealthy and hasn't experienced hardships.] I was kitoed, taken advantage of and forced to wise up. So I did and I started helping young and sheltered people to not make the mistakes I did. Whenever any of them tell me about someone they like, we have to go through their Facebook and Instagram, and sometimes check to see the mutuals they have. If you don't have mutuals, that is a red flag. If the posts are fanatically religious, red flag. It's a long process but it is how I ensure they survive. I also tell them that if anything goes left, they have to call me first. I'll pay whatever money the kitos need and will come pick them up.

Throughout the country – especially in the big cities like Abuja, Lagos and Port Harcourt where the queer community is slowly but steadily trying to create a form of solidarity offline – community leaders like Alex are rising up to protect more vulnerable queer people. The LGBTQ+ community is also using kito tactics against homophobes by creating Kito Diaries. This is a platform which allows people to submit their kito experiences, details of where they happened and sometimes the kitos' names, social media accounts and profile images. It also contains information on the kitos' bases of operations and locations that have high kito activity. Over the past few years, Kito Diaries has become a relatively large database.

While this has likely saved lives, it has not eradicated kitos. The LGBTQ+ communities in countries like Nigeria, Egypt and Morocco need the global LGBTQ+ community, campaign groups and mainstream media to highlight what is going on. But action is also needed beyond this – catfishing and kito represent a whole new frontier of persecution, requiring a new approach from Silicon Valley. Technology companies must realise that tailored measures are needed to stop attacks by kitos: that could mean better reporting functions, stronger verification processes for accounts, and more education or warnings provided in areas where users are vulnerable. More research into the issue is important, too, and it may be that collaborations between app developers and, for example, Kito Diaries should be explored.

To bring an end to kito activity, or drastically reduce it, it is also important for international advocacy and human rights bodies to apply pressure on the Nigerian government. Nigeria's homophobic laws must change as they make it impossible for queer people who have fallen victim to kitos to seek justice. I'd like to see international bodies partner with organisations like TIERs Nigeria (an NGO that fights for equality here) and Kito Diaries in order to raise awareness and to hopefully make a real difference.

I am twenty-one years old and I was born and bred in Nigeria. So far, I am yet to plan a date with someone from an app and actually meet up with them. This isn't from a lack of interesting or 'meetable' people, it is from a deep-seated fear for my safety. I'm not alone. Queer people in parts of the world like mine should be entitled to basic experiences like safely chatting on apps and going on dates – and it's clear to me that both better laws and digital solutions are urgently needed to make this happen.

* Names have been changed.

---

1 Adam Nossiter, 'Mob attacks more than a dozen gay men in Nigeria's capital', *New York Times*, 15 February 2014, https://www.nytimes.com/2014/02/16/world/africa/mob-attacks-gay-men-in-nigerias-capital.html

2 'Gay men publicly stripped and beaten in Nigeria', Human Rights First, 1 April 2014, https://www.humanrightsfirst.org/blog/gay-men-publicly-stripped-and-beaten-nigeria; https://www.naijaloaded.com.ng/news/nigerian-men-forced-public-angry-mob-port-harcourt-see-photo-video

3 Quoted in Josh Jackman, 'Nigeria police spokesperson tells gay people: Leave or face prosecution', *Pink News*, 23 January 2019, https://www.pinknews.co.uk/2019/01/23/nigeria-gay-police-leave/

4 Mia Jankowicz, 'Jailed for using Grindr: homosexuality in Egypt', *Guardian*, 3 April 2017, https://www.theguardian.com/global-development-professionals-network/2017/apr/03/jailed-for-using-grindr-homosexuality-in-egypt

5 'The trap: punishing sexual difference in Egypt', Egyptian Initiative for Personal Rights (EIPR), 22 November 2017, https://eipr.org/en/publications/trap-punishing-sexual-difference-egypt

6 Russell Brandom, 'Designing for the crackdown', *The Verge*, 25 April 2018, https://www.theverge.com/2018/4/25/17279270/lgbtq-dating-apps-egypt-illegal-human-rights

7 'The digital rights of LGBTQ+ people: When technology reinforces societal oppressions', EDRi, 17 July 2019, https://edri.org/our-work/the-digital-rights-lgbtq-technology-reinforces-societal-oppressions/

8 Mike Miksche, 'Gay dating apps are protecting users amid Egypt's LGBTQ crackdown', *Vice*, 25 October 2017, https://www.vice.com/en/article/pa3pxg/gay-dating-apps-are-protecting-users-amid-egypts-lgbtq-crackdown

9 'Designing for the crackdown', *The Verge*, 25 April 2018

VISIBILITY

'My memories of watching queer people on TV and in music remind me that when you relate to something it is empowering – and when you feel empowered you are able to empower others.'

Mary Beth Patterson, known by her stage name **Beth Ditto**, is an American singer-songwriter and actress. She's well known for her work with the indie rock band Gossip, as well as her solo career. Beth also acts in TV and film.

The 'Visibility' We Still Don't See

BETH DITTO

My earliest memories of queerness come from pop culture.
I was born in 1981, when it felt like queer culture just
was pop culture. This was around the time that 'Girls Just
Want to Have Fun' and 'Material Girl' came out. Prince
was everywhere, as was Annie Lennox and Culture Club.
Boy George was really the first explicitly queer person I
saw on TV; I was four years old. My mom had me young
(even though I was her fourth kid) and she was a 'cool
mom' – meaning we had cable television. I remember we'd
watch MTV, which was brand new to the scene, and that's
where I saw Boy George performing. I was just so enamored
with him. It didn't *not* make sense to me. I never thought:
So that's a boy dressed as a girl? Wearing make-up? It
was almost like it was home.

Not everybody felt that way. Just after I saw my first
images of queer people on MTV the channel was banned
in our town, Searcy, a small place in Arkansas. The county
was and still is influenced by a very conservative Christian
college – you couldn't go to a bookstore and buy a gay or
feminist magazine; you had to ask behind the counter. We
weren't even allowed to have dances! It was the Christian
college who made the cable company drop MTV, and
when they did, those images of Prince, Annie Lennox and
Boy George were the last glimmers of pop culture that I

would see for a while. But they stuck with me. It's like I had a tiny window into queerness in my little developing brain. I took those moments and ran with them. They shaped my idea of what gender is and music is.

As a teenager, these queer images eventually started to creep back in. They had banned MTV but VH1 was still available and I remember watching Rupaul's talk show on it. There was Ellen too, but before her sitcom started they would give you a warning, like a trigger warning, that there was going to be gay content, basically. They made it seem like we were going to watch someone getting murdered. I remember my mom saw that warning and said, 'Maybe we should change the channel,' because I had a little brother. I was like: 'Don't worry, Mom, she's just gay!'

I can't explain my life sometimes. It's not like there was some huge awakening moment for me, as I always knew the kernel of truth inside and I've always seen the world through the same eyes. Being queer was so who I was it seemed to find me or something. I was just lucky that I came from an extremely warm family – crazy as hell but super liberal in a place where most weren't. When it came to my being queer I was more afraid of God than the people directly around me, but I also knew that people in my town wouldn't be accepting of it. That's why I was so grateful that when I was a kid, TV gave me a glimpse into a world that was more free. It showed me what the possibilities were and sparked an awakening in me to look for more. It made me go find punk rock, radical feminist literature, figures like John Waters and Angela Davis. And that showed me that there was even more out there; I just had to keep looking for it, along with the other people out there who wanted it as much as I did ... I knew I had to find my people, not change who I was.

As a teenager, I made a group of queer friends who were so aggressively punk and queer and out of the closet. They taught me two things. Firstly, that chosen family is everything. Someone who shares a history with you, understands what you're talking about without you having to explain it, that is what kept me alive. Secondly, that while media visibility is important you cannot replace face-to-face connection. This was the days before social media – which is of course amazing and there is strength in numbers – but when there are just a few of you together in a room and you're laughing so hard you're crying? And you're not thinking about anything else because you're untouchable, because the space is closed off? That is special. That is tangible.

It was these friends who literally got me my plane ticket out of Searcy when I was eighteen. Once I moved away a whole new world of activism and community opened up. I was working in fast food and sleeping on a fold-out couch for the first year, but we were together and living our truths; it was that simple. It was so free and beautiful. I was living in this house, being queer, immersing myself in queercore, going to punk shows, learning what a femme was, what a butch was, meeting trans people for the first time, hearing about racial justice and going to workshops that taught survival skills – because maybe the revolution was upon us!

From a young age I wanted to do something that involved helping others, but I just didn't know what it would be. Once I left Arkansas, I saw things more clearly. I saw that coming from a place in the Bible Belt, below the Mason–Dixon Line – a place where you're being constantly reminded that God is watching and judging you – I had a duty to show other queer kids from small towns that it is possible to get the fuck out of there. When we started Gossip, this was the message I wanted to put out – that it's easier than you think to escape situations that make you feel wrong or ugly or gross or like you're going to hell, that the world is bigger than you think, that you can be queer and be yourself and be happy. I'd say 'role model' was never a comfortable term for me because I haven't always said stuff in the right way, especially as I don't come from an academic background. I've also changed my mind over the years; we're only human and movements evolve and we keep learning. (Besides, who wants to be quoted when they're turning forty about something they said when they were twenty-one?) But I'm very lucky that I got to make music for a living, and I got to do it being openly queer, being fat and being femme.

In the 2000s, there weren't so many queer role models as there are today. We've especially opened up in terms of gender – the number of people who publicly identify as trans and nonbinary is growing and that's got to expand the way we think about gender in the most amazing way. But I think we still need more. We're still not done. We need more trans men to be visible. More trans women of color. More trans men of color. More butch femme relationships and more real butch visibility. (Because when I watch *The L Word* I am like, *Who* are these lipstick-wearing butches? Where do they exist?)

I think we need to talk about class within queer visibility too. Class is a funny thing – it has different meanings and consequences for each of us. I am from a poor town near Walmart's HQ and living there, you either work as a teacher, in the medical industry or in some huge retail outlet on a zero-hour contract with no benefits. Coming from where I come from taught me that it's important to look at class because you don't have as many options when you're poor and often you're treated like shit, which I also know from when I was a fast-food worker.

Class is a queer issue because queer and trans people face employment discrimination, and a lot of the problems with class in America are to do with the cost of healthcare, which is also a real issue for queer people and disabled people. Many people in the trans community need a way to get hormones – and if you have no work and no health-care then you're paying out of pocket for that. How are you supposed to do it? I have an autoimmune disease and I have to pay $400 a month for healthcare; there are queer people living with disabilities or chronic illnesses who just can't afford that kind of money. So we need to see the stories of poor queer people to truly understand that lack of privilege.

I'd say too that we haven't seen enough change when it comes to visibility of the many kinds of queer bodies out there. I think, in a sense, that fat visibility and queer visibility need to go hand-in-hand. Like being queer, when you're a fat person you have to be more creative. That comes from necessity. You come up with all of these incredible ideas for how to exist, unlike people who have the idea that they can just go and buy something that's ready-made for them. Body positivity was a lonely place for me when I was talking about it ten, fifteen years ago. A lot has improved since then but we still do not see enough 'fat' bodies. Does it need to change more? Definitely!

One of the problems with the body positivity movement is that magazines and advertising campaigns are sticking to a beauty standard that's as close to being 'pretty' and thin as possible. There's an acceptable big body that doesn't reflect the body I see on myself every day, or on my friends, and that's not okay. There are still very few fat people visible, especially men. This movement is not inclusive if we only see individuals who fit into a narrow idea of beauty. It definitely won't teach queer people of all sizes to love their bodies, which is important when queer bodies are so marginalized anyway.

Finally, I want to see what our realities look like, what we do every day. When you think about pop culture, you don't really see it: us getting up, brushing our teeth, going to work, calling our partner, dealing with depression, sometimes being hilarious, sometimes not being hilarious. There's not enough of it. The media is giving us breadcrumbs to reflect the change they see in the world or to react to our activism. I'm not so much talking about queer-centric television shows where day-to-day life is the specific topic, but the rest of it. I'd like our days to be shown as we live them – where we're not these people on the fringes, or people who go home and all we're thinking about is how we're queer. I just want to see queer people being human, not constantly living their fucking oppression all the time.

In some ways, the world is getting more accepting for LGBTQ+ people, but that doesn't mean that role models are any less important. 'Queer' is a big umbrella, with so many different needs and aesthetics and opinions and values – so we're always going to search for whatever speaks to us. Especially as, even if we are gay, or bi, or trans, life isn't *just* about being gay, or bi, or trans. That's why we've got to move past one-dimensional representations and for everyone to understand that there's more to us than stereotypes, and more to us than just our gender or sexuality. Maybe we need a role model for another reason – because we're bad cooks and Martha Stewart doesn't make us feel good!

My memories of watching queer people on TV and in music remind me that when you relate to something it is empowering – and when you feel empowered you are able to empower others. As human beings we need others, we need people who look like us to be visible in every part of public life, we need to see the lives we deserve so that we can know those options are available to us.

'Early on in my career, I was faced with a choice: did I want to create the kind of visibility I had needed to see when I was younger?'

Holland – real name Go Tae-seob – is South Korea's first openly gay K-pop star. His debut single and video, 'Neverland', released in 2018, got 1.6 million views in twenty-four hours and now has over 13 million views and counting. It features the first same-sex kiss in a K-pop video. He took his name from the Netherlands, the first country to legalise same-sex marriage.

Don't Be Afraid to Be the First

HOLLAND

It was in 2010 that I realised that I was gay. Back then, South Korea was even more conservative than it is now. While, for me at least, the process of accepting my sexuality was quite natural – and I felt no denial or sorrow about it – I was concerned about how I would cope with the closed society around me. Anything LGBTQ+-related was a taboo subject and not openly discussed. People didn't bother developing their own opinions about LGBTQ+ rights because it just wasn't a topic on the agenda. The actor-comedian Hong Seok-cheon was the only openly gay celebrity in Korea at the time. A beloved and witty TV personality, he had come out on Korean television in the year 2000. It had caused a public outrage, and he was subsequently fired from his TV network and advertising work. Eventually, when he managed to rebuild his career, he came to represent the LGBTQ+ community in a way that seemed acceptable and humorous, so that the public could embrace him. It offered a little hope, yes, but at thirteen, I couldn't really relate.

I didn't come out at home, but I did confide in someone at school. There was a boy I had a crush on, and one day I told him how I felt. 'I'm gay and I think I have feelings for you,' I said. 'I don't expect you to accept it but I just wanted you to know.' He didn't take it very well. He also decided to tell all the other kids at school about my sexuality. From that day on I went through what felt like endless incidents that would – or at least should – be considered totally unacceptable now. I was called names, sexually assaulted, and dragged to the bathroom or empty storage cupboards to be bullied during breaks. It wasn't only the other students who were causing me problems, but also the teachers and school staff who didn't know how to deal with the bullying. Instead they just did nothing.

My family had no idea what I was going through because they didn't know that I was gay. They only found out when I started making music as an openly gay musician and talking to the press about my sexuality. They later told me that they felt incredibly sorry for not knowing what had been happening to me at school, and for not having my back. Now, though, they are fully supportive of who I am and my career. I wish I could have talked to them to begin with, and maybe my school years wouldn't have been so tough. I am still affected by it, and every time I have to go past the school, I have an anxiety attack. I'm scared to visit the neighbourhood. Being bullied left me depressed for years, but I don't know that I'd change the past, because so much of what I do today is connected to that time.

I didn't take a traditional path to becoming a K-pop star. Instead of majoring in music, I studied photography. I had a brief experience as a trainee at a Korean entertainment company while a teenager but I quit because I felt I would have to lie about my sexuality to be successful. I had always dreamed of becoming a musician, I just wasn't ready to really follow those dreams. It was only once I became an adult that I started soul-searching, figuring out who I want to be and how I want to be known by others. Eventually, when I decided to try to be a musician, it wasn't only because it is what I really wanted to do, but also because

I knew I had certain messages to convey through my music. So I set up a one-man entertainment company. I juggled multiple jobs to raise funds to create my first album. I taught myself how to compose songs, how to do my own marketing and how to produce music videos.

Early on in my career, I was faced with a choice: did I want to create the kind of visibility I had needed to see when I was younger? It was not part of the initial plan for me to kiss a boy in the video for my first single, 'Neverland'. But while we were making it I decided that I should show the way I love. I told the director what I wanted to do and he expressed his concern: the video would be rated 19+ in South Korea if I included this kiss, meaning that no one under nineteen would technically be allowed to watch. It would also be restricted on mainstream television and online video channels for its direct depiction of same-sex affection. I didn't know that this would be the case and I was outraged. That outrage encouraged me to move ahead with including the 'controversial' scene in order to raise awareness about censorship here, and to publicise how unfair I think it is. I took the opportunity to make my message clear: our love is just like anyone else's and the law shouldn't treat it differently.

When the video came out, many people in South Korea were shocked as most of them hadn't seen a man kiss another man in a scene before. But I received more positive responses than I expected: some people told me that it was beautiful or that it was just the same as any other kiss. It split opinion, and that is exactly what I wanted; for me, the most important issue facing the LGBTQ+ community in my country is simply that LGBTQ+ people's lives and experiences need to be more widely talked about. That's why I put another same-sex kiss in my music video for 'I'm Not Afraid', later the same year.

*

LGBTQ+ topics are still usually considered too sensitive to talk about in South Korea, and when they are discussed, that discussion is often very negative. Take, for example, when, during the COVID-19 outbreak, a gay man tested positive for coronavirus after visiting several clubs in Itaewon, an LGBTQ+-friendly party neighbourhood. Immediately after this, authorities discovered over one hundred new COVID-19 cases linked to iconic gay clubs in the area. What happened next really demonstrated public opinion about queer people: after a major Christian media outlet covered the story, people took to social media to unapologetically shame, blame and attack the whole LGBTQ+ community. It was clear that the issue was no longer coronavirus, but queerness. LGBTQ+ rights activists including myself were left despondent. It felt like all the progress we had made in recent years had collapsed, but it was also a reminder of why we have to keep fighting.

As long as LGBTQ+ content is restricted in South Korea I will keep trying to be visible and build a reputation. K-pop is a beloved part of our culture, especially for young people. I feel a sense of responsibility and pressure as the first openly LGBTQ+ K-pop artist, as every action or musical decision I make could be taken by others to represent the whole Korean LGBTQ+ community. It is never easy to be gay in our entertainment scene; I am sometimes discreetly mistreated behind the scenes and there are people out there who more openly disapprove of me having a place in K-pop. It's almost like people are waiting for me to do something wrong, but I will keep trying to set a positive example, and to create depictions of our love.

I'm determined to do this because I believe that more awareness could lead to more support for LGBTQ+ kids, and that is critical. I believe parents should be more open-minded: we have to build a culture where parents offer their children comfort and a home under any circumstances – only through seeing same-sex love in the media will they get used to the idea over time. Better visibility will hopefully provide comfort to kids themselves, too. Looking back, when overcoming the dark times of being bullied at school, the biggest source of comfort I found came from musicians who publicly supported the LGBTQ+ community: pop stars like Troye Sivan, Madonna, Lady Gaga and Celine Dion. These people inspired me to help LGBTQ+ kids who are struggling like I did when I was younger. If I had found a Korean role model to look up to as a teenager, I would have felt empowered. Finally, I also do this work to prove to my childhood bullies that I deserve to be loved and that they were wrong.

As time has gone by, I can say I have become stronger. I am more mature now and able to love and embrace myself. If I had a message to my younger self, it would probably be what I often tell my fans: don't try to conform. Remember your beauty blossoms when you believe in it. Just be yourself.

'I want a future for those living with HIV that is life-affirming, that is open to possibility, that is limitless.'

Mykki Blanco, the artist persona and stage name of Michael David Quattlebaum Jr, is an internationally renowned musician, performing artist and LGBTQ+ activist. Mykki is releasing two new musical projects as well as a poetry book in 2021. Mykki lives in Paris.

Seen & Unseen: Living Between Two Stigmas

MYKKI BLANCO

Self-worth is a tricky thing. Is it nature or nurture? It seems some people are born with large amounts of it. Some are raised and nurtured by their parents or guardians to acquire and cultivate it. Others are neither born with self-worth nor acquire it at all. I have at times yearned, wished and hoped I had been born with self-worth, and yet my life trajectory has made me realize that perhaps, for mystical soul-affirming reasons yet to be revealed, I was born into the latter category. Securing self-worth has been a daily journey, and it is one that I find you must turn into a life practice.

High-risk behavior. I am sure everyone who lives with HIV as I do, or works with HIV patients or advocates for the rights of those living with HIV, has heard or knows what the phrase means. There are millions of people who have been born with HIV, a situation completely out of their control. There are millions of people I am sure who, when telling their personal account of contracting HIV, have an honest story of being surprised at their diagnosis or unaware of how they got the virus, but that is not my experience.

Whether I dress it up and put a bow on it or use all the fancy words in the world, I know that I have HIV today because of my behavior in my early twenties; it was my behavior, driven by my lack of self-esteem and my internal dialogue. The ways in which I spoke to myself and the beliefs I had about myself in my most private of moments characterized the decisions I made. But my tale is not a complete sob story. As I sit here writing, my intention is not to depress the hell out of you; there is enough pain in all of our lives, and I have transcended many of the things that once caused me pain in both my personal life and professional career. I am writing this because I want to talk about the taboo, personal aspects of the self we're so often told not to.

As queer people, we do not want to contribute to the already toxic narratives heteronormative society has carved out of our lives. Whether by clichés, rumors or lies, sometimes the realities that we have lived are too textbook; cinematic in their exactitude in how they fit into society's often dangerous mythologies of queer folk. Sometimes the cause and effect of truth is too perfect, outlined crisp like fresh pressed linen. This creates an almost certain task for many; the job of overcoming these judgments and living our own truths. For the record: I'm speaking about my own experiences, no one else's, but I hope this illuminates the cycles of shame and secrecy that many of us find ourselves trapped in.

Looking back, I can see how the cycle started for me. I was sexually abused as a child and this painful and traumatic event that I experienced in my youth – without proper therapy and counseling afterward – led me toward high-risk behaviors. This was catalyzed by the fact that sometimes, as a queer person, we are not given examples by society of a life lived with happy endings and positive outcomes. I reflect on my teen years when my curiosity about sex, which is healthy for any teenager, developed into compulsive sexual behavior. Growing up alongside the arrival of the internet as a tool for mass communication and connection, I would sit on the computer in my small town and scroll online gay chat rooms to find older men for sex. While doing an extensive book report during high school, I discovered by accident that a state college library bathroom was a cruising spot for the college students; when not involved in some after-school activity, I would frequent it at least twice a week to have a sexual encounter of some kind. It didn't occur to me then, being fourteen, fifteen, sixteen, that these older men were taking advantage of me.

These patterns of sexual behavior continued into my twenties when I went to college in Chicago and then to study in New York City. I would fall into deep depressions of feeling unloved, feeling ashamed, and yet still engaging in hook-up situations that led to disappointment and sadness. I assumed what I was doing was 'what it is to be queer' because no one ever steered me in another direction or showed me an alternative. The loop of trauma was my normal – until, one year before I contracted HIV, I started a relationship.

The guy I was dating was positive. I'll call him 'David'. I would later find out that I was the first guy David had dated after becoming positive. It was this experience that, I know, helped to save me from plunging deep into even darker self-destructive acts, both then and after my own diagnosis. He was young like me. He was cool, stylish, extremely healthy. I would watch him take his medication every morning to lower his viral load and make him undetectable (a person who is undetectable cannot transmit the virus). He would call me after he had gone on a long run, he could drink me under the table, and he had a network of really close friends and family. But people still gossiped.

Even the close friends and friends of friends who deemed themselves 'extremely open-minded' and 'completely non-judgmental' gossiped. David and I dated for a few months but then the relationship ended naturally and amicably. We are still very good friends to this day.

Something good that my sexually compulsive behavior around that time had instilled in me was that I regularly got tested, every three months. Part of my compulsiveness had also manifested as a neurosis around not catching STDs. (I know that probably doesn't make sense because the simple answer would have been to not engage in the behavior in the first place, but I am merely telling you, honestly, how my mind worked then.) I had gone into the health clinic for my routine check-up as usual. I remember when the nurse read my diagnosis out to me: 'Michael, you have tested positive for HIV.' Tears started falling down my face ... I remember scanning my mind and seeing the situations I had been in – sex parties in Brooklyn, in Harlem, a guy I had met on Craigslist, group sex that I had been invited to on a pre-Grindr site called Adam4Adam. I thought about the guy, who after wearing a condom for the first round of sex, complained that it was too tight and asked if he could not wear one. I thought about the bowl of rum and punch and the marijuana joints that had been passed around ... I was no victim. And I remember as I was leaving that clinic, tears still running down my face, I did not ask, 'God, why me?' but, instead, 'God, what have I done to myself?' So much good was happening in my life, how could this be happening to me right now? No, I thought, I'm not going to let this stop me, my dreams are happening, my dreams are manifesting. I've seen how healthy David is, I know this is not going to stop me.

I only told my mother, David and one other friend, one of my closest, and it remained that way for the next year.

I knew my love life wasn't over but it mutated in a way that was even more unhealthy. I felt there was no way I could ever be open about my status in the way David was – especially as this was 2011, before things like PrEP were common knowledge or even promoted in the media, before the Center for Disease Control declared that 'undetectable is untransmittable.' I became immersed in a late-night culture of sleeping with men who were positive – men using hard drugs with sex, which at that time was completely alien to me. It felt filled with shame, and hiding, and self-destruction. I knew I had to get out of that world quick, and I did, to focus on my career.

It seemed to me at the time that if I was going to succeed at what I loved doing, I had to keep my status secret. Rap music was fun, so I had to be fun, I had to have swag – I was already one of the only gay rappers to ever exist openly and I was rapping in drag. I mean, the only example I had of an entertainer who had come out as HIV positive was Eazy-E and he had died shortly afterwards, and I knew Magic Johnson was HIV positive. But I was very young and don't recall the reception either of them received from America, especially from Black America – were people accepting, welcoming or understanding? I told myself that as long as I was open with the people I was intimate with, and swore them to secrecy, everything would be okay. So life went on and my career excelled while, subconsciously, a part of me was slowly withering.

In the very beginning, standing up for HIV awareness and against stigma felt too much like a badge and a weight. I was afraid that suddenly all of my art, all of my music, all of my work that has so much to do with how I navigate the world would just be labeled through the narrative: 'Oh, this is the HIV artist.' But I decided to come forward about my HIV status because I realized if I was going to live a healthy life, a life with meaning, and the authentic life that I idolized, I would have to come into the light of my own truth. For me, that meant disclosing my status.

Writers and journalists were – as predicted – not kind to me in the two years after I revealed that I was living as HIV positive. Every time I released a new song, a music video or did anything within the public sphere that focused on my music alone, the tagline would always be 'HIV+ rapper Mykki Blanco.' It was as if my status had to be front and center in the audience's mind, as if to judge me only on my artistic merits was no longer good enough. It was a painful time, but I kept forging ahead and my professional life became easier. After a while, I saw that being open about my diagnosis had weeded out the people who had kept my company for superficial reasons, and had brought me closer to those who truly love and respect the essence of who I am.

Oftentimes I wonder what my career would be like if our society didn't have such rigid dogma around the stigma of being HIV positive. I don't know if it will happen during my lifetime, but my vision for the future is that society will let go of this stigma. Imagine a world where doctors and nurses and medical clinics can finally feel as if they can give preventive care without fearmongering. A society that wilfully acknowledges the advancements made in HIV medical care. A government-funded publicity machine that shares the scientific evidence that people on effective treatment for HIV cannot pass it to another person, given that hundreds of thousands of people still do not know what the word 'undetectable' means.

All of this and more is too selectively hidden from the public health agenda, skipped over time and again. It's as if society has chosen to stick to a twenty- or thirty-year-old script on HIV, one that recalls the dark days and keeps HIV-positive people out of the light. Instead, I want a future for those living with HIV that is life-affirming, that is open to possibility, that is limitless. My friend David, by being open and visible about his HIV status, propelled me to know that visibility around being HIV positive is so important. It's important because when people see that you are comfortable with who you are and the life that you've chosen to live, it can transform the lives of other people living with HIV for the better.

Fifty years ago, my queer forebears led the movements for our liberation with messages of ending stigma and embracing who we are to help create a future free of shame for LGBTQ+ people. But we're still not done. So many of us carry shame for many different reasons and life experiences. When that shame is amplified because of the stigma of HIV it becomes even more isolating. What has helped me in my life is seeing my mistakes and missteps as paths and detours to a deeper sense of growing. Becoming open about my HIV status and my history of sexual abuse has enabled me to be someone who breaks the lineage of silence and ridicule surrounding both.

I believe that if we could see more people who lived between two stigmas, and actively made more space to hear from those people, we could combat feelings and cultures of shame like those I have experienced. That so many continue to experience. We could create a world free of stigma that will allow anyone, even those of us born with no self-worth, to flourish, to thrive. A future that allows us all to live the best and fullest of lives.

'I wanted to give the agency back to asexual people so we could represent ourselves and show the diversity of our community, so we could get our faces out there.'

Yasmin Benoit is a model, aromantic-asexuality activist, speaker and writer from Berkshire, England. In 2018, she started the hashtag #ThisIsWhatAsexualLooksLike to improve asexual visibility.

Ace of Clubs

YASMIN BENOIT

It was the height of the summer in Soho. The tube was sweaty, the streets were busy, and I made my way from my quiet town outside of London to see my pop-up bar for the first time. It was impossible to miss it. A black, grey, white and purple flag hung outside the black building, with the words 'ACE OF CLUBS' printed onto the window in violet letters. I was bursting with pride and excitement as I stepped inside – there was a huge asexual flag painted on the wall, the pillows and bean bags fitting the colour scheme in the seating area, drinks named after asexual puns in the free bar, and my #ThisIsWhatAsexualLooksLike hashtag with a human-sized frame so that people could take their picture with it in the photo corner. The venue, and the two-day event, was everything I had hoped it would be.

The occasion was a beautiful blend of insightful discussion and carefree drunken fun. Downstairs, we had a cinema for a screening of my asexuality documentary, followed by a Q&A with the cast. There was a panel event, and a cake-decorating corner (a nod to the running gag in the asexual community – 'I'd rather eat cake than have sex'). Then the alcohol started to kick in. We were singing Queen songs at the top of our lungs, debating whether Nicki Minaj was better than Cardi B, ordering irresponsible amounts of pizza, and video-calling our non-asexual friends to relish in the fact that we were united like a long-lost family. From the outside looking in, it was just a party, just a bunch of people hanging out, who happened to have something in common. In Soho during Pride season, it would seem commonplace.

But this was different, and it meant much more than your average party, because nothing like this had happened for asexual people before. Even Budweiser had noticed the lack of Pride events for us. When it was announced that they were sponsoring Pride in London that year, they approached me with the idea of creating an asexual bar and wanted to sponsor the project. I am aware that some people in the queer community are dubious of corporate sponsorship, but I decided to take them up on their offer because there is so little visibility and opportunity for asexual people.

It was the first time a large company had sponsored anything for the asexual community, and without their help, that monumental weekend wouldn't have happened. Not only was it a positive step in asexual visibility, it was an unforgettable memory for asexual people who could finally feel united and recognised outside of the internet, outside of our own bubble.

When the doors first opened, in came asexual people of different ages and backgrounds, some with friends, some alone (although not for long). One of the first people to arrive was a girl around my age who said she had never been around other asexual people before, but she had heard about the event on my Instagram and wanted to come. Most extraordinarily, a male model had come all the way from Trinidad, after his friend on the island had sent him a link to an article about the event. As I am also Trinidadian, the coincidence was insane, and we became great friends almost instantly.

Despite all of the activism I do, it was rare to meet other Black asexual people. There were more aces (shorthand for 'asexual people') of colour at Ace of Clubs than I had seen at any other occasion (not that there had been many occasions). In a community that is usually represented by white asexuals during our fleeting moments of visibility, people told me that seeing a Black asexual woman at the front of the project made them feel seen. Even though it was the first time we had met, my friend from Trinidad and I hastily planned to go to UK Black Pride together to celebrate our queerness and our West Indian heritage.

Throughout the night, I often had to remind myself that it wasn't all a bizarre, far-fetched dream. Their hostess wasn't a seasoned Londoner, a quintessential part of the queer scene, a party girl or even a social butterfly – despite the impressions that could be derived from my social media. I was your local friendly neighbourhood goth, who was unusually Black and unusually asexual.

I never really had to 'come out' as asexual or aromantic (I don't experience romantic attraction either) because I didn't pretend to be anything else. I noticed my lack of orientation when those around me realised that they did have one – i.e. in early puberty. But it was just another quirk to add to my list, I wasn't particularly concerned about it, until I noticed other people's reactions. At first, the assumption was that I was a 'late bloomer', or that I was just too young to have an orientation, even in my twenties. As time went on, though, people began to theorise that there had to be something psychologically or physically wrong with me:

'She's probably a lesbian and hasn't realised.'
'That isn't uncommon in psychopaths.'

'Maybe you love yourself too much.'

'You just haven't found the right person yet.'

'Is it a hormone issue?'

'But do you masturbate?'

'So you reproduce with yourself, like a flower?'

'Are you a paedophile but you don't want to admit it?'

Considering that most people didn't know what asexuality was, they sure did have a lot of opinions on it. In 2019, a Sky News Data Poll found that while half of the public thought they could define asexuality, 75% got it wrong.[1] As for how many asexual people there are, while there hasn't been a lot of research conducted into asexuality, it's commonly cited that about 1% of the population is asexual. In a 1983 study, Paula S. Nurius found that, in a non-random sample, 5% of men and 10% of women did not report feeling sexual attraction towards men or women, and she classified these individuals as 'asexual'.[2] In 2004, Anthony Bogaert conducted a nationally representative study into asexuality in Great Britain, with 18,876 respondents.[3] He found that 1.1% of the sample said that they had 'never felt sexually attracted to anyone at all'. Similarly, in a 2015 YouGov poll, 1% of the 1,632 participants answered that they had 'no sexuality'.[4] However, it's often thought that the percentage is higher – especially when you consider that the YouGov poll found no asexual men, when I've met many.

Even if asexual people do only make up 1% of the population, if we apply that to the whole world, then that's 75 million people. Less than 2% of the world's population are believed to be ginger, but most people still know a ginger-haired person. There's a similar percentage of transgender people in the US, and the visibility and awareness for trans people has increased exponentially in recent years, while asexual visibility has improved only marginally during my lifetime. That invisibility has wide-reaching, damaging effects.

The Asexual Community Survey (2018) found that for nearly half of the ace respondents (44.4%), others had attempted to fix or suggested cures for their sexual and/or romantic orientation.[5] This was followed by 30.2% of aces reporting that they had been verbally harassed because of their orientation, 33% of aces who had suffered online harassment, and 18.5% of aces who had been excluded from social activities. These are experiences that I can personally vouch for, but the asexual community is too invisible for others to take notice. Despite the leaps our society has taken when it comes to talking about the diverse nature of human sexuality, despite the positive impact of feminism, the boldness of sexual liberation and queer culture infiltrating the mainstream, asexuality has been left behind.

I realised that the discrimination and abuse came from a lack of understanding, and that if more asexual people didn't do something to change that, we would have to keep dealing with the ignorance. That was why I decided to use the platform I had gained through my work as a model to raise awareness for asexuality. Considering that I was a young Black woman who spent a significant amount of time having my photo taken in lingerie (when you're a model under 5'10 with D cups, that's your pigeonhole), I didn't expect people in the community to want me as a representative. What started off with volunteering at the UK Asexuality Conference in 2018 quickly snowballed into my becoming an unlikely face and voice for our experiences and needs, appearing in LGBTQ+ campaigns and giving seminars at workplaces, universities and even the House of Commons.

As part of this, I started speaking at international Pride events, which felt especially meaningful because it was when I went to Pride at fourteen that I first saw an asexual flag in real life and met other asexual people. In a field filled with hundreds of people, there were two openly asexual people – a homoromantic (romantically but not sexually attracted to the same gender) married couple who I would end up appearing in a documentary with, years down the line. I've been going to Pride festivals ever since. In 2019, the same year as Ace of Clubs was launched, I marched through London waving a giant asexual flag with the Budweiser float and even strolled in purple and black at the front of Prague Pride's parade as a special guest next to their mayor. No one has ever challenged me at these events or questioned whether I should be welcome. But as an activist, I have become increasingly aware of how asexual inclusion at Pride – or in any queer space – is a surprisingly contentious issue.

Misconceptions and confusion around how asexuality fits into the LGBTQ+ movement run deep, with questions like: Do asexual people belong in a community centred around sexuality? What does a group that is too invisible to be systematically oppressed have to complain about? These questions miss the point. I've never seen Pride as being *only* for those who experience sexual attraction to the same sex – it's a space for those who don't fit the heteronormative box. Many asexual people see it that way too. We don't want to tell other people how to express their sexuality, we just want to celebrate ours (or our lack of it) at an occasion dedicated to that. We have our space in the parades, our little groups on the outskirts of the occasion, but we're never truly included. It's a microcosm of our space in society. You'd never know that asexuality has existed for as long as human sexuality. It isn't part of social consciousness, it isn't included in sex education, and it's still largely ignored in queer media and representation.

There are a lot of us out there, all over the world, as diverse as any other population. It's just hard to tell, even if you are browsing the forums. It's hard to feel it when you've never encountered another asexual person in real life. That's why, in 2018, I started the #ThisIsWhatAsexualLooksLike hashtag, inspired by #ThisIsWhatAFeministLooksLike. It came from a personal place. I've been open about my orientation (or lack of it) since I was a kid, and people would come up with any excuse to debunk what I said. As I've grown older, one of the most common things I heard was 'You don't look asexual,' to which I'd respond with: 'What does asexual look like then?' I soon realised that people picture androgynous, sexless nerds, or at the very least, a homely, frumpy-looking person. They fell back on the old tropes of what society tells us is unattractive, assuming that we are asexual because no one would want us anyway, so default and uninteresting that people barely notice us.

I wanted to give the agency back to asexual people so we could represent ourselves and show the diversity of our community, so we could get our faces out there, not just usernames and cake emojis. I was amazed by how much it took off. It was trending on Twitter (a year before I'd even made an account) and I heard that posts about my activism were being reblogged thousands of times on Tumblr. There are a lot of people who just don't understand my approach, but for every anonymous account who called me names, I had far more positive messages:

> 'As an ace myself who has struggled with accepting myself, you've helped me feel more comfortable in my own skin and accepting my femininity.'
> @madeku.art

'*I'm a indigenous Latinx person as well and the intersection of bodies of color and asexuality is often subject to intense judgement and criticism. Keep being the best asexual role model I have ever found, please!*' @em_the_future_librarian

'*I'm aroace [aromantic asexual] and seeing your art, Yasmin, really helped me through accepting I could appreciate the aesthetic of lingerie and leather without feeling sexual attraction towards others.*' @cyber_chartreuse

'*I just want you to know that you are doing a great thing for the community, you are being so brave and I'm so proud our community has someone like you to represent us and prove aphobes wrong. Thank you.*' @_x.kitkat.x

There is a lot more work that needs to be done. That's what motivates me to keep going and push for the change that we need to see. While the event was a success, it was just one important moment in time and a step in the right direction. While the hashtag was successful, there is so much more room for positive asexual visibility in the mainstream media. Our perpetual invisibility up until now means that the asexual community is at a stage where we can shape our narrative, especially now that the world is starting to taking notice. I want to see asexuality included in sex education in schools. I want it to be included in conversations about human sexuality to the same extent as homosexuality, bisexuality and the other orientations. I want our understanding of sexuality to expand further than the idea that you must be sexually attracted to either men or women. I want asexual people to be able to enter queer spaces – physical or virtual – without worrying that they'll be told they 'don't belong'. I want asexual spaces to be commonplace. I want asexual people to be allowed to exist without others trying to correct or harass them. I want everyone to know that we aren't broken, we aren't a problem, and we're not here to ruin anyone else's fun. I want asexual people to feel every day like they did at Ace of Clubs – like they fit, like they're welcome, that they're not just okay, but more than.

---

1 Charlie Bell, 'Asexuality explained: Sky Data poll shows widespread lack of understanding', Sky News, 4 February 2019, https://news.sky.com/story/asexuality-explained-sky-data-poll-shows-widespread-lack-of-understanding-11626697

2 Paula S. Nurius, 'Mental health implications of sexual orientation', *Journal of Sex Research* 19.2, pp. 119–36, May 1983, https://www.jstor.org/stable/3812493?seq=1

3 Anthony F. Bogaert, 'Asexuality: prevalence and associated factors in a national probability sample', *Journal of Sex Research* 41.3, pp. 279–87, August 2004, https://pubmed.ncbi.nlm.nih.gov/15497056/

4 Will Dahlgreen and Anna-Elizabeth Shakespeare, '1 in 2 young people say they are not 100% heterosexual', YouGov, 16 August 2015, https://yougov.co.uk/topics/lifestyle/articles-reports/2015/08/16/half-young-not-heterosexual

5 '2017 and 2018 asexual community survey summary report', 29 October 2020, https://asexualcensus.files.wordpress.com/2020/10/2017-and-2018-asexual-community-survey-summary-report.pdf

'Instead of demonising trans people, the British press should be focusing on the major battles that trans and nonbinary people face today.'

Juliet Jacques is a writer and filmmaker based in London. Her first book, *Trans: A Memoir*, was published by Verso in 2015. Her new book, a volume of short stories called *Variations*, is published by Influx Press.

Transphobia and the UK Media

JULIET JACQUES

Ever since American transsexual woman Christine Jorgensen hit front pages in December 1952, under the headline 'Ex-GI becomes blonde beauty' with 'before and after' photos, newspaper coverage of trans and nonbinary people has often been salacious, sensationalistic and spiteful. The British press – mostly, but not exclusively, tabloids – can be unacceptably intrusive and lacking in empathy, but I would argue that its treatment of trans and nonbinary people over the last decade has been particularly bad, and often abominable.

It may sound strange to complain about the media, in a time when trans and nonbinary people appear in magazines such as *Dazed* and *Vogue*, TV shows like *Euphoria* and *Pose*, fashion and advertising campaigns, and are visible all over Instagram and Twitter. But the 2010s were also the decade of the high-profile Leveson Inquiry into the 'culture, practices and ethics' of the British press that heard evidence of the frequent 'outing' and humiliation of individual trans people, and the smearing of us as a group.

It was a decade of hostile coverage that began just after Germaine Greer's 2009 *Guardian* article that called trans women 'some kind of ghastly parody' and referred to 'a man's delusion that he is female' and peaked around 2017, when tabloids ran stories about Ian Huntley – who was convicted of murdering two ten-year-old girls in

2002 – transitioning in prison, which turned out to be entirely false.[1] It seemed to me, at least, that the Huntley story was the nastiest thing the press could make up about us, associating trans people with one of the country's most notorious killers, and in doing so, implying that the motives of transitioners were inherently suspect. But if the coverage couldn't get any *worse* (and I would never rule it out), it could become more incessant – and it did. Towards the end of the decade, I watched what appeared to be a sustained campaign against trans visibility in many of the UK's newspapers, at a time when much-needed reforms to the Gender Recognition Act were being proposed – reforms which would have formally recognised nonbinary identities, and allowed trans people to self-identify in order to gain legal gender recognition rather than have the approval of two doctors.

If I could change one thing for LGBTQ+ people, it would be the way the mainstream media – especially the print media – treats trans and nonbinary people. This matters because there is a huge population who don't pay attention to fashion magazines, Netflix or social media, but are instead influenced heavily by conservative-leaning TV and radio, and especially newspapers. Consequently, transphobia in the media affects how people approach us, especially as many don't knowingly meet openly trans people and so have their views shaped more by articles and reports than by lived experience. It's a worldwide problem: there are major issues – not least the murder rate for trans people, especially in the global south, with 130 killed in Brazil and 63 in Mexico between October 2018 and September 2019, for example – that need to be more widely reported and discussed.[2] I'm focusing on the UK here, however, because that's where I have spent my entire life. I am one of many British trans people who feel disgusted by the way our country's media treats us, and also to have actively tried to improve the situation.

It's revealing that while I instantly suspected the Huntley story to be bullshit, I couldn't face engaging with it, let alone call it out on social media or in my journalism. I agonised over whether the best tactic was to ignore it, given that so many newspapers were all making it *unignorable*. When the story was shown to be false, only a couple of newspapers publicly retracted it and the correction never had the same impact as the original story.[3] In any case, I couldn't address the issue in the two national publications for whom I had written between 2010 and 2015 – the nominally left-wing or at least liberal *Guardian* and *New Statesman* – because the appearances of 'gender-critical' feminists in their pages made it impossible for me to justify contributing without devoting all my energy to countering the views of this strand of feminism. I was all too aware that these columnists were refusing to accept trans and nonbinary people's stated identities, and that their pieces were gaining significant attention in a media economy based around clicks, and click-bait. Bored and burnt-out, my response was to quit.

This may sound like a depressing state of affairs – and in many ways it is, coming after at least ten years of activists and writers struggling both to work within the mainstream and to set up alternative outlets. But it should also remind us that social struggles have no final victory or defeat, and that the work done in the last decade will inspire the next generation, providing them with lessons to learn and successes to build upon.

Towards the 'Transgender Tipping Point': 2010–2014

By the end of the 2000s, several important provisions, such as recognition of gender reassignment and the right to hormones and surgery via the NHS, had been enshrined in British law – albeit with some significant caveats, notably the Gender Recognition Act 2004 failing to provide for anything beyond 'male' and 'female', and the Equality Act 2010 allowing women-only spaces to exclude trans women despite 'transgender' being a protected characteristic. After this legal progression, British trans activists shifted their focus towards the media in response to the sustained negative coverage, which ranged from wildly incorrect articles on the cost of NHS reassignment services to tabloids outing individuals (including children).[4]

Approaches varied: some activists felt we should refuse to engage, instead setting up our own online and offline spaces and publications as trans people had throughout the 1990s and 2000s. Some felt that pressure groups such as Trans Media Watch, established as a Facebook group in 2009, should publicly call out transphobia and work privately with editors and journalists to share resources that might help them to better understand problems with trans representation, and best practice. Others – including myself – wanted to work within the mainstream media, aiming to change the terms of discussion and, hopefully, the nature of those publications in order to break down transphobia in wider society. I won't spend time here on the successes and failures of the *Transgender Journey* series I wrote for the *Guardian* website from 2010 to 2012, documenting my NHS gender reassignment, or my writing about trans issues in various newspapers and magazines over the next couple of years, as I discussed this extensively in my book *Trans: A Memoir*. Instead, I would like to reflect on the first half of the 2010s, which at the time seemed like a period of progress – slow and frustrating progress, with some significant and shocking setbacks, but progress, nonetheless.

In July 2011 there appeared to be a huge rupture in the power of the British tabloid press. It was revealed that journalists from the Rupert Murdoch-owned *News of the World* had hacked the voicemail of Milly Dowler, a thirteen-year-old girl who was then missing, giving her parents hope that she was still alive, before she was found murdered. This became a huge scandal, as the paper was found to have hacked the phones of both celebrities and people who had, often unwillingly, become involved with news stories. The first part of the subsequent Leveson Inquiry into misconduct by the media began in November 2011 and heard a submission from Trans Media Watch. I was intrigued, even excited: for the first time in my life, we were answering back to the press in a more powerful way than an opinion piece, or a letter to the editor.

Trans Media Watch's presentation aimed to show 'the unethical and often horrific and humiliating treatment of transgender and intersex people by the British press', arguing that it was 'a stark and instructive example of what newspapers (often, but not exclusively tabloids) will seek to get away with when no effective formal or internal restraints are in place'.[5] It discussed the 'sustainment of a climate of ridicule and humiliation' for trans people, with routine misgendering, use of 'previous names' and 'before' photos, and the intrusive behaviour towards their families. Along with numerous examples of tabloid articles that had destroyed private individuals' careers and relationships, many stories that collectively demonised trans people were cited. These mocked community support and activist groups, and often focused on convicts who happened to be trans. The presentation also referred to numerous pieces that attacked the provision of sex reassignment surgery on the NHS.

Leveson made his recommendations in November 2012. He suggested replacing the Press Complaints Commission – the industry's self-regulatory body – with a new, independent body. Membership, however, would be voluntary; at the time of writing, it still does not exist. The second part of the inquiry was planned to deal with unlawful or improper conduct within News International – Murdoch's media empire – but was postponed until after prosecutions regarding events at the *News of the World* and dropped six years later. From my perspective, the inquiry seemed to have brought about little improvement, particularly in terms of coverage about trans people. Even I, who remained pessimistic about the possibilities for change while still striving for that through my writing, was surprised and disappointed.

At this point, it looked essential to set up our own outlets, where trans writers could start to build a readership and hold the wider media to account, but the task of producing a mainstream trans, nonbinary and intersex equivalent to popular gay and lesbian magazines was daunting. The community had an awkward relationship to visibility, understandably given their media treatment, and did not have a comparable sense of social cohesion, instead being riddled with infighting. In 2012, Paris Lees founded and edited *Meta*, an online-only magazine from the publishers of *Diva* and *Gay Times*, but it lasted just three issues, and journalists and activists – including another pressure group, All About Trans – mostly kept focusing on the mainstream press. Lees, myself and others contributed op-eds to the *Guardian*, the *New Statesman* and elsewhere. While we managed to highlight problems with trans healthcare, social safety and media representation to a huge audience, we still found ourselves having to argue against more established columnists who wanted to debate the validity of our identities. Even so, we were encouraged not just by space opening up in Britain's liberal press, but also by the emergence of US advocates such as writer Janet Mock and *Orange Is the New Black* star Laverne Cox, both trans women of colour who began challenging racism and transphobia on prime-time news programmes with style, wit and intellect.

By late 2012, editors who had overlooked trans voices could no longer question if the issues we raised were too complicated for their audiences to understand – it was obvious that an emerging millennial feminist culture was *very* interested, with a vocal presence on social media. Some commentators continued to write against us, resisting the language that trans activist writers used to describe their experiences, characterising all trans activists as inherently aggressive, and challenging certain aspects of the healthcare provision for our community.[6] Yet despite the frustration of getting bogged down in circular arguments about these issues, the fact they were being discussed at all was a positive sign.

However, a backlash was brewing. In December 2012, Richard Littlejohn wrote an article for the *Daily Mail* headlined 'He's not only in the wrong body ... he's in the wrong job'.[7] This concerned a primary school teacher in Accrington who had gone back to work after the Christmas holiday as a woman, and her employer had told parents and children to call her Lucy Meadows. She was later hounded by journalists near her home, and in March 2013 Meadows killed herself. Journalist and author Mick Hume published two pieces insisting that Littlejohn and the *Mail* could not be blamed for her death, defending Littlejohn's conduct on freedom of speech grounds, while Roy Greenslade in the *Guardian* was careful to emphasise that 'no clear link' could be made between the coverage and Meadows's death.[8] My feeling was that, at best, it couldn't have helped; the coroner at the inquest agreed, stating that, 'Her only crime was to be different ... And yet the press saw fit to treat her in the way that they did.'[9]

In January 2013, the *Observer* published a piece by Julie Burchill entitled 'Transsexuals should cut it out'. Full of transphobic insults, with a joke about 'having one's nuts taken off', it concluded by warning 'shims, shemales, whatever you're calling yourselves these days' not to 'threaten or bully us lowly natural-born women'.[10] It attracted widespread scorn – not just from trans people and long-term allies, but many others not normally engaged with the issue of trans media representation – and the *Observer* deleted it from their website two days later. The Press Complaints Commission, however, ruled that they could take no action because the piece had not broken their Editors' Code of Practice and individuals' rights had not been compromised.

After this chain of events, there seemed to be a little pause for thought. When Chelsea Manning came out as trans that summer, the *Star* called her a 'traitor' but otherwise she was treated comparatively respectfully.[11] This coverage of an American story contributed to a growing sense that the UK was catching up with the US, where Cox and Mock in particular were becoming the public face of a burgeoning civil rights movement. In May 2014, *Time* made Cox their first ever openly trans cover star, headlining an article about the 'Transgender Tipping Point', at which the trans community could no longer be ignored or denied its rights. Little did I suspect, at the time, that it might not necessarily tip in our favour.

After the Tipping Point: 2014–2019

The next big splash in the US media, regarding trans issues, came in June 2015, when Caitlyn Jenner came out as trans and appeared on the cover of *Vanity Fair*. A former Olympic athlete who had appeared on the hugely popular reality TV show *Keeping Up with the Kardashians*, Jenner became the most famous trans person in the world. However, unlike Cox or Mock, Jenner backed Donald Trump for US president, only retracting in October 2018 after Trump's administration sought to ban trans people from the military and define gender as being just 'male or female based on immutable biological traits identifiable by or before birth'.[12] But this was part of what I view as a wider shift during the second half of the 2010s, when some politicians stepped up their attacks, and 'progressive' outlets who had tolerated transphobia under the free speech banner became more divided. The US branch of the *Guardian*, for example, struggled to find American trans people to comment on Trump's policies – they were boycotting the newspaper after a recent editorial in the UK edition that argued that trans rights were a direct threat to those of cis women.[13] What happened?

Time's 'Tipping Point' feature appeared as 'gender-critical' feminists were kicking back against trans and nonbinary expression in the mainstream press. In the years following, the tabloids ran numerous op-eds that, while not singling out individuals, positioned trans people as the new politically correct orthodoxy against whom they stood alone, despite the near-total absence of trans people from senior political positions or editorial roles.[14] The broadsheet reaction consisted of a stream of comment pieces that stopped short of Burchill or Greer's incendiary language, but provocatively questioned the terms in which trans and nonbinary people discussed their experiences, or the wisdom of allowing children to self-define their gender.[15] A link was also drawn between adult trans women's requests to have their gender identities recognised and instances of men infiltrating women's spaces and compromising their safety.[16] When these pieces inevitably angered trans people and their allies on social media – especially Twitter – these columnists responded by accusing all trans people of being an angry, baying mob.

This culture war drowned out any discussion of trans people's problems with housing or employment, violence and discrimination, the medical system or the media, taking us back into a position where we were endlessly forced to justify our own existences. Understandably, many trans writers refused to get involved in 'debate' on these terms.

My 'tipping point' was a February 2015 op-ed in the *New Statesman*, where I was a regular contributor, entitled 'Are you now or have you ever been a TERF [Trans Exclusionary Radical Feminist]?', reminiscent of the question asked of suspected communists during the US 'witch-hunts' of the 1950s. Taken in isolation, much of the article did not seem completely unreasonable, opening by denouncing transphobia before accusing a 'small subset of trans extremists' of imposing 'their definition of reality, and their political agenda, on everyone'.[17] My problem was that this article appeared alongside a barrage of similar pieces – it didn't feel to me like the power dynamic was as it suggested, and only at its conclusion was it revealed that its byline, 'Terry Macdonald', was a pseudonym. As editors were mostly interested in my personal life, I had spent years publishing intimate details about myself so as to use this as a platform to discuss social issues. For this author to undermine that work anonymously seemed indicative of a wildly unequal balance of power, and reminded me that our ability to operate within the mainstream depended upon the understanding of editors and commissioners.

Over the next few years, the situation became markedly worse. Calls that trans people were silencing their 'critics' and shutting down 'debate' appeared on prominent news websites with ever more frequency. The articles did not appear unreasonable when taken in isolation, but cumulatively, this coverage led to many – myself included – feeling ground down and no longer able to contribute to the *Guardian* or the *New Statesman*. Consequently, our opponents continued to be able to frame the discussions: I turned down a BBC radio discussion about 'comparisons being made between trans people [as a group] and Rachel Dolezal', the individual US anti-racist activist who pretended to be Black; an invitation to 'challenge Germaine Greer from the audience' (unpaid) during a long interview with her on Al Jazeera; and an unusually carefully worded invitation to appear on a Channel 4 programme called *Genderquake*, which would apparently be 'more like a dinner-table discussion' about trans and nonbinary experiences than a bad-tempered debate. When *Genderquake* aired, some audience members yelled 'Penis!' at the trans women involved: all I could do was quietly feel relief that my suspicions had been correct. At the same time, I was furious that I and many others had worked hard to have more nuanced conversations about trans people, only for the *Genderquake* producers to facilitate something so disingenuous and disempowering.

The situation came to a head in autumn 2018, as the Conservative government consulted people about reforms to the Gender Recognition Act, which would streamline the reassignment pathway and allow legal recognition of nonbinary identities. *The Times* ran a host of negative headlines about trans and nonbinary people in general, ranging from 'Trans extremists are putting equality at risk' to 'Children sacrificed to appease trans lobby'.[18] The *Guardian* editorial 'Where rights collide' suggested that the rights of trans women and cis women were fundamentally in conflict with each other, while subtly silencing trans men from its argument by describing their need for the Act to be reformed as 'far less controversial' without going into further detail on that position.[19] It asked for 'further research into the rise in referrals of children to gender identity services' and repeated the talking point about gender self-definition providing 'violent or controlling male prisoners a new opportunity to dominate women by changing gender and transferring to a female prison'.[20] Days later, *Guardian* US journalists rebuked the UK branch, stating that the editorial 'highlighted for us an alarming intolerance of trans viewpoints in mainstream UK discourse'.[21] They emphasised that 'academic studies have confirmed that trans-inclusive policies do not endanger cis people', that trans people suffer significant victimisation in public bathrooms, and that compared to cis people they are three times more likely to be sexually assaulted, five times more likely to be harassed by police and nine times more likely to have attempted suicide.

By March 2020, three trans members of staff had resigned over the *Guardian*'s coverage since that editorial, with one quitting at a staff meeting after the newspaper published a piece by Suzanne Moore that accused trans people of silencing women.[22] As such, the damage to the UK *Guardian*'s standing among members and allies of the LGBTQ+ community, and particularly the trans and nonbinary community, is some way from being repaired.

What Next?

All of this should cause widespread embarrassment. Instead of demonising trans people, the British press should be focusing on the major battles that trans and nonbinary people face today – from the long waiting times for Gender Identity Clinic services, which have been up to three years according to the BBC, to the mental health crisis amongst young trans and nonbinary people, with 45% found by Stonewall in 2017 to have attempted suicide – and endeavour to bring positive change rather than to attack and humiliate.[23]

For cisgender people in mainstream media who want to offer allyship to trans and nonbinary people, there are several options. One would be a stated editorial commitment to trans rights, with apologies for previous transphobic content, and an invitation for us to contribute to their pages – without this, we are back to the situation of the mid-2000s where occasional trans and nonbinary contributors are in the minority in apparently hostile outlets, arguing on unfavourable terms. It would be especially good if trans and nonbinary people were regularly commissioned on subjects unrelated to gender, suggesting to younger writers that they need not be defined solely by their identities if they want to work in the media. It is important, too, for cisgender journalists to take up our causes in a sympathetic and accessible way – given the current near-absence of our voices from more established outlets; writers including Owen Jones and Ellie Mae O'Hagan are already doing commendable work.

However, the last decade has disabused us of the notion that getting a column in a mainstream newspaper will be enough to secure better representation. Instead, some of us have chosen to write for magazines devoted to other subjects – art, fashion, literature or sport – aware that this will not inspire such an intense reaction as directly arguing for our rights in the politics sections of national papers. Others have concentrated on building our cases in new left vehicles such as *Tribune* or the *New Socialist*, which has made its support for us very clear. A vacancy still exists for a good publication or website written about, by and for trans and nonbinary people, perhaps along the lines of gal-dem, a highly successful online and print journal 'committed to sharing the perspectives of people of colour from marginalised genders'. If it was built patiently, through crowdfunding, subscriptions and creative use of social media, it could provide a home for both trans and nonbinary writers, and their readership, the size and passion of which is still frequently underestimated. Maybe this would shame the mainstream press into always treating us with compassion, understanding and respect. And then who knows how politicians – or the wider public, for that matter – might respond?

---

1 Germaine Greer, 'Caster Semenya sex row: What makes a woman', *Guardian*, 20 August 2009, https://www.theguardian.com/sport/2009/aug/20/germaine-greer-caster-semenya; Sean-Paul Doran, Jonathan Reilly and Tom Wells, 'Soham murderer's "new name"', *The Sun*, 14 February 2017, https://www.thesun.co.uk/news/2866040/child-killer-ian-huntley-tells-lags-to-call-him-female-version-of-his-name-ian-as-make-up-frankland-prison/; Isobel Dickinson, 'Sick killer Huntley's wig stunt', *Daily Star Sunday*, 8 April 2018

2 'Countries with the highest number of murders of trans and gender-diverse people in Latin America from October 2018 to September 2019', Statista, November 2019, https://www.statista.com/statistics/944650/number-trans-murders-latin-america-country/

3 Benjamin Butterworth, 'The Daily Star Sunday has admitted its claims that child murderer Ian Huntley is transgender were never true', *iNews*, 11 February 2019, https://inews.co.uk/news/media/ian-huntley-transgender-claims-apology-daily-star-257028

4 Guy Patrick, 'Dad-of-two driver changes gear in sex swap', *The Sun*, 24 October 2009; David Pilditch, '"Half man" gets new breasts (and guess who's paying £78k)', *Daily Express*, 1 January 2011, https:// www.express.co.uk/news/uk/220433/Half-man-gets-new-breasts-and-guess-who-s-paying-78k

5 'The British Press and the Transgender Community', Trans Media Watch, December 2011, http://transmediawatch.org/wp-content/uploads/2020/ 09/Publishable-Trans-Media-Watch-Submission.pdf

6 Simon Hoggart, 'Changing the gender agenda', *Guardian*, 25 June 2011, https://www.theguardian.com/theguardian/2011/jun/25/simon-hoggarts-week; Sadie Smith, 'There's no point in online feminism if it's an exclusive, Mean Girls club', *New Statesman*, 21 March 2013, https://www.newstatesman.com/voices/2013/03/theres-no-point-online-feminism-if-its-exclusive-mean-girls-club; Ed West, 'The transgender taboo is a threat to academic freedom', *Daily Telegraph*, 24 January 2012

7 Richard Littlejohn, 'He's not only in the wrong body ... he's in the wrong job', *Daily Mail*, 20 December 2012

8 Mick Hume, 'Daily Mail and Richard Littlejohn did not kill Lucy Meadows', *Press Gazette*, 10 June 2013, https://www.pressgazette. co.uk/daily-mail-and-richard-littlejohn-did-not-kill-lucy-meadows/; Mick Hume, 'The Daily Mail did not kill Lucy Meadows', *Spiked*, 30 May 2013, https://www.spiked-online.com/2013/05/30/the-daily-mail-did-not-kill-lucy-meadows/; Roy Greenslade, 'Daily Mail urged to fire Richard Littlejohn after death of Lucy Meadows', *Guardian*, 22 March 2013, https://www.theguardian.com/media/greenslade/2013/ mar/22/richard-littlejohn-transgender

9 Helen Pidd, 'Lucy Meadows coroner tells press: "shame on you"', *Guardian*, 28 May 2013, https://www.theguardian.com/uk/2013/may/ 28/lucy-meadows-coroner-press-shame

10 Julie Burchill, 'Transsexuals should cut it out', *Observer*, 12 January 2013

11 Juliet Jacques, 'Chelsea Manning, pronouns and the press', *New Statesman*, 5 September 2013, https://www.newstatesman.com/ media/2013/09/chelsea-manning-pronouns-and-press

12 Caitlyn Jenner, 'I thought Trump would help trans people. I was wrong', *Washington Post*, 25 October 2018, https://www.washing tonpost.com/opinions/caitlyn-jenner-i-thought-trump-would-help-the-lgbtq-community-i-was-wrong/2018/10/25/3c4cd61e-d86a-11e8-83a2-d1c3da28d6b6_story.html

13 Sam Levin, Mona Chalabi and Sabrina Siddiqui, 'Why we take issue with the Guardian's stance on trans rights in the UK', *Guardian*, 2

November 2018, https://www.theguardian.com/commentisfree/2018/nov/02/guardian-editorial-response-transgender-rights-uk

14 See Leo McKinstry, '2017 was the year that the madness of transgenderism finally took over', *Daily Express*, 21 December 2017, https://www.express.co.uk/comment/columnists/leo-mckinstry/895046/transgender-madness-2017-year-insanity; Douglas Murray, 'Good riddance 2019, the year of the woke police', *Mail on Sunday*, 29 December 2019, https://www.dailymail.co.uk/debate/article-7833715/DOUGLAS-MURRAY-Good-riddance-2019-year-politically-correct-woke-police.html

15 See Sarah Ditum, 'What's missing from the transgender debate? Any discussion of male violence', *New Statesman*, 30 November 2016, https://www.newstatesman.com/2016/11/whats-missing-transgender-debate-any-discussion-male-violence; James Kirkup, 'The silencing of the lesbians', *Spectator*, 16 May 2018, https://www.spectator.co.uk/article/the-silencing-of-the-lesbians

16 See Janice Turner, 'Children sacrificed to appease trans lobby', *The Times*, 11 November 2017, https://www.thetimes.co.uk/article/children-sacrificed-to-appease-trans-lobby-bq0m2mm95

17 Terry Macdonald, 'Are you now or have you ever been a TERF?', *New Statesman*, 16 February 2015, https://www.newstatesman.com/politics/2015/02/are-you-now-or-have-you-ever-been-terf

18 Trevor Phillips, 'Trans extremists are putting equality at risk', *The Times*, 22 October 2018, https://www.thetimes.co.uk/article/trans-extremists-are-putting-equality-at-risk-fjv8skwz0; Janice Turner, 'Children sacrificed to appease trans lobby', *The Times*, 11 November 2017

19 Jules Joanne Gleeson, 'On the Guardian's transphobic centrism', *New Socialist*, 21 October 2018, https://newsocialist.org.uk/on-the-guardians-transphobic-centrism/

20 'The Guardian view on the Gender Recognition Act: where rights collide', *Guardian*, 17 October 2018, https://www.theguardian.com/commentisfree/2018/oct/17/the-guardian-view-on-the-gender-recognition-act-where-rights-collide

21 Levin, Chalabi and Siddiqui, 'Why we take issue with the Guardian's stance on trans rights in the UK', *Guardian*, 2 November 2018

22 Suzanne Moore, 'Women must have the right to organise. We will not be silenced', *Guardian*, 2 March 2020, https://www.theguardian.com/society/commentisfree/2020/mar/02/women-must-have-the-right-to-organise-we-will-not-be-silenced; Emma Powys Maurice, 'Yet another trans person dramatically quits the Guardian amid bitter transphobia row', *Pink News*, 3 March 2020, https://www.pinknews.co.uk/2020/03/03/the-guardian-another-trans-person-quits-transphobia-coverage-row/

23 'Transgender people face NHS waiting list "hell"', BBC News, 9 January 2020, https://www.bbc.co.uk/news/uk-england-51006264; 'School report', Stonewall, 2017, https://www.stonewall.org.uk/sites/default/files/the_school_report_2017.pdf

'If we are going to do better, we need to start being iconoclastic about the power dynamics and pitfalls of queer influencer culture.'

Shon Faye is an author, journalist, presenter and sometime comedian, whose work has focused on socialism and transgender liberation, queer people's consumption of pop culture, feminism and mental health. Her first book, *The Transgender Issue: An Argument for Justice*, was published in September 2021.

Trans Influencers

SHON FAYE

In spring 2019, I visited the 2pass Clinic in Antwerp, Belgium, for a consultation about my options for surgeries that promised to boost the femininity of my appearance. 2pass is a private clinic specifically catered to transgender women. Its name '2pass' is an unintentionally comical word play on 'to pass', i.e. to pass as female. In essence, the clinic's implicit promise is that it can help its patients look more feminine; it's principally known as a European centre for facial feminisation surgery, a series of procedures on the skull and soft tissue of the face which promise to reverse the effects of male puberty on a trans woman's facial features.

FFS, as it's known, can cost anywhere between £10,000 and £30,000 depending on the amount of 'work' the woman requires. Because so many people travel from outside Belgium to the clinic it has a guest house with private rooms but communal dining. When I stayed the night before my consultation, I sat down for dinner among the other guests. Being surrounded by four or five other women – all with swollen, bandaged faces and black eyes, some of whom were only able to consume liquids due to jaw operations – combined the macabre and the mundane. At times, it felt like I was watching an outtake from *American Horror Story*.

The youngest patient was twenty-five-year-old Jamie Rose Dee, who, when we met, had just had nine different surgical procedures performed on her face. Dee was with her mother and explained to me that she was documenting her surgery on her YouTube channel, where she has over 180,000 subscribers and on Instagram where her follower count is 153,000. Dee had received a significant discount on her facial surgery in exchange for this advertisement of 2pass to her online disciples.

A year on from her surgery, in summer 2020, Dee and I speak again. She's completely healed since our encounter, as I have been following on her Instagram. Her 'new face reveal' post accrued over 10,000 likes and the accompanying YouTube video almost 400,000 views. I'm intrigued by what it's like to go through something so personal in public. 'It's not something that I've just been clueless about. I know that I'm putting myself out there,' she says. 'I sell parts of my personal life to, in the long run, make my life better. I don't think that I would have physically been able to transition and have the procedures and surgeries without the online following.'

Dee grew up on a council estate in the north-east of England in a community where, she says, most people were unemployed and on benefits. Yet under her online screen name, JamJars, she had a second life as a 'Tumblr famous' icon to a generation of teenagers around the globe – a quick google reveals 'JamJars' has its own entry on Urban Dictionary. 'It was a weird dynamic because I would go to school and just be the Jamie that everyone grew up with. But then I was getting fan letters from people in Australia.' This kind of internet fame at such a formative stage in her life has had a lasting effect on Dee's sense of self. She later moved to YouTube and Instagram and in her early twenties came out as transgender.

I'm only seven years older than Jamie Rose Dee but in terms of the rapid development of LGBTQ+ people's visibility on social media I might as well be seventy years older. Certainly, my own experience of using the internet to express and shape my identity as a trans teen was far patchier, and more dismal. Technically, my first experience of 'identifying' as a woman was in online chatrooms circa 2002 where I would pretend to be a hot, blonde twenty-two-year-old with large breasts in conversations with adult men. Sometimes I would become so engrossed in my nervous curiosity I'd forget I was not, in fact, a bouncy blonde woman. Reminders only came when the men would beg me to appear on camera for them, which would have revealed me to be, in fact, a fourteen-year-old boy with brown hair. A reveal that would probably have been awkward for both parties. A decade later and I joined Twitter, where I followed more and more glamorous queer people, who had new and exciting ways to challenge the gender binary in their appearance or their politics – forcing in me the kind of reflections that would eventually result in my transition.

In the 2020s, there are far more ways to be trans online than the clunky web forums of the 2000s. A lot of modern content, though, revolves around physical transition. Ten years ago, insider information would come from forums with names like *Susan's Place*, where a user might cheerfully narrate the ups and downs of getting electrolysis on her scrotal sack prior to vaginoplasty. Now, things are a little more glossy: the trans YouTuber is a subgenre of its own in which glamorous-sounding names like Gigi Gorgeous, Nikita Dragun and Jamie Rose Dee herself share slick face-to-camera content about the physical and mental demands of hormonal and surgical transition.

I've relied a lot on YouTubers in my own transition and find myself addicted to the form: a pretty girl's gleaming veneer smile cheerfully narrates some of the most extreme body modification known to humanity. Some trans women find following other, very beautiful, trans women on Instagram depressing or intimidating – but I was relieved, early in my transition, to fill my daily consciousness with this type of trans beauty, in a world where we are still largely seen as monstrous and encouraged to internalise this harmful self-image. The chief benefit of the explosion in trans content creation has been cutting out the middleman of the mainstream media, which has historically misrepresented, abused or exploited trans people.

Yet the democratisation of power, platform and audience that social media seemed to promise a decade ago turned out to be a chimera. Women, people of colour and LGBTQ+ people who gain any kind of following online are now apparently expected to endure unprecedented levels of abuse and harassment in exchange for their platform. Jamie Rose Dee tells me that vast swathes of online hate have been part of her daily reality since she was fifteen years old and she expects it. 'I take it as part of the job,' she concedes.

Abuse is perpetrated to silence people or at least cause self-censorship, so it is, obviously, one of the largest limitations on LGBTQ+ self-expression online. But everyone knows abuse is a problem. What is less often questioned is the subtler, stifling effect of homogeneity: a lot of the biggest trans content creators tend to look and sound the same. For trans women, the standards are strikingly similar to the standard for cis women in the mainstream media: whiteness, thinness, conventional feminine aesthetics all dominate.

It's not just about beauty standards. When it comes to such a small minority whose safety in public space so often relies on having a 'satisfactory' appearance for cisgender people, the similarity of the aesthetic takes on a political character: it presents a homogenous view of what being trans is, what it means and what it looks like to a wider audience in a way that becomes necessarily reductive. '[It's] just regurgitations of the same old story that makes us boring and dead and *safe* to read about,' writes Kai Cheng Thom in the foreword to *Fierce Femmes and Notorious Liars: A Dangerous Trans Girl's Confabulous Memoir.*[1] She was referring to the trans autobiography as a literary form, but I think the sentiment rings true for much of the content created by big name trans influencers online, too. What, according to Thom, is 'the same old story' being told over and over again? '[I]f you're good and brave and patient (and white and rich) enough, then you get the big reward ... which is that you get to be just like everybody else who is white and rich and boring.'

The rise of the online 'influencer' – essentially a high-profile Instagram user, typically a young female, whose services are engaged by big brands to market products to their followers – has introduced a capitalist incentive to what might have otherwise just been seen as a shallow popularity contest. There's money to be made here and, for trans people, there's a particular attraction for selling parts of their lives in exchange for financial access to healthcare in a society in which trans healthcare is not valued by the state and remains unobtainable for many. It is also worth remembering that the employment market still remains closed to many trans people. Conditions are so hostile that one in eight trans people in Britain has been physically attacked while at work.[2]

Capitalism is always insidious but in online influencer culture, one of its most insidious mechanisms is the hiring of people from marginalised or minority communities in order to present a facade of corporate social justice. LGBTQ+ pride, fat liberation, Black Lives Matter and feminism are all radical movements which have proven ripe for corporate misappropriation. As writer Huw Lemmey puts it: 'Consumer capitalism operates through the recuperation of aesthetics, dynamics and culture of social struggle, but usually at a safe distance.'[3] In the case of trans people, there is a co-option of the stories and hardships endured by individual trans people as a marketing ploy: transphobia is not here understood or presented as a systemic injustice endemic to capitalism; it is a personal misfortune, a 'backstory' which can be triumphantly overcome at the individual level, with the help of brands and consumption.

Stories like Jamie Rose Dee's, as a working-class trans woman who privately funded her transition, are held up as inspiring. While that may be true, they should come with the caveat that they are exceptional. They also mask the fact that the surgeons are often themselves brands, and their clinics are profit-making enterprises. Gender affirmative healthcare is envisioned only as a luxury private service for trans people to strive towards when, in reality, trans healthcare is a human right that should be available to all.

Of course, I don't blame influencers for operating cannily within this environment. I, too, have written articles or done panels or worked with brands out of desperation to fund my own transition. But the question remains about whether the individualised promise of empowerment that now reigns online is actively inhibiting collective liberation for all trans people by means of distracting them from the material conditions of their oppression. I think, regrettably, it's all a bit of a dazzling sideshow.

A select few trans individuals' ability to exchange their online visibility for a degree of material comfort perpetuates a narrative that visibility equals safety. However, this is simply not the case for trans people in Black and brown communities, especially those who work in the criminalised economies of drugs or sex work. As writer Alex V. Green notes in a 2019 longread for Buzzfeed News, for many trans people of colour, 'visibility doesn't translate to acceptance, but greater attention, scrutiny, and restriction'.[4] I agree: clearly, for all the visibility and autonomy the internet has brought trans people, it hasn't made all our lives safer, either online or off.

Even where the internet has been important in trans communities for guaranteeing anonymity or physical safety, it is now increasingly an arena for state surveillance of LGBTQ+ people, especially sex workers. Tumblr, the platform on which Jamie Rose Dee first achieved online fame, barely exists as an LGBTQ+ online space anymore thanks to a wide-ranging ban it imposed on its users in December 2018 which restricted so-called 'adult content'. The rules changing in this way led many queer and trans users to feel policed and they simply left. Restrictive legislation against online sex work means that trans sex workers, the trans people statistically most likely to be murdered, are forced to flee to ever more dangerous environments.[5]

Visibility is not the revolution many of us hoped it would be. But I am not completely pessimistic about the future; if we are to have better ways to express ourselves online then we need to stop idealising the internet as an apolitical space where the individual can forge their own path to prosperity, comfort, community, sexual liberation or love. This is just more capitalist mythmaking, a digital regurgitation of the American Dream that queer people should refuse to buy into.

In a short space of time between my adolescence and the generation of trans young adults coming of age now, the internet did indeed transform trans representation in unimaginable ways. Trans people went from being universally ridiculed on television and forced to hide from intrusion by the tabloid press to hugely visible, liked and even held up as beautiful online. If things can change that much between when I grew up and when Jamie grew up, for the next generation I'd like to see us go even further and focus more on using the internet as an instrument for structural change as much as a tool for individual advancement.

Offline politics and online politics influence one another and improvement in the material conditions of trans people's lives 'irl' – in real life – would help us online, too. For example, free and accessible healthcare for trans people would relieve the financial pressure on young trans creators to exchange their candour for decent care or be forced into ever more imbalanced labour relations with brands who use them to sell products. Less of a reliance on brands as agents of change and more on using the internet creatively for grassroots activism instead of 'influencing' would help bring the benefits currently enjoyed only by the handful of the prettiest and luckiest into common ownership.

On a lighter note, I also want the internet to give us more ways to express ourselves aesthetically. When I look at how my own appearance and style has evolved in my ten years on Twitter and seven years on Instagram, I've frankly got more boring. Somewhere along the line I must have realised I got more praise and less abuse for looking like a Marks & Spencer-clad PTA secretary than I did dressing like a genderqueer Courtney Love. It would be nice for us to have more honest community conversations about the pressure Instagram creates for us all to look and be a certain way and about who is setting those, often impossible, expectations. This is complicated work but the benefits of greater connection and community the online space can still offer us, I believe, makes it worth it.

If we are going to do better, we need to start being iconoclastic about the power dynamics and pitfalls of queer influencer culture. Even better, we need to surrender our myths of individual empowerment to find creative new ways of doing collective politics online. The internet has been the most powerful tool we've ever had when it comes to queer representation. Let's think strategically about how we use it in the future in ways that really do liberate us.

1 Kai Cheng Thom, *Fierce Femmes and Notorious Liars: A Dangerous Trans Girl's Confabulous Memoir* (Montreal: Metonymy Press, 2016)
2 'LGBT in Britain – Trans Report (2018)', Stonewall, January 2018, https://www.stonewall.org.uk/lgbt-britain-trans-report
3 https://twitter.com/huwlemmey/status/1268167808665432066
4 Alex V. Green, 'Trans visibility won't save us', BuzzFeed News, 4 December 2019, https://www.buzzfeednews.com/article/alexverman/trans-visibility-wont-save-us
5 Boglarka Fedorko and Lukas Berredo, 'The vicious circle of violence: Trans and gender-diverse people, migration, and sex work', TvT Publication Series, vol. 16, TGEU, October 2017, https://transrespect.org/wp-content/uploads/2018/01/TvT-PS-Vol16-2017.pdf

DATING, LOVE AND FAMILY

'More tolerance of grey areas would make self-discovery easier for many of us ... I am not going to apologise for fluidity.'

Naoise Dolan is an Irish writer. Her debut novel *Exciting Times* was a *Sunday Times* bestseller, and her work has appeared in the *London Review of Books*, *Granta* and *Vogue*.

Know Thyself, or Don't

NAOISE DOLAN

As a queer novelist, I veer between motives. One is to depict LGBTQ+ people as individuals, as complicated, and the other is to make them as universally likable as possible. Expectations also weigh on me, from cisgender heterosexuals who read my work anthropologically ('Whatever are the gays up to now?') to those who wish to see themselves. I try to please everyone. Three words in, I remember I can't. Art has starved the community of visibility, so we might understandably snap when served things we can't eat. Still, unexamined 'relatability' is corporate. It reduces experience to branding. It's admirable to give LGBTQ+ readers someone to root for, to show us winning, but it's not the only worthy aim. You might want to do other things it's incompatible with. Representation is a wedding gift list: it works best if we all choose different things, and less well if we all come with spatulas. I serve up terrible people and trust other writers will offer role models. None of my characters are direct analogues of me or anyone I know, but they are messy and conflicted because that's life as I know it.

The way I have described my own sexuality is complicated, too. I only call myself 'queer' or 'gay' now. I know I'm sapphic, but whenever I have specified lesbian or bi, the label has soon felt like a target. There are many reasons for that. I first encountered labels as slurs levelled at me against my wishes, and I suffered trauma from anti-autistic ableism and sexual assault. All of this made me both desperate to understand myself and completely unable to do so. Rather than letting my past define me negatively, I now embrace fluidity as part of who I am. But it took me a long time to get there.

Let's start with school. Can you remember which year your primary class discovered the word 'lesbian'? I can, because the general riposte was to call me one. Kids screamed it at me, so I denied it. I was a runt. I was terrified of flying basketballs, more so of people, of loud noises and rule-breaking and any more social disapproval than I already faced for my obvious desire to hide in my sock until adulthood. So I said, no, I'm not a lesbian.

In my teens, I realised I liked girls. I thought: Well, it would be wrong to have lied about not being a lesbian, so I guess that makes me bi. I wish there were more to it than that. But I was fourteen and didn't know my arse from my elbow, and that wasn't my fault. My parents rationed my internet, and the books around me didn't offer frameworks for describing myself. The first queer writing I read was from Emma Donoghue, Sarah Waters and Oscar Wilde. They changed my life and possibly even saved it, but they don't usually discuss contemporary labels. (In Wilde's case, cadavers are generally silent on the topic.) Later I'd find Audre Lorde and James Baldwin, and later again young queer writers working now. At the time, though, I was on my own.

So when a friend asked on messenger, 'Are you gay?', I didn't want to say no. I typed, 'I'm bi.' It sent and was fact, and my mother yelled from the kitchen that my time was up. A whole identity, and I really couldn't take this one back.

That's one of those memories you don't want to air in mixed company, because to say a bisexual person is 'really something else' is biphobic: bisexuals often hear that they must really only be attracted to one gender. I would never want my experience to be taken as generally representing bisexuality. It just happens that in my particular case, I fumbled for a term that was queer, but that was different to the ones I'd had slapped on me. That reasoning felt dishonest, but nothing was honest in my teens. Publicly I stayed entirely closeted. Privately I told a few people I was bi, and often got the usual 'gay-in-denial' or 'straight-seeking-attention' responses – the former more than the latter, since I was still a designated lesbian in the broader Dublin secondary school miasma. If I'd imagined selecting my own label would free me, I was wrong. The policing only took a different form.

God, you couldn't pay me to be sixteen again. Why couldn't I come out when it was something lots of the other kids were saying about me anyway? And why the rush to define a sexuality that was still pretty much entirely theoretical? At that age I wholly, resoundingly did not fuck. A cocktail of mental illnesses soon left me biochemically unable to crave much of anything, and my body was all of me, although I urged it not to be. When I did start sleeping around, I felt nothing and wanted nothing, and only did it because I thought I had no choice. With all that to work through, and with intense social pressure to deny how I was feeling, knowing myself became even harder.

When I moved from school to university, it was no longer in the surrounding collective conscious that I'd been called a lezzer for eight years. I was what I had wished for, had cried myself to sleep wishing for: assumed straight. I promptly hated it. Dutifully, though, I got with men. College was the first place I'd remotely fitted in, and I was desperate to shore up my acceptance. I really can't say if there are circumstances in which I'd have wanted men sincerely. Having spent my formative years numbing my ability to process the world, I'm amazed I can still tell if it's raining or not. And because, to me, identity comes from your past, I'm still getting there with labels.

All of this has been further complicated by the autism diagnosis I got last year. It was never an 'invisible' disability, it's just that I'd learned to hide it from those who were already bullying me. My efforts – mimicking the gestures, speech and overall behaviour of those around me – 'worked' to make me eventually less repulsive to ableists, i.e. virtually everyone. That's not pejorative. It's just true. A tiny example: if you say someone doesn't make eye contact, 99% of people will assume you mean they're dodgy. It hurts me to meet most people's eye. Again, I'm not exaggerating. Pain is what my nervous system does with that input, so I intuitively flinch, just as I avoid cacti, needles and the face of Nicolas Cage. Also, when I do try to fake eye contact, I have no instinct for timing: I look over too often or not often enough. The whole sorry fandango freaks me out so much that I'm sure I come across shiftier than if I'd been allowed to look away. Eye contact is one thing. Imagine dealing with that across all aspects of interaction.

I can't separate queerness and autism, because they both come from the same brain that tells the rest of my body what to do. I still don't know how to express myself without deliberately performing, and that means I have no fixed identity. I can't easily distinguish between the behaviours that came from masking my sexuality, and those that came from masking my disability.

So you can see why I'm figuring things out. This process would go more smoothly if I could behave authentically now, but my need to hide didn't come from nowhere. It came from homophobia and ableism. There's nothing irrational about my social inhibition: it's a learned response to stimuli. There are still many scenarios where I'm punished for 'being myself', so maybe I want society to change first. Maybe I'd drop the mask if it were safe. I am furious about this, because constant performance saps my energy from the things I actually want to do in life.

I've lived in many cities and don't want to generalise. Some spaces I've found keen to police identity, others have accepted fluidity, and many are in between. My guilt and imposter syndrome over labels haven't come from individual malice, but from a society that collectively pressures people to define themselves before they're ready, often without meaning to. While I've chosen here to outline some of the experiences that have made me the way I am, I shouldn't have to offer this information to strangers before they'll respect my identity. Other fluid people have their own stories, and their own right to privacy. More tolerance of grey areas would make self-discovery easier for many of us. I wish I'd had room to breathe when I was a kid. I wish the concept of sexuality hadn't come to me through bullying, and I wish my approach to my identity hadn't been shaped around reacting to that discrimination. I can't get those years back, but I want that space now, and I want to allow other people theirs.

I am not going to apologise for fluidity. I'm compelled to embrace the one thing I know I am, which is: hard to pin down. I don't want queer to be a compromise or a 'please update your laptop'. It might apply for the rest of my life, and that's fine. I know little about myself for reasons largely beyond my control, and I'm going to keep learning. Still, my lack of clear category is something I choose to own. What's queerness if not saying, this opacity could be for ever and it's mine?

'The first step in building a kinder queer community is learning to love ourselves for who we truly are, not punishing ourselves for who we have "failed" to be.'

Amrou Al-Kadhi is a drag queen, writer and filmmaker based in London. They are the author of the multi-award-winning memoir *Life as a Unicorn*, which is being adapted for television by NBC-Universal in America. Their screenwriting credits include *Little America*, *The Watch* and *Hollyoaks* and they are currently developing several new projects for TV and film.

Single and Fabulous?

AMROU AL-KADHI

Like all human beings, I'm riddled with insecurities – but chief among them is the fact I'm thirty this year and have still never been in a long-term relationship. I'm cringing just writing this down (cringing hard, folks). Now, if you're not aware of my work – and it's OK, I can handle it if you aren't (sobs in bathroom) – I'm a bit like Carrie Bradshaw, if Carrie was a six-foot Iraqi drag queen who downs antidepressants instead of Cosmopolitans, and instead of scoring dates with rich, hot men like Mr Big, scrolls on Grindr home alone next to my satanic puppy.

It's odd, not much makes me shy; singing about Allah on stage while thrusting a stiletto into my ass doesn't induce so much as a butterfly flutter, and I find putting the often grim, sometimes absurd truth of my family history and sexual mishaps out in the open almost mundane. But the fact that I've never convinced a man to love me long-term ... well ... it makes me want to curl up like a pathetic little armadillo. When I see a queer couple in a long-term relationship, it genuinely feels like sci-fi to me. It's so foreign to my way of life that it leaves me burning with questions: So, wait ... you just show all of yourselves to one other all the time with no consequences? Are you not constantly on eggshells that a flaw will slip out and they'll see the real you? Do you not live in terror that the other person is imminently going to leave you?

I think anyone who has suffered trauma can hold these questions; but I also think that the trauma I've experienced as a result of being queer has amplified them in my brain. Psychologically, as queer people, we're given a lot to battle with (that's on top of the regular existential crap that comes with being human). Figuring out how to love yourself amid the torrent is a bit like trying to swim freely in a pool filled with custard. And that's before you even enter a partnership with another queer person, who might *also* be carrying the weight of years of sometimes subtle, sometimes overt societal shame and stigma. How the hell does that work?! To *my* shame, I've never been able to get there. What, then, are the hurdles that we face when it comes to forming strong and caring relationships with others in the LGBTQ+ community, and how might we take them down? I'll try and answer this by telling you about my own experiences.

My mother – gorgeous, hilarious, loving and on this occasion devastatingly harsh – once said this to me: 'I'll never have to worry about coming to your wedding, because you will never convince anybody to love you.' Cute, right? I was twenty, and we were doing our weekly catch-up where she'd ask if I had suddenly reversed my 'decision' to be gay. It seemed to me that for mama, my being queer was intrinsic to my being unlovable. And so I internalised the belief that the societal rejection of my sexuality went hand in hand with my inevitable rejection by all prospective partners.

Adolescent puberty happens at a time when the brain is still maturing, with your desires conditioned in tandem with new neural pathways – for me, and millions of other queer people, my desires were warped by malign forces. I was taught from as young as I can remember that my being gay would lead to a lifetime in hell. In Islam, hell isn't just an idea – it's a very real destination for sinners, and one we are taught to tangibly conjure up in our head every day; a place where punishments include drinking boiling water, consuming 'fruits' that rip up your insides, and non-stop torture with absolutely no way out. Though reminiscent of any Berlin fetish club worth its salt, hell for me was a terrifying and certain prospect, leading to recurring nightmares where Allah himself was binding me to a slab of hot metal and ripping off my testicles with a scythe. Quite camp really. When I finally reached adulthood and left home, I thought I had flushed this way of thinking out of my system. Then I started dating.

When I was at university, I fell for a gorgeous young man, who I kissed for the first time on a historic bridge as the sun was rising following a night of endless champagne (think *Brideshead Revisited* plus one token Iraqi). We went on a date, and it was wonderful. Romantic, passionate, sexy, full of laughter, hope and prospect. Here was someone ready to love me, against all the odds. And I adored him. So when he texted me asking for that prized second date, it surprised even me that I couldn't respond. I desperately wanted to, but whenever my hands went to type a reply, I felt sick in my gut – a lifetime of expecting punishment because of my desires was manifesting in physical aversion. I ignored the text, and did the thing most typical of assholes – I ghosted him. I've been on the receiving end of ghosting a few times; not only is it maddening, but the silence becomes a wormhole in which you start reflecting on everything you did to deserve being tossed aside.

A few weeks later, we bumped into each other at a London nightclub. Ever the gentleman, he was attentive, patient and charming (looking gorgeous too, to add insult to injury). Even though it had been my dream to gain this kind of genuine affection, I became so irrationally stressed that I went to hide in the loo and suffered a panic attack. I subsequently had to run home, leaving him there without so much as a polite goodbye. It was bizarre – as if my desires were at war with my brain. I so wanted to be with him, but my now deep-set thought patterns were screaming that not only was it sinful, but that him actually liking me was a fallacy. I mean, how could a guy as nice as him actually want someone as worthless as me? And so, because of the cruelty I had once endured, I treated him with cruelty, and ignored him for the rest of my student years. I ran into him at a party during my final term, where he told me about the intense impact of my behaviour. I feel guilty about it to this day.

Through a lot of therapy, a lot of conversations with other queer people, and, dare I say it, a lot negative experiences – I've learned that it's not just my own poor psychological grammar that's to blame for all of this. That there is a bigger problem at play. If homophobia in my family left me feeling unlovable, the LGBTQ+ community, to *its* great shame, hasn't always been kinder. Perhaps then, improving the relationship we have with ourselves is contingent on the interactions we have with those around us.

The gay 'male' community (in which nonbinary and trans people of course operate) is a melting pot of infinite inherited and learned traumas, and can be a cesspit of toxicity. This is especially the case if you are not white, masculine and cisgender. I'm Arab, femme and nonbinary. *Result*. Queer people like me have had to get used to men on dating apps insulting us with: 'Straight acting only'; 'I don't fuck sissys'; 'NO ASIANS'; and my personal favourite: 'I don't sleep with fags.' THEN WHAT ARE WE ALL DOING HERE, HUN?! The cumulative effect of these comments led me to avoid putting photos of myself in drag on Tinder – it's a brutal fact that this will lead to fewer matches. What is this cruelty doing here?

Many gay men are led to believe that their sexuality is their emasculation – and so, within gay spaces, they enjoy a kind of hypermasculinity, an embodiment of the thing they were told was out of their reach. There is finally the chance to leave a childhood of feeling like a failure behind; when reminded of their 'failings', they often react with cruelty. Many gay men also reject anything that looks like otherness, believing that 'I grew up feeling like an outsider, so now I should get to feel like an insider as much as possible.' Added to this is the impulse to attack any marginalised groups within the queer community who they see as potentially threatening their bid to conform.

I too am culpable. I can't deny that I am seduced by the idea of being married to a white, cisgender, masculine gay man, with the associated safety of a white picket fence. It shames me to admit this. But after an entire life of being told I was worthless, winning the devotion of an Adonis gay would feel like the greatest trophy of all, and the ultimate 'fuck you' to all the critical voices in my head. It is generated by a childhood desperation to feel legitimate, and the deluded belief that 'earning' what the world denied me would somehow mitigate my shame. It took me years to learn that this too was an illusion.

This came to the fore in a brief romance I had with one such Prince Charming. I was doing a drag performance at a festival, and Mr Darcy was in the audience. Once I finished, he came to find me backstage. I was excited – this textbook hunk has seen me in all my femme brown glory, and still wants me? Is this a mirage?! It felt like I'd hit the jackpot: someone like him didn't care that I was femme or brown (I know how this sounds, by the way). I came to learn, however, that he wanted me so much *because* I was femme and brown. As somebody who embodied the zenith of the gay male hierarchy, he apparently assumed that I would be a submissive person, that I would willingly sacrifice all my power because I had the privilege of wearing him as my medal. Anything that destabilised this dynamic was not tolerated. He looked furious when he learned I made more money than him and when I challenged him intellectually. As a femme brown queer, my social forth-rightness upset the pecking order that we all silently acknowledge in the gay community. When he dumped me, he said it was because I was 'too difficult'. With some hindsight, it seems to me that his way of coping with shame was through upholding the traditional 'masculine' role in any relationship. His stand-in wife speaking up shattered this fantasy.

I've since learned that validation will never come through winning the attention of men who 'tick the boxes', but only through embracing and celebrating my own iden-tity. My failed relationships often entailed my operating like a chameleon, adjusting who I am to accommodate the egos of others. But that strategy's doomed to fail, for the relationship is premised on a self-belittling fiction.

The first step in building a kinder queer community is learning to love ourselves for who we truly are, not punishing ourselves for who we have 'failed' to be. I've embraced the idea that my queerness is not the absence of something, but an abundance – of having something the world that excluded me doesn't. For me, this shift in my behaviour came from embracing drag as a lifestyle, not just a second closet which I tap into a few nights a week. Drag is an unapologetic celebration of the self, one that upends the flaws society might perceive in you, so I try to practise the level of power I get from my drag performances in my everyday life. One exercise I enjoy doing at home is dressing up in drag and then walking as slowly as possible across the living-room floor, treating every step like a cinematic event. It can feel as if space and time are bending. I now teach this exercise on beginner drag courses – it's all about living for the sheer majesty of yourself, even when doing the most mundane of things, like breathing or napping. We may live in a world that doesn't exalt us – so why not let our queerness exalt us as it should?

This has brought me to a much better place. I've recently put my iconic drag photos on dating profiles. It leads to fewer swipe-rights, that's for sure – but at least I know that if they do like me, they're doing so knowing about *all* of me. In any case, I've come to see my single status as something tied to my queer identity in a way that's empowering; in having a more loving relationship with myself, a partner is not an imperative – it would just be a bonus, should the right one come along. My hope going forward is that as queer people, we stop recycling the rejection we've individually amassed onto our own community, and instead treat one another with kindness and compassion. It's tough enough out there.

'It's imperative and urgent that we begin to not only erase trans dating stigma, but also support and promote positive images of the people who love and care for us.'

Peppermint is an actor and singer. She was the first trans woman to create a principal role in a Broadway musical. She's been involved in the fight for LGBTQ+ equality for decades.

On the Stigma of Dating Trans People

PEPPERMINT

When I was a kid, the only trans women I remember seeing were on *The Jerry Springer Show*, a trashy daytime tabloid talk show. The same thing would always happen: Jerry would bring on a woman and she would talk a little bit about her relationship. 'But ...' she would say, 'I have a big secret.' Then her lover would come on so that she could confess to them – on national television – that 'I was born a man' or 'I'm trans' or 'I'm not really a woman.' Often, the lovers would be disgusted, or even react by beating the woman up. One time, I remember, the guy hit the woman with a chair. That was the reaction – it was never a conversation, only violence.

Those memories have shaped how I approach a man and talk to a man – they inform every decision that I make when meeting a prospective partner. Given that this is what I grew up watching – what so much of America grew up watching – it's probably no surprise that the majority of my dating experiences have been what I would call 'negative', that in my dating life I've faced a lot of (for lack of a better word) 'bullshit'.

I identify as a straight trans woman. My perspective on dating when you're trans is specifically about heterosexual relationships between trans women and 'transamorous men' – a term that many in the community use for the men who date trans women. The fact that there is a term at all is telling; dating trans women is still highly stigmatized. It's seen as abnormal.

Over the years, most of the focus and conversation when it comes to trans issues has been on transgender women themselves, whether it's the surgeries that we've had, how we dress, what we used to look like versus, you know, our Transformation Tuesday! There's been very little focus in the media – film, television, books, any type of public resource – on the overall livelihood of the person, and certainly not on positive relationships among trans individuals and the people who love them.

When we talk about trans dating, we usually only talk about the trans person. And if we do talk about the partner, it's mostly in the context of something negative: either targeting him because 'he likes trans women – he must be gay!' or, more often, discussing the horrific cases when trans people have been murdered by their partners. Now, I'm not a criminal investigator, but based on the stories I've seen, violence against trans women and particularly trans women of color in the US is regularly committed by somebody who has been romantically or sexually involved with the victim. Go to the website of the Anti-Violence Project – a charity that tracks these murders in the US – and you will see that this is true; often the perpetrator is the partner.

This negativity is all we tend to see in the media, but it's not just trans women who see it – it's men who date us too. If what they're seeing is violence towards trans women and men *killing* trans women, then subconsciously, that has to affect their opinion of us and their behavior. Certainly, what we are not seeing is the general idea that it's good or okay to be dating us. And that's a problem.

If there is an epidemic of trans women being murdered at the hands of their lovers or sexual partners, then it's imperative and urgent that we begin to not only erase trans dating stigma, but also support and promote positive images of the people who love and care for us. We must show people how to do a better job, and how to be gentle, kind and respectful.

I look back at my dating experiences and one thing I notice is that a lot of them are marked by secrecy. Myself and a certain partner would only exist in my apartment, because they didn't want their roommate or anyone else to know. Once, I had a first date with some dude and on the date he said: 'Well, I'm glad we didn't meet in public because I could never date you. You basically have the body of a linebacker.' All of this says to me, 'You're not worthy of being seen with me.' It forces our relationships into a kind of closet, and sets up the pretense that we are going to operate in a compartmentalized world where a guy won't share his real phone number, say, or his real name.

This behavior, I believe, is rooted in homophobia – and that's not to say that transphobia isn't real. I think transphobia is often a *type* of homophobia. If society feeds certain men the idea that trans women are really men, they think it makes them gay to date us, and that is, in their minds, the worst thing that they could be called. Seeing another person give up their – at least perceived – masculinity to comfortably identify as a woman also offends their own masculinity, and reminds them of the other terrible thing that they could be called: a woman. To me, transphobia is a blend of homophobia and misogyny, wrapped into one.

People tell me, 'It's not transphobic to say you don't want to date trans women, it's just a type.' Here's what

I'd say to them: there's a really thin, blurry line between preference and prejudice. People say: 'I don't date trans women, I just couldn't do it. There's no trans woman who could ever turn me on.' I think that a lot of people would defend that sort of speaking. But if you simply substituted the word 'trans' for 'Black' or 'Asian' or 'disabled', then that sort of talk would be seen as more discriminatory and prejudiced. It is, for instance, unquestionably a blanket statement to say you could never date any Black woman. In essence, there's only one reason why you couldn't date all Black women, seeing as though all Black women are not identical. The only thing that all Black women have in common is the fact that they are Black. And if that is the only reason that you are excluding them then it is, by definition, racist.

Similarly, all trans women are not the same, we don't all look the same, and we don't all behave the same in a relationship. So if that is the only factor that you are using – that we are trans – then you are saying two things. Firstly, that you're going to instantly judge all trans women and paint them with the same brush, which is discrimination. And secondly, that you don't think trans women are 'real' women.

One place we see this play out a lot is on dating apps – partly because they're mostly image-focused, so you swipe people based on their picture, and also because people seem to act on their prejudices more when they're hiding behind a screen. I've been using one dating app for a few years, and early on, my account was inexplicably deleted. As I don't believe that I mistreated anyone or violated the app's terms or conditions, I can only assume that I was reported when other users discovered that the woman they swiped right on – and whose profile says in capital letters 'I'M TRANS' – was, in fact, trans. What was I supposed to do beyond writing it on my profile? Send them a tele-pathic signal? If you see my picture, and you swipe right, that's on you. If you don't read my profile, and you decide to have a conversation with me, that's also on you. What this experience brings up is the issue of disclosing – that's when, whether and how you choose to say you're trans. Disclosing is sort of coming out on an individual-to-individual level. In an ideal world, you wouldn't have to disclose but I guess we don't yet live in that world.

Disclosing is a personal decision, so it's important for each person to make it for themselves. I'm sure that there are some people who make a different decision on different occasions – but because I live a fast-paced sort of life and I don't have time to psychologize people who don't have anything to do with me yet, I put it all out there upfront. For me, the question is: If you're going to have the misfor-tune of matching with someone who will react negatively, when do you want that reaction to come? I want to avoid all of that later on. I want people to know early that, yes, I'm trans. This is who I am. And if you want to talk to me, then you need to treat me with respect right from the start.

When I haven't disclosed, I've found that men have been able to get off the hook with bad behavior, using this as an excuse to shift accountability for their decisions and actions. Historically, men have been allowed to say: 'Oh God! I was just going with the flow – I didn't realize she was trans!' – like it wasn't his fault that he mistreated us, or, in some cases, murdered us. In many US states, there is still something called the 'trans panic defense', whereby trans women are positioned as the perpetrators in court for 'tricking' men into thinking they are cisgender, as though that explains away the man's subsequent act of violence. Like it all had to do with the element of surprise. If until recently courts of law endorsed the idea that shock or panic was an excuse for people to harm us, then isn't that sending out the message that violence is a reasonable reaction to have?

Another problem disclosing brings is that we run the risk of attracting people who are just going to fetishize our transness. This means that often when folks do like you as a trans person, they're focused on having sex with you and nothing else. We are seen as exotic sexual encounters who are not relationship-oriented. Of course, it's fine if individuals only want casual sex and not a relationship, but it's more than a coincidence when every single interaction starts to be like that.

In some ways, it makes sense that this happens when you consider that a lot of people only see us literally as a category on a porn site – at least until recently, when media visibility began to improve a little. I'm not demonizing porn, and I'm not demonizing sexual attraction, but really, it doesn't take very long to get the sense that you are an object when a person starts listing off what they want from you sexually, without asking you what your preferences are. Or when they are so excited by whatever they're getting from this situation sexually, they're not even aware that you are no longer enjoying yourself.

Fetishization does not support a healthy sexual connection. It does not support conversations about consent, what is acceptable and what is not, or whether you've each been tested. Too often the only conversations around STI and HIV testing is the man asking the trans woman if she has been tested: 'As long as the trans woman has been tested, then I can do anything I want.' This disregard for our needs and safety happens because a lot of people think of a trans person as a fetish, an object, a throw-away experience.

For me, this treatment often has a negative effect and causes me to put up emotional walls, and other trans women I've talked to have experienced the same. It's made me assume that men are going to cancel and flake on me on a first date. It's made it hard for me to open up to people. But it's been getting slowly better, which is a sign that the world is getting better. Recently, I've had nice exchanges with men letting me know from the get-go that they've seen me disclosing that I'm trans and can respect it. How they do that varies, but along with saying I'm trans in my dating app profile, I say that I love ice cream, and sometimes a guy will say: 'I read your profile and I love ice cream too.' That's him telling me that he accepts who I am and that my being trans is not going to be the focus of the conversation. We'll just have ice cream, and it'll be great.

While things are gradually improving, a lot more can be done to tackle all of the issues above. To start with, there's the media. We've come a long way since those depictions on *Jerry Springer* and there have been positive media representations. Take the show *Transparent* – I'll highlight the writing and leave aside the allegations regarding one of its actors – which showed the complexities of trans dating. And then, more hopefully, there's Angel's relationship in season 2 of *Pose*. It's TV, so it of course has drama, but the relationship doesn't always come back to Angel being trans, and we see someone who loves this woman, unabashedly, saying: Can I support you? I love you. I'm here. That's just so rare to see. We need more of it! As gatekeepers, people in the media need to find and create positive stories of romantic, loving relationships that value trans individuals without centering on their transness, or that celebrate (rather than denigrate) their identities.

On top of this, we still really need some positive examples of trans dating among people in the public eye. If there were more high-profile people who felt comfortable enough to share their relationships with the world, knowing that they would be supported and not ridiculed, that would create a big shift. In the last ten years, we've arrived at a place where it's not acceptable to publish articles outing trans people. Now that we've done this, I hope we can get to a place where no one is ever 'outed' or ridiculed for dating a trans person.

As for our day-to-day lives, it's important to focus on individual relationships. A lot of trans people I know are dating other trans people because they 'get' each other. That's good! I would love a beautiful trans man to strike up a conversation and ask me on a date. (It's not that I can't ask a man on a date, but I'm just praying that some universe brings him to me!) But I would also like us to be able to date people who are not trans, and for them to show up for us. From conversations I've had, it seems that within the trans community – and particularly among trans women of color – our partners aren't yet supporting us as much as they could. Maybe that's because we haven't made space for them or they haven't created space in their lives to fully support us. That's a real shame, though. I want to see our partners acknowledging the things we are up against – whether it's politicians' discriminatory comments or the high rate of violent crimes against us, to talk about it, and to become a part of the solution. There's only one trans woman that I know whose partner spoke out about these subjects in public and that trans woman was on the cover of *Time* magazine! That's excellent, but I want to see everyone being uplifted and praised in the same way.

To make this happen, I think people will need to risk being more open. I know that it's scary, but there is strength in numbers. While it is not rare for cis people to date trans people, we need to create the space in both the media and our everyday lives so that this can be more visible. Don't assume that someone's partner is not trans. Don't be surprised when a trans woman introduces you to her cisgender boyfriend. Don't be surprised when you learn that he's heterosexual. Accept straight partners of trans people coming into gay bars. If you know someone who's a trans woman, and you invite her over to your family holiday dinner, ask her if her partner would like to come too. If you have a friend who is a cisgender heterosexual male, and you find out he is dating a trans girl, invite her to watch the game with you and all the other couples. Bring her into your circle of friends. Invite her as his guest to a wedding.

Of course, eliminating transphobia in general will help eradicate trans dating stigma over time. But I don't think we need to conquer the wider issue of discrimination before trans people can have more respectful encounters. We can start now.

So, to cis people, I would say: Remember that you would be lucky to date a trans person. The world is not always kind to trans people, so we have put a lot of thought, time and energy into getting to a place where we're living our truth and are happy. Many of us have faced prejudice, lost our jobs or our families, and struggled to get to wherever we are today. In my eyes, that's character-building – it means that we're not only thinking about ourselves, but also the effect we have on other people. Transitioning has meant that when I go into a room, I am conscious of my behavior, of my emotions, of what I'm projecting into the world (it's almost like a spidey sense). And I'm not alone in that. I believe that I've become more sensitive and attentive, and that any person would benefit from being with someone who has done all of this work.

To my trans siblings, my message would be this: Don't accept less. Find someone who makes you laugh and who you can argue with (and win these arguments!). I want you to find someone who feels as overjoyed and excited about you as you do about them, and who doesn't mistreat you.

As Dr Angela Davis says: 'If we want to develop an intersectional perspective, the trans community is showing us the way ... This community has taught us how to challenge that which is totally accepted as normal.'[1] We trans and nonbinary folks hold an understanding and communication that exceeds convention. There is such power in that. Although you may feel misunderstood, you are powerful.

---

1 In an interview with Dark Entries Records. Available at https://www.facebook.com/DarkEntriesRecords/videos/4049025058500829/

'So many in the LGBTQ+ community have fought for same-sex marriage to be recognised, but it feels like no one is fighting for disabled people to have access to those rights without compromising our independence.'

Andrew Gurza is an award-winning disability awareness consultant whose written work has been featured in several publications and anthologies, continuing the conversation about queerness and disability. Andrew is the host of the *Disability After Dark* podcast. He/they are thirty-six, use a power wheelchair and live in Toronto, Canada.

Happily Ever After Isn't Accessible to Me

ANDREW GURZA

In 2005, when same-sex marriage became legal in Canada, I can remember the excitement in the air. There was a sense of renewed hope within the LGBTQ+ community that was intoxicating. As a young queer person, this felt like a big step forward, but as a disabled queer person specifically, I knew deep down that little would change for me.

In 2012, my best friend called to tell me that she was getting married. I was, of course, so excited for her. We chatted on the phone for hours and hours about what her dress would be like; her hot fiancé, and what it would be like for her to take these next steps. Amid all my excitement and joy for my best friend's life-changing moment, I'll admit that, sat in my wheelchair on the phone, there was a part of me that felt an unmistakable pang of sadness. As I get older and inch closer to my forties, I see more wedding and baby announcements than ever before, old friends reaching those new milestones that we're all expected to meet. Each and every time, no matter how happy I am for them, I know that the idea of 'happily ever after' may not be a part of my story as a queer disabled person. While I am coming to terms with it, it hasn't been easy.

Before we even consider walking down the aisle to meet the person of our dreams, many of us will first walk down the street to our local watering hole in the hopes of meeting someone right (or, if we're super honest with ourselves, someone right now). Imagine for a moment though, if alongside all the regular anxiety and trepidation that comes with dating and/or hooking up, you had to constantly contend with the fact that you couldn't actually get inside the bar or club where your future partner was waiting for you. This is a really big issue for disabled people trying to date, and is even more pronounced when you are both disabled and queer. So many queer spaces haven't been designed with any kind of accessibility in mind; there are very few ramps, elevators or push buttons to be found in LGBTQ+ spaces, and not only is that ableist* as fuck, it is also a huge barrier for someone to see just how smoulderingly sexy I am, and isn't that a shame?

And, even if you could (through some miraculous feat of engineering) get into the queer club or bar where your Romeo was waiting with bated breath, you'd quickly discover that he might have an issue with ableism he needs to work through. Picture it: there you are in your sexy power wheelchair just waiting for him to approach you, and when he doesn't you wheel up next to him hoping for sparks to ignite, and something magical to happen between you. You've watched this scene in your favourite romantic comedy over and over, so it's bound to work, right? Instead, those beautiful eyes of his look at you with a pitying sadness as he says, 'Yeah, I don't think this will work, I'm not really into guys in wheelchairs.' Le sigh.

The next avenue in your queer crippled† quest for love, might be to hop on the internet superhighway. No worries

---

* Ableism is the discrimination of disabled people in favour of able-bodied folks and is a system of actions, language and implications that undermines disabled people.

† I use the word 'crippled' as a disabled man, as a form of reclamation for myself. Others who are not disabled should not use it without a disabled person's permission.

about access there. A few points, clicks and you'll find someone in no time. For some disabled people, this is the case – I have friends who have had flings through chat rooms, and others who have met their soulmate through Skype. Unfortunately, even with these successes, ableism often still finds a way to bring out the digital dickheads on the apps. I can't count the number of times guys have said the most hurtful things to me: 'You'd be so cute if you weren't disabled,' 'Did your accident hurt your dick?', 'You are so courageous, but I couldn't ever date someone like you' ... the list goes on. Ableism is everywhere disabled people look, and it feels undeniably rampant in the queer community no matter if your bar is physical or virtual. All of these experiences take their toll on you as a queer disabled person – they are continuous, constant and down-right painful reminders that you don't belong here, that there is no place for your disabled body in these communities that pride themselves on accepting everyone. Yeah, sure, they'll accept everyone if 'everyone' refers specifically to white, able-bodied gay men who have abdominal muscles and keep up a regular gym routine. Ugh.

Let's imagine just for a minute though, that someone saw you as their Palsied Prince Charming, and they wanted to take that next step with you and explore not just dating, but moving in and marriage. Even as I type that, the idea sounds too good to be true. You've finally found someone who sees how your disability is a beautifully perfect part of who you are, and wants to take that journey with you. A picket fence, a service dog, 2.5 kids. If that were to happen, maybe I could call my best friend and she could help me plan my nuptials. But alas, as a disabled queer person whose primary income comes from social assistance programmes provided by the government, the dream I have of moving in with a boyfriend or significant other or others may have to stay just that – a dream never to come true.

Here's why: In countries like Canada, the US and the UK, if a couple decides to move in together or get married, with one partner living on a disability payment, the system (you know, the one supposedly set up to help disabled people) combines their respective incomes. This affects the disabled person's eligibility for benefits, often meaning that payments – particularly to do with employment and housing – are reduced to an unlivable amount or, in some cases, halted altogether. If I'm honest, this feels like one big ableist slap in the face, and every time I think about it my heart shatters into a million little pieces. It's because of rules like this that I feel that my singledom as a queer disabled man is just that much safer. If I stay single and live alone, I won't have to be financially dependent on a partner – which could lead to their eventually resenting me and leaving – and might instead be able to survive on my monthly payments. It makes me fearful of building a bond with anyone in the queer community because I know that unless I land a dream job making six figures overnight, it's unlikely that anything could go further than a few dates or hook-ups. And how exactly do you bring that up on a date? 'So, listen, it's our six-month anniversary, and there's something I have to tell you ...' Not exactly, the romcom happy ending, is it?

I have a great support system: amazing family, the best disabled community I could ask for, but even with all that, I recognise these relationships cannot compare to a romantic partnership, and I'd be lying if I told you it wasn't really, really lonely for me at times. I love that in 2021, queer people across so many countries can have the option of officially getting married – whether or not they take that choice, it's important that it's there. That they can totally take advantage of it if they want to is a huge step forward. That's why as a queer disabled person it hurts me even more; so many in the LGBTQ+ community have fought for same-sex marriage to be recognised, but it feels like no one is fighting for disabled people to have access to those rights without compromising our independence.

So, the question becomes: what can we do to fix all this so that queer disabled folks can actually daydream about their disabled futures? We need to start at the beginning. We need to go to those queer spaces and confront our ableism and recognise that the LGBTQ+ community has a huge problem with it that must be addressed. We need to work on changing our ableist language, and calling others out when we see ableism in our everyday lives. For instance, please stop using phrases like 'special needs' to describe a disabled person. Language like 'special needs' erases the importance and the impactfulness of the disability community, and it is particularly insulting when you use it after a disabled person has asked you not to. We need to engage with disabled community members and learn what we can do to help them feel included and not like an afterthought (a great place to start is by reading the work of disability rights activists like me online). We need to check in on our disabled friends more often, just because we want to, not because we want to be seen doing a 'good deed'. We need to hold queer fundraisers for ramps, buttons and elevators in queer spaces, just like we do for AIDS/HIV research. We need to remind the queer community that disabled people are a part of it, and are deserving of a seat at the rainbow table.

From there, we need to open up all our levels of government to disabled people and commit to making our political organisations all the more inclusive ... I'd love to see more disabled heads of state and chiefs of staff, but I especially want to see a disabled person appointed as the lead on social assistance and benefit programmes. This would, I hope, ensure that rules like the one affecting marriage and disability are appropriately revised and improved to reflect the lived experience of disabled people. In the meantime, personally I'd like to see the LGBTQ+ community halt all marriages in support of disabled communities. I think people ought to be outraged enough to boycott, but arranging impactful campaigns and continually working for change is also important.

Maybe, if we make these changes, and queer folks stand up against the ableism that harms their disabled peers, it will act as the ramp disabled people need to make 'happily ever after' accessible after all.

'Our pregnancies, or our other experiences of having children, might not look like other people's – but that can be a good thing.'

Levi Hord is a trans theorist whose work focuses on embodiment and histories of trans medicine. They have spoken internationally on the intersections of trans rights with other social justice movements, and have worked with several advocacy organisations as a researcher and writer. They are currently a PhD candidate at Columbia University in New York.

Pregnancy Beyond Gender

LEVI HORD

When I was growing up, I always imagined having my own children. But even as I acted out elaborate family scenes with my 'gender-appropriate' Barbie dolls, I never imagined having said children in a straight relationship. Nor did I dream of being a mother. My childhood make-believe sessions featured a group of best friends collectively raising twins in the Dreamhouse, Barbie as surrogate to the lovely folks down the street, or Ken being devotedly supported through his own pregnancy by his partners. I had no idea that there was anything abnormal about this. I thought I was doing what every child did: playing house, making families. This was before I was taught, as children are, that there is only one proper way to have a family, and it looked nothing like my Dreamhouse.

I guess you could say that there was a part of my desire to have children that never fit into that version of 'normal'. Most kids are expected to grow out of this phase, where imagination dictates their dreams rather than social propriety. I never did. However, I began to keep my memories of this childhood play private, sensing that they were in conflict with how the people around me lived their lives. They became a secret fantasy, an incredibly queer vision my young self had concocted of my future. It felt like radical possibility.

As I turned away from dolls and towards books, I realised that I was far from the first to have imagined worlds where things worked just a bit differently. The first time I read Marge Piercy's work of feminist science fiction *Woman on the Edge of Time*, published almost fifty years ago, it seemed incredibly natural to me that the society in the book – where gestation is technological and where all genders share the responsibility of chestfeeding children – would be free from gender discrimination. This woke me up to the fact that the fixed association of pregnancy with cisgender women's bodies was the root of so much oppression – the root of unequal access to work, to income disparity, to lack of freedom over one's life course. Equally thrilling was Ursula K. Le Guin's 'Coming of Age in Karhide', which featured beings whose biological sex could change once a month as a catalyst for reproduction, allowing each body to participate in these acts of creation in every imaginable way. Gendered power dynamics were virtually absent in Karhide; biological bodies were not tied to gendered destinies, but were free to become several different things.

As a young, queer feminist, both books got me thinking about how opening up reproduction beyond gender might dislodge patriarchy at one of its very foundations, improving things for cisgender women as much as it would give freedom to all others who wanted to carry pregnancies. Feminist science fiction captured and politicised what I had always thought of when I pictured having children. It reminded me of the radical possibility I had imagined when I was younger. As I read these things, my vision of what it would look like if our bodies did not restrain us began to solidify.

However, as I came out as trans, my relationship with the idea of pregnancy remained private. Through the cultural images I was receiving, I learned that for many people, my transmasculinity seemed to go hand in hand with the assumption that I would never want to be pregnant, even if I did want a family. Pregnancy, after all, is one of the most feminised processes a person can undertake. It was antithetical to who I was meant to become. The perceived wrongness of my desire to give birth to my own children was confirmed when I revealed it to people, only to be met with confused looks and concerns that my gender identity would negatively affect any child I could have. For most of the world, 'trans' and 'pregnancy' fail to fit together neatly: one is a process that challenges proper sexed and gendered existence, while the other is supposedly a process that whole-heartedly confirms it.

The more deeply I engaged in these debates, the more I discovered that this tension between pregnancy and trans-masculinity is not a coincidence. It is built into the medical histories of transgender identity, through doctors' biased and harmful ideas about what being trans meant. In fact, long before Piercy and Le Guin were writing, medical institutions were shutting down possibilities for trans lives – and trans reproduction – based on their own imag-ined ideas of what made trans people authentic.

When hormone therapies and gender-affirming surgeries started to become standardised post-1950, cisgender doctors felt the need to define transgender identity through official diagnostic criteria to ensure that they were giving medical care only to those of us who would be able to pass as 'normal' men or women. These criteria, though doctors claimed they were 'objective', served to restrict people from accessing healthcare if they did not fit seam-lessly back into the gender binary. From the very beginning, one of those keys to supposed authenticity has been a *complete* rejection of one's assigned gender, with no suspicious exceptions. This has meant that, for the past couple of decades, admitting as a transmasculine person that the idea of pregnancy is not repulsive could result in being denied transition care.

Even today, this admission can block the pathway through the gender identity clinic system and towards medical transition. It is one of the reasons that I have made the difficult choice to delay my own transition. Currently, to access hormone replacement therapy or chest masculinisation surgery through the NHS, I would have to go through multiple assessment appointments, where there is potential for clinicians to deny these based on their understanding of what trans people should and should not want. If I ever wanted to change the gender marker on a passport, I would need a letter from a doctor testifying that my change in gender is *permanent* – something less likely to happen if my doctor believed that my becoming pregnant would make me less masculine, or less trans. Though both transition and pregnancy are part of the future I imagine for myself, they often only seem possible when held apart.

Until just a few years ago, it was still legal in twenty-two European countries, including France and Finland, for transgender people to be medically sterilised before receiving legal recognition of their genders. This is a process that prevents all types of reproduction. In 2017, this was found by the European Court of Human Rights to be a significant human rights abuse. However, sterilisation is still the case in countries such as Japan, who upheld the mandatory removal of reproductive organs in a 2019 ruling. At the root of this practice is a eugenic idea that we have seen weaponised against many marginalised communities: the idea that people undesirable to the nation's image should not be allowed to pass on their genes.

Trans people, perhaps unsurprisingly, have never coincided with the image of ideal citizenship. At a deeper level, this forced sterilisation signals to us that trans people do not have the right to desire more from life than just to be allowed to live.

Even in countries that do not force sterilisation as the gateway to recognition, reproductive justice issues for transgender people persist. If you've been through medical transition, you've likely received information about the preservation of your fertility – information that is usually half-heartedly offered as a bid against medical malpractice accusations, and which is under-researched.[1] Most options for preserving fertility involve storing eggs or sperm which, paid for out of pocket, is unaffordable for a vast majority of trans people who still experience economic disparities due to things like workplace and housing discrimination. No trans person I know has been offered safe or reliable information about how to adjust hormone regimens to start the process of conception. This is still largely unthinkable to doctors.

This interference in our fertility and reproductive rights, as well as the institutionalised discrimination we face when we choose to become pregnant is not unique to trans communities. Disabled people also still face forced sterilisation, as do Indigenous populations whose lands have been colonised, as do prisoners. To cite just a few examples, people declared disabled by a doctor in Spain can still be sterilised against their will, and often experience additional coercion by family members. As recently as 2017 a number of Indigenous women in Canada were coerced into sterilisation in hospitals by being prevented from seeing their newborns until they agreed to it. In the US, an investigative report revealed that 148 prisoners were sterilised without consent in California between 2006 and 2011, despite formal eugenics laws having been struck down.[2] These human rights abuses are ongoing and widespread. They link us to broader lesbian, gay, bi and queer communities who experience fertility discrimination in the form of reliance on expensive, medicalised processes to have children. They also link us to any cisgender woman who is not in control of her own fertility, does not have access to sex education or contraception, who is forced into a pregnancy, or who is forced to terminate one.

For trans people, I believe that part of the work that needs to be done is a re*thinking* of the possibilities for reproduction in our lives. Our pregnancies, or our other experiences of having children, might not look like other people's – but that can be a good thing. This process of rethinking reproduction is already happening, and it goes far beyond what I initially experienced as childhood fantasy or the stuff of science fiction. It is oriented around deeply personal acts that link together the power in how we experience gender and the power in the act of creation. Growing into trans communities, I discovered I was far from the only person who desired to break down the barrier between trans identity and reproduction. People have been doing so for decades, for many different reasons, and in various different ways. This narrative is already being rewritten.

One example of rethinking the meanings of pregnancy through a personal experience of gender is trans men who experience their pregnancies as fundamentally masculine processes. This is sometimes linked to admirable qualities of masculinity, especially the role of providing for and protecting one's family in every sense. Pregnancy, as a process in which the body is a vehicle for care, protection and nurturance, can be the first step towards cultivating the values that one wants to bring forth as a father. Gestation can be a masculine act, as can birth, as can chest-feeding. Our experiences of our bodies are always filtered through gender, and pregnancy is no exception.

The same can be said for trans women and transfeminine people. Because we currently lack the technology to allow trans women to safely carry pregnancies, their relationship to the concept of pregnancy is often overlooked. It is not absent, however, but present and powerful and just as reflective as those who have the ability to gestate. Some who participate biologically in conception do so by pausing hormone therapy in order to be able to produce sperm. This process involves negotiating fluctuating hormone levels, bodily changes, the waves of emotion that come with all of this, in the framework of sacrificing one's bodily stability to participate in the act of creation. I can think of few other experiences that could be so aptly described as pregnancies, and indeed have often been narrated as such by transfeminine people.

Trans people who participate in reproduction introduce more than just children to the world: they introduce us to these myriad new interpretations of what reproduction can mean.

One of these new interpretations includes thinking of pregnancy as a type of transition – in fact, a type of transition intimately linked to gender. Many pregnant cis women have reported that they notice people treating them differently and interacting with their bodies in a more gendered way, as if the very fact of their being pregnant makes their status as 'woman' hypervisible. This shift, many women say, has made them more reflective about how they appear to other people as a gendered person in the world, and has sometimes made them think more deeply about their own gender identity.

Most trans people are already *very* familiar with such experiences, and have engaged in a lot of this reflection about how the changes our bodies undertake create our genders for other people to perceive. There is power in thinking of pregnancy as another type of gender transition, or even just as a moment of heightened reflection about what gender means to us. For trans people, pregnancy can be part of an already ongoing negotiation of gender. But for people who aren't trans, thinking through pregnancy as a gendered transformation can be powerful, too. Like transition, pregnancy is something that causes shifts in our self-perception. It can reveal how we are all implicated in the creation of life, of social structures, of families, and of futures. It can be a moment to notice and take stock of the way we are treated based on the appearances and abilities of our bodies.

Comparing the processes of pregnancy and transition links us all to the larger fact that what we do with our bodies becomes part of who we are in the world, and that we can be intentional about how we relate to the social concept of gender. It reveals how unimaginative mainstream thought about gender can be, and offers us another way to begin thinking through it. At the very least, the comparison gives many of us the common ground of being able to recognise how such processes of creation – whether the end product be a gender or a baby – can *really* throw your hormones out of whack.

The early stages of my transition have involved a lot of slow thought. I spend a lot of time reflecting on how I relate to each part of my body as it is and as it could be. Looking towards a specific transition – the transition of my body towards masculinity, in material ways – has caused me to reinterpret my body as something that holds multiple potentials. For me, pregnancy is one of these potentials. Something that my body can undertake, something that I can become, another potential transition that I look towards.

My explorations of gender have, in the same way, changed how I view the meanings of pregnancy. Relating to pregnancy through trans experience, I recognise that the meanings society assigns it are just one possible interpretation. This interpretation seems natural because it has built up over the centuries, linking together social norms about what it means to be a proper woman and a proper citizen. But there is nothing about this interpretation that binds me to it. The things that I do with my body are mine to name, at least within the realm of my own life.

Pregnancy beyond gender might seem like just as much of a fantasy as the ones I used to spin with my Barbies. However, the number of trans, nonbinary and genderqueer people carrying pregnancies is steadily growing.

The UK, for example, is home to the Trans Pregnancy Project, the first international study of trans people who have been or are pregnant, and pictures are continually emerging of the scope, scale and joy of our reproductive practices. For every trans person whose pregnancy has been sensationalised in the media, there are dozens more whose acts of creation have gone unnoticed by the broader public, but whose privacy makes them no less radical. For every persistent attack on our reproductive agency, there are individual healthcare practitioners and midwives working to educate themselves on our needs. Though trans and nonbinary youth still lack crucial information about reproductive safety and choice, they can imagine lives fuller and more variant than we could have decades ago.

Trans pregnancies are happening, and I feel as if I am witnessing a future – one that I was told was incompatible with my identity – come to life in vibrant ways. There are also technologies being worked on, such as womb transplants and stem-cell-driven reproduction, that could massively change the way that we reproduce as a species. If any of these technologies ever come to fruition to be used by everyday people – which is unlikely now, but may be possible for future centuries – we will have even more cause to start thinking about pregnancy outside of the constraints of gender, sex and sexuality.

This progress, however, is slow. One thing that I think we can do better at, within all of our communities, is claiming the possibilities of pregnancy without using traditional ideas of gender to restrict them. Pregnancy can be a radical force that we can claim in our transness. It can help us create worlds and futures that have been denied to us. This starts – as most change does – with the ability to imagine differently.

---

1 See, for example, Leena Nahata et al., 'Understudied and under-reported: fertility issues in transgender youth – a narrative review', *Journal of Pediatrics* 205, pp. 265–71, February 2019, https://pubmed. ncbi.nlm.nih.gov/30293639/; Shira Baram et al., 'Fertility preservation for transgender adolescents and young adults: a systematic review', *Human Reproduction Update* 25.6, pp. 694–716, November–December 2019, https://academic.oup.com/humupd/article/25/6/694/5601536

2 Corey G. Johnson, 'Female inmates sterilized in California prisons without approval', *Reveal News*, 7 July 2013, http://www.revealnews.org/article/ female-inmates-sterilized-in-california-prisons-without-approval/

HEALTH AND SOCIAL CARE

'A mental health crisis affects far too many LGBTQ+ people: queer people's lives literally depend on tackling it.'

Owen Jones is a writer and author who was born in Sheffield and grew up in Stockport. A *Guardian* columnist since 2014, he has written three books: *Chavs: The Demonization of the Working Class*, *The Establishment: And How They Get Away With It* and *This Land: The Story of a Movement*.

Anti-LGBTQ+ Bigotry Is Seriously Bad for Your Health

OWEN JONES

Many queer people have their own story about their struggle with mental distress: here is mine. I was sixteen when I was prescribed antidepressants – the long-suppressed but growing realisation about who I really was had suddenly led to a moment of crisis. If I took them on an empty stomach, I'd sometimes be hit with excruciating heartburn, scoffing bread to try and suppress the pain, slumped in a ball on the sofa to wait it out. I was desperate not to be gay – like many of us, I grew up hearing 'gay' bandied around as the ultimate insult: to be labelled with it meant loneliness, rejection, social death. I didn't know any younger gay people, either. How I'd come to realise this compounded the sense of turmoil: I'd fallen in love with one of my best friends, a dead end which suddenly seemed to foreshadow a life of unhappiness and solitude.

The reality turned out very differently. The nightmarish life that seemed to beckon never came: I lost sleep over fears that would never be realised. When I came out, I had loving friends, straight and queer; loving relationships with the same ups and downs as everybody else, and that's just with my two cats. I can write, proudly, about LGBTQ+ rights and our aspirations and challenges. Other queer kids had far worse experiences than my own: with more support, we could have spared them a huge amount of avoidable anguish.

The continued failure of society to fully accept LGBTQ+ people as we are, and as we say we are, inflicts immeasurable mental harm, often from a very early age. Mental distress, such as depression and anxiety, is considerably higher amongst LGBTQ+ people than it is for the population as a whole; with it comes an increased risk of suicidal ideation – which is tragically all too often acted upon – and self-medication, such as the abuse of alcohol and drugs. A mental health crisis affects far too many LGBTQ+ people: queer people's lives literally depend on tackling it.

Homophobia is ingrained in Western culture. It was exported to colonised lands across the world, and even when it was partially decriminalised in Britain in 1967, Lord Arran – who co-sponsored the legislation – declared: 'Lest the opponents of the Bill think that a new freedom, a new privileged class has been created, let me remind them that no amount of legislation will prevent homosexuals from being the subject of dislike and derision, or at best of pity.'[1] His pessimism seemed confirmed by what came next.

In Britain in the 1980s – as elsewhere – the HIV/AIDS crisis fused with already entrenched homophobia, cementing an image of gay and bisexual men in particular as dangerous, diseased outcasts with a deadly affliction caused by their depraved or sinful (or both) sexual acts. Mainstream media outlets and politicians alike portrayed gay and bisexual people as sexual predators, as brainwashers of children, as transgressors of the laws of biology, as being defined by mental illness, as compelling the majority to redefine because of the whims of a tiny minority. All of this was internalised by a generation of LGBTQ+ people. In an effort to deploy a moral panic against her Labour opponents, Margaret Thatcher decried children 'being taught that they have an inalienable right to be gay', and drove through Section 28 which forbade the 'promotion' of homosexuality, de facto banning LGBTQ+ issues from being taught in schools. The law remained in place until 2000 in Scotland and 2003 in England and Wales.

As a gay man born in 1984, Section 28 was in place throughout my time at school, and the Britain I knew was deeply and unapologetically homophobic. According to the British Social Attitudes Survey, homophobic bigotry peaked in 1987 – I was three – when 64% of the population believed same-sex relations were 'always wrong', 11% opted for 'mostly wrong', and 8% said 'sometimes wrong', with just 14% declaring 'not wrong at all'.[2] When BBC soap *EastEnders* aired the first gay kiss in 1989, then *Sun* writer Piers Morgan denounced a 'homosexual love scene between yuppie poofs' (comments for which he apologised three decades later).[3]

By 1999 – as I neared the end of high school – nearly half the population still believed same-sex relations were always wrong, with only just over a quarter opting for 'not wrong at all'.[4] Many LGBTQ+ people who are now in their thirties struggled with their sexuality as teenagers in what remained a largely hostile climate, with life-lasting consequences.

Because of the struggle and sacrifice of LGBTQ+ people, attitudes have manifestly changed. As of 2019, just 10% opt for 'always wrong', 6% for 'mostly wrong' and 6% for 'sometimes wrong', while two-thirds agree that it is 'not wrong at all'.[5] But that still means millions of people continue to object to same-sex relations, and many will not admit to their prejudices. On average, one in every five LGBTQ+ people grows up in a family which openly does not entirely accept them; and every one in five people they pass in the street may believe there is something innately wrong with same-sex attraction.[6] In addition to this, a 2017 study found that two out of three LGBTQ+ people do not feel safe holding hands with their partner in public, and those who *do* find the courage to hold hands with a loved one, or show any affection, may be met with disapproval through a glare, a muttering of disgust, or even abuse or the threatening of violence.[7]

LGBTQ+ people continue to live under an authoritarian regime of prejudice; its informers are everywhere. Depending on how they present, gay and bisexual people can sometimes cloak themselves to avoid prejudice and discrimination: more than a third report hiding that they are LGBTQ+ at work.[8] But LGBTQ+ people appear randomly and sporadically: statistically they are unlikely to grow up in a family with other LGBTQ+ people; they will not have parents and siblings who have a shared culture and understanding of a common oppression, offering solidarity and passing on resilience. When they start to have a sense that they are different, they are mostly alone, with some exceptions, largely unable to draw from the direct experiences of close relatives. What's more, other children can pick up on differences at an early age and act upon them. 'Some LGBTQ+ people are more gender-nonconforming as children,' explains Dr Kate Rimes, a clinical psychologist. 'Some are bullied by being called gay or other insults, like being "sissy" or too "butch" as a girl from a very young age, often before they're aware of sexual orientation, before puberty. They realise they're different and internalise negative perceptions, even if they don't understand if they're gay.'

While LGBTQ+ people have been coming out at ever earlier ages as general acceptance grows, that poses a double-edged sword: younger teenagers are more vulnerable than their older peers and may need more emotional support when facing adverse reactions. Today, according to LGBTQ+ charity Stonewall, 99% of young gay people report phrases like 'that's so gay' being bandied around the playground; 96% hear words like 'poof' and 'lezza'.[9] While there are teachers who offer desperately needed help for their LGBTQ+ students – a whole four in ten LGBTQ+ teachers themselves have suffered bigotry in the workplace – research by Stonewall in 2017 found that fewer than a third of bullied LGBTQ+ pupils reported teachers intervening during bullying.[10] Anti-bullying policies are often inconsistently applied and zero tolerance can be lacking. Some young LGBTQ+ people may witness hostile or indeed abusive responses to fellow students coming out and decide to remain firmly in the closet as a consequence.

The response of parents can inevitably have even more lasting consequences. According to Dr Rimes, because of a popularised message that LGBTQ+ children will be okay – that they will be loved, that 'it gets better' – when they don't get that response, it can be all the more shocking. The cliché is of parents in denial, of their children simply going through a phase, of refusing to accept it. 'That's very distressing to young people, it comes across as their parents not loving them,' says Dr Rimes. '[Parents] should always say "I love you anyway" if they then have to express their worry about the impact of coming out – they need to say "I love you".'

Where LGBTQ+ people live has an impact, too. Perhaps surprisingly, the evidence suggests that mental wellbeing for LGBTQ+ in London is lower than outside the capital.[11] This may be because it is hard to make personal connections in a metropolis afflicted by high rents and a costly standard of living, and many LGBTQ+ people who arrive in London are fleeing less accepting small towns and villages, with all the accompanying resulting distress. Helen Jones, the CEO of LGBTQ+ mental health charity MindOut, is based in Brighton and Hove, one of the LGBTQ+ heartlands of Britain. 'LGBTQ+ people think it's great when they get here, especially when they're fleeing difficult, unsafe or abusive circumstances,' she tells me, 'and they come to Brighton to get a better life, but then they find it a very tough and very expensive place, especially if they don't have friends or money. For a lot of people that can feel like the end of the road.' For LGBTQ+ people who find themselves identified by hostile neighbours – who may abuse them or even graffiti their property or smash their windows – the housing crisis may make it difficult for them to move to somewhere safer. Strikingly, a quarter of young homeless people identify as LGBTQ+, many fleeing intolerant families with nowhere to go.[12]

On the streets, reported homophobic crimes have doubled over five years.[13] But it is trans people who have suffered the most of late: anti-trans hate crimes have trebled – the vast majority are not reported to the authorities – and the British media have, intentionally or not, contributed to a moral panic against trans people disturbingly similar to that previously endured by gay and bisexual people (for more on that, read Juliet Jacques's piece in this book).[14] A shocking 83% of trans people have suffered name-calling and 60% threats and intimidation.[15] As well as in wider society, bigotry and racism is rampant within LGBTQ+ communities and spaces: according to research by

Stonewall, for example, half of BAME LGBTQ+ people report discrimination from fellow LGBTQ+ people.[16] It is clear that our mental health and wellbeing is imperilled not only by the prejudice of the heterosexual world.

All of these combined factors have conspired to create a mental health crisis for LGBTQ+ people. 'Lifetime rates of depression and anxiety are between two to three times higher for LGBTQ+ people compared to straight or cisgender people,' says Dr Liadh Timmins, a psychologist who specialises in LGBTQ+ health; 89% of trans people report considering suicide, while more than one in four have attempted to do so.[17] That leads to self-medication: drug use among gay and bisexual men in England and Wales is estimated to be three times higher than among straight men; among lesbian and bisexual women it is four times higher compared to heterosexual women.[18] Research has also found that a quarter of bisexual people have considered some form of self-harm within the last year, also reporting higher levels of mental distress than gay and lesbian people all round.[19] There are other aggravating factors: LGBTQ+ people of colour, those in poverty, those with disabilities, those with HIV, those who are older and more isolated – all will suffer even more acute levels of mental distress. The evidence, too, suggests that bisexuals suffer higher rates of depression and anxiety, partly because of prejudice within as well as outside of LGBTQ+ communities.[20]

How to solve this crisis? In the long term, there is only one viable solution: to overcome patriarchy, a system which aggressively and violently punishes deviations from gender norms assigned at birth. For men, for example, homophobia represents gender policing. Straight men who deviate from supposed masculine norms – perhaps they don't get into enough fights, or talk about women in certain ways, or lack athletic prowess – are liable to be on the receiving end of homophobic abuse, told to 'man up' and 'stop being such a poof'. These were words and phrases I heard bandied around with abandon growing up – including, shamefully, sometimes by myself. Nothing is as unmanly – or, indeed, 'gay' – as talking about feelings.

In the here and now, investment in expanded mental health services is desperately overdue. Under the Conservative-Liberal Democrat Coalition government of 2010–2015, supposed parity of esteem was promised between mental and physical health services. But mental health services still receive inadequate funding, and there have been cuts to school counselling services, and to support for those with an abusive relationship with drugs and alcohol.[21] Between 2013–2014 and 2017–2018, 70% of English councils cut drug and alcohol services.[22] Proper investment will help those most vulnerable, including LGBTQ+ people.

That must surely include specialist LGBTQ+ mental health services. According to Helen Jones, LGBTQ+ people wait longer to seek help for mental distress; there is also a specific stigma of how 'we are still, in some ways, desperately trying to prove that we're alright to the rest of the world'. Her charity, MindOut, has only ten counsellors who often find themselves catering for people across the country: additional support for such organisations is needed right now. Services catering specifically for LGBTQ+ people have been reduced because of post-financial-crash austerity and reversing this vandalism is an urgent priority.[23]

LGBTQ+ community centres are also critical. London is a rare example of a Western capital which still – at the time of writing – lacks one. As things stand, many LGBTQ+ people are required to go to spaces centring on alcohol and sometimes where there is an expectation of seeking a sexual relationship. New centres would offer support, particularly for those who are questioning and vulnerable. As well as these vital centres, focusing on LGBTQ+-inclusive education at an early age, and introducing tougher policies on homophobic, biphobic and transphobic bullying could prevent lifelong damage being done to young people.

To achieve these demands, LGBTQ+ people must do what we have always done to secure rights and freedoms: organise and fight. Collective struggle and showing solidarity with each other will, itself, challenge the mental distress imposed upon us by societies which must be compelled to fully accept us as we are. Only when we build a world which no longer centres on patriarchy and profit, rather than human need, will LGBTQ+ people truly be free. Until that day, there are many demands we must make to improve our needlessly harmed mental wellbeing.

---

1 https://api.parliament.uk/historic-hansard/lords/1967/jul/21/sexual-offences-no-2-bill

2 British Social Attitudes 30, NatCen, 2012, https://www.bsa.natcen.ac.uk/latest-report/british-social-attitudes-30/personal-relationships/homosexuality.aspx

3 Nick Duffy, 'Piers Morgan apologises for anti-gay article attacking EastEnders over "yuppie poofs"', Pink News, 29 January 2020, https://www.pinknews.co.uk/2020/01/29/piers-morgan-the-sun-eastenders-yuppie-anti-gay-michael-cashman-g2/

4 British Social Attitudes 30, NatCen, 2012, https://www.bsa.natcen.ac.uk/latest-report/british-social-attitudes-30/personal-relationships/homosexuality.aspx

5 https://natcen.ac.uk/blog/over-the-rainbow

6 Ibid.

7 Olivia Petter, 'Two-thirds of LGBT+ people fear holding hands in public, survey finds', *Independent*, 3 July 2018, https://www.independent.co.uk/life-style/lgbt-holding-hands-public-fear-uk-government-survey-penny-mordaunt-a8428381.html

8 'Stonewall reveals coming out at work still a problem', Stonewall, 26 April 2018, https://www.stonewall.org.uk/about-us/media-centre/media-statement/stonewall-reveals-coming-out-work-still-problem

9 https://www.stonewall.org.uk/sites/default/files/tackling_homophobic_language_-_teachers_guide.pdf

10 Lily Wakefield, 'Four in 10 UK LGBT teachers have experienced homophobia, biphobia or transphobia at work', *Pink News*, 26 February 2020, https://www.pinknews.co.uk/2020/02/26/lgbt-teachers-uk-homophobia-biphobia-transphobia-schools-lgbt-inclusive-education-discrimination/; 'School report', Stonewall, 2017, https://www.stonewall.org.uk/sites/default/files/the_school_report_2017.pdf

11 'Personal well-being and sexual identity in the UK: 2013 to 2015', ONS, 9 May 2017, https://www.ons.gov.uk/peoplepopulationandcommunity/wellbeing/bulletins/measuringnationalwellbeing/2013to2015

12 https://www.akt.org.uk/

13 Ben Quinn, 'Hate crimes double in five years in England and Wales', *Guardian*, 15 October 2019, https://www.theguardian.com/society/2019/oct/15/hate-crimes-double-england-wales

14 Ibid.

15 https://www.stonewall.org.uk/sites/default/files/trans_stats.pdf

16 'Racism rife in LGBT community Stonewall research reveals', Stonewall, 27 July 2018, https://www.stonewall.org.uk/news/racism-rife-lgbt-community-stonewall-research-reveals

17 https://www.stonewall.org.uk/sites/default/files/trans_stats.pdf

18 https://londonfriend.org.uk/official-data-confirms-lgb-drug-use-much-higher-than-heterosexuals/

19 'LGBT in Britain: bi report', Stonewall, 2020, https://www.stonewall.org.uk/system/files/lgbt_in_britain_bi.pdf

20 Lori E. Ross et al., 'Prevalence of depression and anxiety among bisexual people compared to gay, lesbian, and heterosexual individuals', *Journal of Sex Research* 55.4–5, pp. 435–56, November 2017, https://www.tandfonline.com/doi/full/10.1080/00224499.2017.1387755

21 Alice Ross, 'Schools cutting mental health services to plug funding gaps, warn MPs', *Guardian*, 2 May 2017, https://www.theguardian.com/society/2017/may/02/schools-mental-health-services-funding-gaps-mps-report; David Rhodes, 'Drug and alcohol services cut by £162m as deaths increase', BBC News, 11 May 2018, https://www.bbc.co.uk/news/uk-england-44039996

22 'Breaking point: the crisis in mental health funding', TUC, 19 October 2018, https://www.tuc.org.uk/sites/default/files/Mentalhealth fundingreport2_0.pdf
23 Owen Jones, 'Why London's LGBT communities need their own base more than ever', *Guardian*, 21 June 2018, https://www.theguardian.com/commentisfree/2018/jun/21/lgbt-london-community-centre

'If we were equipped with better education as kids and teenagers, then as adults we'd feel more comfortable speaking about our mental health, our sex lives and our sexual health.'

Olly Alexander is the lead singer of Years & Years. He is an English musician, songwriter, LGBTQ+ advocate and actor, starring as Ritchie in Russell T. Davies's TV series *It's a Sin*.

Sex?! Relationships?! PrEP?!

OLLY ALEXANDER

Gay sex was mentioned once at my secondary school; it was during a history lesson about the Second World War. My teacher described the gruelling conditions the soldiers faced, how hard and dangerous life was on the battlefield, before revealing that so far from home and without any women 'some of the men had sex with each other'. Of course, we were all scandalised. Amid the giggles and screeches of 'GAY!' and 'That's GROSS!' I remember sitting in stunned silence, imagining these men reaching for each other in the filthy, perilous trenches. It was both sexy and terrifying. Other than this indelible moment, my school taught us that queer people did not exist, but we knew they did. They lived as rumours and stories about this teacher or that pupil, they hid in crumpled notes and names scratched out on the battered desks.

Homophobia was both explicit and casual. I learned that almost any person, thing or situation that was embarrassing or wrong could (and would) be called 'gay'. Any boy's behaviour deemed suspicious enough got them named and shamed in marker pen on the toilet cubicle wall. I dreaded seeing my name among them. I started secondary school in 2001 – two years before Section 28 was repealed across the UK, so it's not surprising the environment was the way it was. As a teenager, I embarked on my own reluctant queer education of sorts, taking a one-foot-in-one-foot-out approach. I convinced myself the odd furtive exchange in a Habbo Hotel chat room, or reading *Giovanni's Room* and watching *My Own Private Idaho* didn't necessarily mean I was *actually* gay, it just made me interesting.

I watched a lot of television too, sneaking in *Queer as Folk* at a friend's house and obsessing over John Paul and Craig's storyline in *Hollyoaks*. I remember a song from an episode of *Family Guy* called 'You Have AIDS' that got drunkenly repeated at a party. I sang along. When I did start having sex with other men it was with huge anxiety and I feared any sexual encounter would result in me contracting HIV. Looking back, I see that shame was at the heart of this anxiety, but at the time I didn't understand it. I felt implicated in something terrible and that some inevitable punishment would be deserved. I was afraid.

Just before my nineteenth birthday, a year after I had left my mum's house and moved to London, a GP prescribed me antidepressants and advised me to start therapy. After years of concealing how I was feeling, too ashamed to admit I was self-harming as well as bingeing and purging food, I started wanting to take better care of my health. In the beginning, I had many encounters with different doctors, counsellors and therapists; it took me a while to figure out what worked for me and what didn't.

For the longest time, I was convinced something was intrinsically wrong with me. Growing up gay in a world that prefers straightness can do that to you, but it's not just my sexuality that made me feel this way. It was my daddy issues, my brain, my body, my DNA. Shame is toxic and it likes to get in the way of almost everything. My mental health did improve though, and my hyper-anxious trips to the clinic became less stressful. By the time things started taking off with Years & Years I had put my most damaging self-destructive behaviours to bed. I'm not pretending that my mental health is glorious all the time, though. I have the occasional dark patch, I still take meds, and I speak with my therapist once a week.

My relationship with another medication has been just as fraught, and just as informed – I think – by what you might call internalised homophobia. In 2017, PrEP – which stands for pre-exposure prophylaxis, and is a daily pill that can help prevent HIV – was made available through an NHS trial to about 10,000 people in England. This caused quite a bit of contention. Some people were not happy that the NHS would be funding a drug that supported what they saw as a 'certain lifestyle choice', and talked about how 'the gays having dirty unprotected sex' should really know better. There's a lot to unpack in the responses to the PrEP trial and why giving people more options to protect themselves and each other is so controversial, especially when you consider that studies have shown PrEP to be 'highly effective in preventing HIV as long as the drugs are taken regularly'.[1] I think it suggests we haven't come as far as we might hope since I was at school, in terms of social HIV stigma.

For this reason, when I started taking PrEP in 2018, I'm embarrassed to admit that I did not speak with a healthcare professional first. At the time I told myself I was just too busy but I came to realise that I was afraid to talk about it. Despite all the trips I'd taken to the doctor's office for my mental health, talking about sex and prevention filled me with panic, and at the time I didn't know about helpful websites like prepster.info or iwantprepnow.co.uk, and the incredible organisation the Terrence Higgins Trust, which disseminates information about PrEP where it can sometimes be lacking.

Recently, I played a gay character in a TV show created by Russell T. Davies called *It's a Sin*. Set in the 1980s, the story unfolds as a group of friends' lives are turned upside down by the arrival of a deadly virus. It's a fictional drama but much of it drew on Russell's own life, and hearing him speak about that time and researching the stories and lives was an experience I'm profoundly grateful for. It helped me understand a bit better where we've come from, where we are now, and how the LGBTQ+ community was impacted by HIV. Today, HIV is no longer a death sentence thanks to effective treatment, better understanding and PrEP. It's difficult to overstate what a huge difference this has made. Looking back on how much I learned from the show, and how many conversations the programme sparked, I can see how much room there is for improving public awareness – not just about what happened in the '80s, but about HIV today.

The barriers to greater understanding and awareness are many and significant – given that there's still a huge stigma surrounding HIV and queer people that is often perpetuated by the media. In 2019 former Welsh Rugby captain Gareth Thomas was forced to publicly announce his HIV status before tabloid journalists did so being just one example. However, changes in the availability of PrEP are a positive sign. In March 2020, the UK's health secretary announced that PrEP will finally be made widely available on the NHS in England. It has been provided in Scotland since 2017 and Wales since 2018, and now Northern Ireland as part of a pilot programme. I'd like to see this happen everywhere. Too many people deemed at risk still don't have access to treatment, care or prevention. This has to change. I want queer people and people in high-risk groups in all countries to know what their options are and feel able to talk about them.

All of us suffer the scars of adolescence no matter how we identify – awkwardly navigating sex and how to take care of ourselves and our bodies is part of growing up (I'll let you know when I figure all that out). Learning how queer people have been marginalised, medicalised and politicised throughout history has given me a context for my own experiences and to better understand those of others. There's a lot about what we're taught in schools that needs to change (learning about the legacy of the racism and destruction of British colonialism, for starters). If I had a child, I would want to show them that lots of different identities and relationships exist and that they all deserve respect. In secondary school I would absolutely want them to be educated on how to look after their mental health and how to have sex safely and enjoyably. If we were equipped with better education as kids and teenagers, then as adults we'd feel more comfortable speaking about our mental health, our sex lives and our sexual health.

Teaching kids that queer people are real is not radical, neither is including LGBTQ+ experiences in sex education – it just makes sense. We don't arrive at adulthood armed with all the knowledge we need to thrive in the world; making mistakes and learning is a lifelong commitment, but we can try and help young people give it their best shot.

---

1 'Update on commissioning and provision of Pre Exposure Prophylaxis (PREP) for HIV prevention', NHS England, 21 March 2016, https://www.england.nhs.uk/2016/03/prep/

'Maybe if we learn about the importance of diversity, self-reflection and communication in our sexual lives, we'll see that these things are essential in other areas of our lives too.'

Sasha Kazantseva is a blogger, journalist and sex educator from Russia. She lives in Saint Petersburg and identifies openly as a lesbian. In 2017 she started the blog *Washed Hands*, which offers information and advice about sex for lesbians, trans and nonbinary people, on topics like consent and healthcare. She also co-edits *O-Zine*, a magazine spotlighting queer artists and publishing positive stories about queer people across Russia.

Queering Sex Ed

SASHA KAZANTSEVA

It's 2001, I'm fifteen years old, standing in the Moscow subway in the evening, headed to my father's work. There's a real treasure waiting for me, a teenager of the early 2000s: a bunch of computers connected to the internet. By my calculations, most of my father's colleagues will have already gone home and I'll be able to use one of the machines. I'm going to google 'lesbian sex articles'. I want to learn a lot about lesbian sex.

How can I have sex with a girl? Do I need protection? Should I visit a gynaecologist? Googling 'lesbian safe sex' that night in the empty office, I find only two articles in Russian: one apparently written in 1993 (wow), another one dated 2001. I don't yet know that they will stay the only two search results for this request in Russian for a very long time. The third one will finally appear seventeen years after the last – in 2018, when an online magazine publishes my own 'lesbian safer sex guide'.

Sex, sexuality and gender have been filling my head with questions from a young age: 'Why do princesses in books always meet princes, not other girls?', 'What if I feel I'm not a girl and not a boy?', 'When I climb a gym rope to get pleasing sensations – is it called "masturbation"?' But the only thing I learned from adults is that these questions are 'inappropriate' and 'shameful' for some reason and that I'd be punished for asking them.

Talking about sex was a great taboo in my family, and it was the same at school. In Russia, we have never had anything like 'sex ed lessons'. I was about ten when my curiosity led me to start reading sex columns in teen mags, the 'Reproductive System' section in the anatomy atlas, sexology textbooks which I hid in my room under stacks of clothes. I thought I knew a lot about sex – more than my classmates, more than my parents. But everything I found was about straight sexuality and straight bodies, about 'norms' and 'standards', about very limited ideas of what is 'supposed to be' and what is 'the right way to do' things.

It's probably the shame I felt as a kid that encouraged me to run sex ed seminars in my twenties, at a camp for teenagers that my friends and I organised. Here, we openly discussed sex, sexuality, health, LGBTQ+ identity and gender – the topics which are rarely raised in schools or at home. Of course, among dozens of adolescents, there were those who identified as queer or were in a process of self-identification. Talking to people both in groups and privately, I strived to support my young friends.

'We should stop talking to teens about all this queer stuff,' my colleague says at our planning session for a new vacation camp. 'Now it will be too big a risk for us and for the project.'

It's 2013, and the Russian 'propaganda law' has just been adopted. According to this new law, nobody should mention LGBTQ+ issues to underaged persons – 'to protect children from information promoting the denial of traditional family values', as the document specifies. Nobody can yet say how this law is going to be implemented (other recent Russian laws have shown us that this is unpredictable). But many queer people are alarmed and afraid of persecution.

'Well, what if some guy asks me if I consider an LGBTQ+ person to be equal to a straight person?' another colleague asks.

'Really don't know ... Change the topic. Just don't answer,' replies the first colleague.

In the days leading up to the approval of the propaganda law independent media were suddenly publishing more sympathetic features about LGBTQ+ people, seemingly recognising the injustice of the new law and that such articles would likely be banned once the law came into force. That year, many Russian queer people, especially families with kids, who had money and opportunities, left the country. Most of us stayed, though – now with heavier silence and greater tension in our lives than before.

It's 2018. I'm getting my regular HIV test at one of the local HIV organisations, and a specialist is filling in a standard form. I have been running a blog about queer sex called *Washed Hands* on the blogging platform Telegram – popular in Russia and some Asian countries because bloggers can stay anonymous and there are no comment options available – as well as publishing my articles regularly in a Russian lifestyle magazine called *Wonderzine*, known for its feminist perspective. It's the beginning of a turning-point year when several Russian media outlets start to cover queer people's lives more broadly than ever before. A 'critical mass' of queer content appeared on social media, which in turn influenced other forms of digital and print media. It seemed the Russian government had other priorities beyond monitoring queer articles, so it became easier for editors to take risks.

The doctor, in his early thirties like me, draws my blood. We need to wait several minutes for the result. He has already asked me the usual questions about whether I have a boyfriend and if I use condoms – assuming I am straight, of course. I've corrected him, and now he makes small talk: 'Really, I don't understand why lesbians have any need for protection,' he says. I'm not surprised. It's not the first time I've heard it. My friends and followers have had similar experiences with medical specialists they decided to talk to openly, with comments like 'If you have sex with another girl you just can't get STDs' or 'You don't need to go to a gynaecologist if you're a lesbian.' It's common for transgender people I know to be told to 'stop pretending' or to 'turn back before it's too late' by their GPs, while gay men I talk to avoid visiting doctors even when they have major problems, due to fear of experiencing homophobia.

Most of us Russian queers feel that we can only come out to special 'friendly doctors' who are recommended to us by other LGBTQ+ community members. But even if you manage to find a 'friendly specialist', they still hardly know how to treat queer patients. Nobody tells doctors how to deal with LGBTQ+ people here – how to communicate correctly, what health risks we have and what protection we may use. 'Only once during my university studies, in the fourth year, did a lecturer mention homosexuality, just a few phrases – and that's all for education about queers,' says my gynaecologist friend. All of the knowledge that doctors get is about straight cisgender people and penile–vaginal sex. This is all the more a problem because we have an HIV/AIDS epidemic in Russia at the moment, with more than 1 million positive people recorded, while 37,000 people die from AIDS annually. Experts have attributed it to the inaccessibility of information, particularly about sexual health and protection. Not to mention that we still have no public statistics on the health of queer women, as well as of transgender people in the country.

Sex education is important because it's about essential rights – the right to be healthy, and the right to safety, both physical and psychological. But this means far more than just 'get tested and visit your doctor'. It means more than just increasing one's sexual comfort and pleasure, too.

Everybody has a body, even if we're different in so many other ways, I thought when I started my blog. All of us are able to feel pleasure or to feel vulnerable and ashamed, so what would happen if we paid more attention to this similarity? Wouldn't we feel more connected and be better able to understand each other as well as ourselves?

I believe, then, that the best kind of sex education should involve exploring yourself, your interactions with other people, and their needs. Maybe if we learn about the importance of diversity, self-reflection and communication in our sexual lives, we'll see that these things are essential in other areas of our lives too. Maybe this will even allow us to bring about wider social change. How would a different and better sex education work? Here are five points on what it should teach us:

Self-reflection
Sex education should begin with the question 'What do I want?', a question that encourages us to be attentive to our inner 'yes' and 'no', and to realise our needs and personal boundaries. Unlike most areas of our lives, sex is a unique sphere which is never about 'have to' (if it is, then it is not called sex) – it's only about you and your partner's wants and your mutual comfort. That's why it's perfect for training the skills of self-reflection.

Diversity

When you reflect on your own sexual interests, you may assess some of them as 'weird'. The fact is, though, that many things we consider 'weird' turn out to be things we're just not well informed about. That's the problem of 'silence' when it comes to sex: many of us are only aware of a limited range of experiences or ways of behaving, and these serve as the norm to us.

What is sex? Sex will be different with different people. Sex may not involve penetration, sex may not involve genitals. Sex may be solo, sex may be multi-partnered. Sex may be super kinky, sex may be very simple. Providing there is consent and you are communicating, sex is almost all that you consider it to be. Sex education should help us to accept our peculiarities and differences, to broaden our horizons about ourselves and others, and to be generally more open-minded about our bodies and our sexualities.

Communication

Talking about sex – vocalising private experiences that are often hushed up – is a perfect opportunity to improve the way that you speak with others. When you recognise that just like you, someone else is trying to seek out the words to describe their desires it makes for better communication. When you start open dialogues, free from stereotypes, it's better communication. Respecting consent – that's about better communication, again. If more people with different needs, experiences and cultural codes start to understand one another and to find a way to enjoy interacting, imagine what our society could be like.

Vulnerability

There's nothing difficult about saying that you're excited about your new sneakers or that you feel sad when a gadget you have just bought gets broken. For many, shopping is a daily topic of conversation; we have lots of words to use about it and we feel free to use them. But when we start to talk honestly about sex – especially in cultures where sex is connected with guilt – we may feel embarrassed and vulnerable. It's no wonder, since sex is stigmatised, standardised and shrouded in shame.

Feeling like this isn't, perhaps, the situation that we'd *choose* to be in – but we are in it, so can we at least get something out of it? Yes! By being open about our vulnerability and talking to each other, we can grow closer. We can embrace this feeling together, learn to trust and, hopefully, become braver.

Overcoming unnecessary taboos

Some acts and topics are, of course, rightfully seen as taboo and unacceptable. But others are unnecessarily made taboo – and sex is definitely one of them. We often look at these sorts of taboos in the same way, going through doubt ('Why does anybody even need to talk about it out loud?'), guilt ('It seems like it's really shameful to vocalise it!') and the lack of lexical constructions ('How will I describe it? Does it sound weird?').

When a person successfully overcomes an unnecessary taboo, it can be incredibly liberating and life-changing. So what happens when these kinds of taboos are overcome by the whole of society? How can it move the culture forward? I'm really interested to know!

When I was a teenager, I thought that the reason I couldn't find enough information about queer sex was because I wasn't seeking it out properly. So I thought that I should keep looking. But as I became older, I realised that nowhere is there a surplus of queer sex education; that LGBTQ+

people (not just in Russia, but in other countries too) may not be aware of their sexual health, may be afraid to go to the doctors, and are mistreated when they do (or even face violence).

In fact, this affects everyone, not only LGBTQ+ people. Many of us are not provided with basic tools for understanding our own needs and unique traits, or for talking about sex. Instead, we may feel ashamed of our bodies, of our desires and of who we are. When I realised this, I knew that it's not about tracking down sex education – there can be so little to find – but about creating it, improving it.

For me, being queer is about having a sincere dialogue with yourself, about exploration, about searching for answers to all the 'Who am I?' and 'What do I want?' questions. And so I see sex education as an inevitably queer thing. It's about attentiveness to the variety of people's qualities, about inclusion, about acceptance, about diversity. Most importantly, it's about honest contact with yourself and others through the type of open-minded communication that I would love us to have in all spheres of our lives. By making personal changes we can, potentially, bring about the broader transformation of society. I want all queer people to have access to sex education that respects them, and even more than that, I want a queer approach to sex education for everyone.

'So many hoops, so many gatekeepers, when the person who ultimately knows what's best for me is me.'

Fox Fisher is an award-winning artist, filmmaker and author. Fox is co-director of the film company My Genderation along with their partner Owl. Together they co-created *Trans Teen Survival Guide* and *Trans Survival Workbook*.

Navigating Trans Healthcare

FOX FISHER

During my childhood in Saudi Arabia, where my parents had moved us for work, I was considered a trouble-maker. I refused to conform to gender stereotypes. I would let my older sister cut my hair all short and wonky and I told the American soldiers who arrived during the Gulf War that my nickname at home was Ralph.

Playing by some trees one day, I got involved in an unripe banana fight with some boys I didn't know. One boy threw a stone and it hit my face, drawing blood, soaking my white shirt. I had to get stitches across my left eyebrow. Each boy was frogmarched to my house to apologise. I remember them all saying: 'I thought you were a boy. I would never have done that if I thought you were a girl.'

I felt like no one truly understood me at that point. I had wanted more than anything to be seen as one of the boys and to have that taken away from me hurt way deeper than having a rock thrown at my head.

My family moved back to the UK during my teenage years, which were shrouded in angst, recklessness and very little respect for myself. During my mid-teen years I came out as a lesbian and embraced my queerness. When I got to university I became the chair of the LGBTQ+ student society, kept up an active LGBTQ+ social life and organised several protests. But regardless of the fulfilment this gave me as a queer person I never quite felt at ease.

At the end of my twenties, I was at a crossroads. I was living in Seattle, working at the British Consulate, and I began experiencing panic attacks. Having buried my gender issues, I assumed it must be because I wasn't being creative enough. The day I returned from the US to embark on an MA in Design, one of my dearest friends and soulmates died by suicide. Her death triggered something in me and I realised that I had to start being true to myself and stop running away from what was really bothering me. I felt like I owed it to her to live my life to the fullest, and most importantly, owed it to myself. I'd always walked the line between male and female in terms of how I expressed myself and had attempted to embrace my androgyny and body as best I could. But no matter how hard I had tried to love myself, nothing had worked. For years, my fear of not being believed if I told people who I really was had held me back from coming out. But finally, I pushed aside my fear and disclosed to a close friend that I was trans. She didn't freak out. She listened to me.

I made an appointment with my GP so I could start taking testosterone. My GP tried to discourage me, saying it would take a very long time until I'd get anywhere, and I'd probably be disappointed and perhaps I would be better off trying to accept myself and my body as I was. Been there, tried that. I switched GPs and was referred to a psychologist who then referred me to the Gender Identity Clinic in London. At this point I had already had a lifetime of distress and confusion and my mental health was really shattered. Having to fight to get the healthcare that I needed was frankly terrifying and endlessly frustrating.

I just wanted support, and after ten years of deliberating over transition I was champing at the bit to start hormone therapy. A friend, a trans man, a saviour, offered me his injectable testosterone left over from his prescription. It was dangerous to take someone else's prescription (which I don't recommend anyone does), but I was desperate, and so I gratefully accepted. Two months later – during which time my voice had started descending and fat re-distributing, and I could see my actual self emerging – I was nowhere near getting my own prescription of testosterone from the NHS. I was still waiting for my appointment at the Gender Identity Clinic.

I turned to websites that didn't require a prescription for hormones, featuring big men flexing their big muscles. As my oestrogen levels returned, I began splashing cash I didn't have on testosterone creams, gels and injectionables. I had no professional guidance and the products didn't work at all, which made matters worse. Eventually, despite not really being able to afford it, I went to a private doctor and was given a private prescription for testosterone. Thankfully my GP honoured it.

Back then – around 2010 – the NHS didn't have the strong track record of top surgery results that it has today, so I decided to seek out private surgery. After many years of binding my chest, this decision felt empowering. I had taken part in a mainstream TV series on being trans, and through my social media following I was fortunate enough to be able to raise half of the cost through an online fundraiser. Top surgery was cheaper in the US than in the UK at the time, so I travelled to Florida to have one of the best surgeons in the world do it.

After a commemorative photo shoot at the shadiest bug-infested hotel in Miami, I flew home. Back in Brighton, I noticed a bad rash on my torso so I went to A&E. The nurse initially said there wasn't really anything they could do for me as I had had private surgery. After I broke down due to stress, though, they finally agreed to treat me, and I found out I was having an allergic reaction to one of the creams I had been given for aftercare. It was tough, yes, but the results of the surgery were even better than I had expected, and the timeframe in which I was able to access it really helped to protect my mental health and allowed me to move on with my life. I was also fortunate enough to have a supportive and loving partner who helped me get through this difficult time.

Ten years on from when I first told my GP about being trans, however, I am still struggling to access further surgery through the Gender Identity Clinic. It sometimes feels like I am stuck on the spin-cycle of a washing machine – there's always another assessment and it's really demoralising. I also have to travel a long way at expensive peak times to these often pointless assessments, but I'm one of the lucky ones – clinics are few and far between and people have to travel from all over the UK to get to them. While quality of care in the UK has improved, it's clear that improvements still need to be made when it comes to trans-related healthcare.

It is common for trans people here to wait eighteen months for an initial appointment at a gender identity clinic, with some having to wait three years, and that's just the beginning of the treatment process.[1] This is on top of needing a diagnosis of gender dysphoria and having to show that you've been living as yourself for two years. To try and secure faster treatment, lots of trans people turn to fundraising sites, like I did, to find money for private care. Others seek hormones and medication online on the black market, which can be incredibly unsafe as there is no medical advice or supervision. Personally, I know count-less trans people whose mental health has severely suffered due to the fact that they can't get help quick enough from gender clinics.

With increasing numbers of people trying to access trans-related healthcare on the NHS, waiting times are only going to get worse without additional resources.[2] There is also a lack of awareness and training that is affecting the level of care. GPs are able to prescribe hormones in certain situations while people are waiting to be seen at gender identity clinics, which could provide some short-term solutions if the right training has been given. The majority of GPs, however, are reluctant to do so and report delays in receiving advice from gender specialists.[3] Then, when you reach a clinic, there is a focus on binary experiences of being trans – that is, fitting in with the clinic's idea of what constitutes a transgender man or a transgender woman – that creates issues and mistrust for anyone who doesn't identify with those strict categories. Further training is needed on this too. Fear of having treatment delayed meant that, until recently, I didn't disclose to my medical practitioners that I identify as nonbinary transmasculine; I also felt unable to correct them when they used the wrong pronouns for me.

Two big recent changes have also had a worrying impact in the UK. In September 2020, women and equalities minister Liz Truss announced that plans for trans people to get improved legal gender recognition (sometimes referred to as 'self-identification') in a reform of the Gender Recognition Act would not go ahead. Instead, the only changes proposed were to reduce the cost of a gender recognition certificate – which allows you to change your birth certificate – and to move applications for certificates online. This was a huge disappointment to me and many others, particularly as news coverage mentioned that around 70% of responses in a public consultation on the Act were in favour of self-identifying.[4] I felt that the withdrawal of any meaningful change was due to how hostile the media is towards trans people.

Following on from that, in December 2020, the High Court for England and Wales ruled that children under sixteen were unable to give consent to taking puberty blockers and to understand what this treatment could mean for the long term. This meant that under-sixteens would require a court order to be allowed to start puberty blockers – a devastating blow, not just for those on waiting lists, but also for those already in the care system. In response, families started to crowdfund online so that they could arrange private care. I had decades of depression and anxiety as I struggled with my gender and, for me, this could have been reduced if care had been available when I was young. Meanwhile, the Gender Identity Development Service has said that puberty blockers are a 'physically reversible intervention: if the young person stops taking the blocker their body will continue to develop as it was previously', and a new study shows that blockers have significant positive effects when it comes to trans young people's mental and physical wellbeing.[5]

In March 2021 it was announced that children could access puberty blockers with their parents' permission, and then, in September 2021, the law limiting under-sixteens' access to puberty blockers was thankfully overturned. However, the despair and anxiety that the earlier ruling has already caused is really concerning and I know that I'm not alone in worrying about it – it was received with horror by the trans community of which I am a part. Mermaids, a leading charity that supports transgender, nonbinary and gender-diverse children and their families, wrote on their website that: 'Hormone blockers ... is an internationally-recognised treatment which has had a hugely positive impact on many young trans people ... We believe this judgment will be seen by future generations as a moment of betrayal.'[6] Again, it seems highly likely to me that pervasive anti-trans propaganda has been affecting the conversation, and in my opinion, the ruling marked a dark day in the history of the UK's ill treatment of transgender people.

It is interesting to compare the situation in the UK to other countries. In the US, President Trump removed a regulation against sex discrimination in healthcare in June 2020, meaning that insurance providers could now deny coverage for gender-affirming treatment to transgender people. This added to the difficulties faced by the community there around how health cover depends on your ability to afford insurance, and how many trans people struggle to get jobs that either come with insurance, or help to pay for insurance, due to stigma and discrimination. Fundraisers are much more common in the US than in the UK because of this – every week I see countless new ones for those desperate to pay for aspects of their medical transition. President Biden has since reversed Trump's policy. However, throughout 2021, several states proposed bills to restrict trans people's access to healthcare. According to a report by the Human Rights Campaign, in 2021, forty-eight bills were proposed to prevent transgender youth from receiving age-appropriate healthcare that affirmed their gender identity choice.[7]

In Iceland, where my partner is from, the picture is brighter. In a fundamental change to healthcare for transgender people, they're adopting an informed consent model that focuses on the individual's approach to their own gender rather than on medical professionals' opinions. This means that transgender people will no longer have to go through excessive and intrusive medical assessments of whether they are trans or not. Specialists will of course still pay proper attention to people's health before and during treatment, but the model gives more straightforward access to important services, including hormone therapy, facial feminisation surgery, top surgeries, breast augmentations, post-surgery aftercare and hair transplants. It is a really important step in respecting and valuing trans people, and recognising that they are in charge of their own life and health.

For the UK to really create a more equal and fair society for transgender people, I believe that three concrete changes are key. The first change is to do with funding: the government and health authorities need to allocate money for full services that support all trans people. Every area of support – social, psychological and medical – needs to be properly funded so that everyone can access these freely and without long waiting lists.

The second is to move to an informed consent model like Iceland's so that trans people in the UK are no longer subjected to a lengthy and humiliating diagnosis process. They shouldn't have to jump through hoops based on arbitrary, outdated ideas about gender and expression to prove themselves.

Thirdly, healthcare services need to recognise the importance of providing for younger people. We live in a world where trans people are finally able to be themselves at a much younger age. With support and access to care where needed, trans kids may be able to avoid mental health issues and distress, and blossom and be themselves.

When I took the plunge to start testosterone, I was stepping into the unknown to take control of a situation. After years of having gendered expectations thrust on me, I'd worked out who I was from knowing what I wasn't. So many hoops, so many gatekeepers, when the person who ultimately knows what's best for me is me. Through my treatment I was able to connect with who I really am, and in turn be able to connect to others more authentically. That's fundamentally what trans-related healthcare is about – and so it isn't only to increase the wellbeing of transgender people, but also to create a more whole, open and free society for everyone.

---

1 'Transgender people face NHS waiting list "hell"', BBC News, 9 January 2020, https://www.bbc.co.uk/news/uk-england-51006264

2 Sarah Marsh, 'Transgender people face years of waiting with NHS under strain', *Guardian*, 20 November 2019, https://www.theguardian.com/society/2019/nov/20/transgender-people-face-years-of-waiting-with-nhs-under-strain

3 Nicola Davis, 'Trans patients in England face "soul destroying" wait for treatment', *Guardian*, 26 February 2019, https://www.theguardian.com/society/2019/feb/26/trans-patients-in-england-face-soul-destroying-wait-for-treatment

4 Tim Shipman, 'Boris Johnson scraps plan to make gender change easier', *Sunday Times*, 14 June 2020, https://www.thetimes.co.uk/article/boris-johnson-scraps-plan-to-make-gender-change-easier-zs6lqfls0

5 https://gids.nhs.uk/puberty-and-physical-intervention; Jen Christensen, 'Puberty blockers can be "life-saving" drugs for trans teens, study shows', CNN, 23 January 2020, https://edition.cnn.com/2020/01/23/health/transgender-puberty-blockers-suicide-study/index.html

6 https://mermaidsuk.org.uk/news/analysis-of-the-high-court-judgment-on-access-to-puberty-blockers/

7 https://eu.usatoday.com/story/news/2022/01/20/2022-anti-trans-legislation/6571819001/

'It's not just surgeries that need to change when it comes to intersex rights, it's the way in which the medical lens is applied to intersex people from the moment we are born.'

Hanne Gaby Odiele is a Belgian model who lives in New York. They publicly disclosed that they are intersex in 2017 and have spent the years since campaigning for intersex rights as well as continuing to model.

The End of Forced Intersex Surgeries

HANNE GABY ODIELE

'We're too cute to be binary!' That's what some of us intersex people say to each other. Gender and sex have been viewed on a spectrum for thousands of years in many cultures, particularly Indigenous cultures, but today we have pretty narrow and binary ideas around what it means to be male or female. To be intersex – as we generally understand it now – means that your anatomy does not fit what is considered typically male or female. There are around thirty terms for different variations in being intersex; for example, it can be to do with your hormone levels, having ambiguous sex characteristics, or your chromosome make-up. And it's much more common than you might think: it's estimated that up to 1.7% of the population are born intersex, about the same amount of people who are born with red hair or green eyes, or roughly the same number of people who are twins. Intersex people come in every shape, size, ethnicity and gender – just as any person of any sex can have another gender identity, it's the same with intersex people: there are trans intersex people, cis-identified intersex people and nonbinary intersex people.

Most of us will know someone who is intersex, but the person might not even know it themselves. We don't necessarily know because there's a lot of shame placed on it; people don't always want to talk about their anatomy or their private parts, and also a lot of doctors tell us not to talk about it and it becomes taboo. In some cases, doctors don't even tell you that you're intersex. This is what happened to me.

I have androgen insensitivity syndrome, one variation of intersex characteristics. I found out that I was intersex when I was reading through a magazine as a teenager, in Belgium. The article was about an intersex woman who could not have periods and had undergone several surgeries but didn't really have an explanation for it. I knew I couldn't have periods and I knew I couldn't have kids, but I had never heard the word 'intersex' before. As I read the article I realised: This sounds like me. So I went to show it to my doctor and he said: 'Ah, yes, you finally found out.' It's strange and concerning that I didn't know the truth about my body, but back then I was just happy that I finally knew the name of what was going on.

After I read the article I was able to find a community. There was an organisation in Holland I contacted, which is when I spoke to other intersex people for the first time. It was great to not feel like an anomaly; it made me feel less alone in what I was going through and I was also able to talk to my parents about it more. They found out at the same time as me. Until then, they'd been told by my doctors that I was the only one experiencing what I was experiencing – a total lie. Androgen insensitivity is not *super* common but it's not the rarest of intersex traits at all. And these days I know a lot of people with it, through the activist work I'm doing.

On some level it felt liberating to have all of this new information, to meet these people, but suddenly I started working in the high-fashion modelling world and got caught up in my career – which, at the time, I felt demanded I live as a cis woman. Combined with shame and trauma from surgeries I had, my identity and community were not something I explored further for a while.

It was around 2015 or 2016, when I was twenty-seven and living in America, that I started to re-engage with intersex issues. Back then people in the public eye were really starting to talk about trans rights and in the modelling community we had people like Hari Nef and Andreja Pejic speaking out, improving trans visibility. I started reading intersex forums again and there I read about a twelve-year-old girl who had osteoporosis because of intersex-related cosmetic surgeries years earlier. It wasn't until I engaged with the forums that I realised that the surgeries were still happening often and to many people around the world. I thought: Why is no one talking about this?

First I started talking to my friends about it, then I contacted the community again, specifically an advocacy group called interACT: Advocates for Intersex Youth. With their help I began to educate myself more and more, started to write a press release, and then I gave an interview to the press in January 2017. It had taken about a year and a half for me to gear up to feel ready to disclose that I was intersex publicly, and although I was a little scared at first, I knew that I had to do it, both personally, to conquer the shame placed on me, and politically, to improve visibility and increase awareness.

The responses were pretty much all positive: a lot of people had never heard of intersex, so it was good to be able to start conversations and educate people, and from within the community there was a great response. That was what was most important to me. In fact, once the information was out in the world, it was the most relieving experience ever. For years, it was like I was living with a secret and now I felt like I didn't have to hide it anymore. It felt like a rebirth.

If I could change one thing for intersex people it would be to end unnecessary intersex surgeries on children. They're cosmetic, aiming to make people's genitals look like a 'normal' female or male; doctors all around the world are still performing them every day. Procedures include clitoral reduction, vaginoplasty or removal of functional testes, and often the children these are inflicted upon only find out later in life that they happened at all, far too late for them to make the choice for themselves. While it's mostly about looks, the consequences from each surgery can be around for ever – for instance, losing sensitivity, not being able to use the toilet properly, and many other impacts. I'm not against surgeries altogether, just surgeries that are not consensual and not medically necessary. People can choose for themselves when they are old enough; the person just needs to be fully aware of the options and their implications. And yet this is often happening to people at a young age without their consent. When parents consent, it's sometimes because they might not know that their child can have a happy and healthy life without surgery, as many of my friends do today.

Over the last few years, I've been protesting against these surgeries. I joined the Intersex Justice Project (IJP), a US-based advocacy group, in protest outside Lurie Children's Hospital in Chicago and outside NewYork-Presbyterian Hospital. In 2021, I took part in a similar protest in Belgium, too. We are hoping that hospitals themselves will change from the inside – so far, most haven't, but at the end of July 2020 Lurie Children's Hospital apologised for performing these surgeries and promised to stop while a report into their approach was carried out. Our direct actions are intended to make positive changes like this but also to raise awareness, as lots of people – particularly medical students – have no idea that this is happening in their own hospitals.

We haven't seen many changes in the years that I've been campaigning. In California, the law was nearly changed to ban unnecessary surgeries, but in January 2020 these efforts failed in the State Senate. While I feel like we haven't been very successful with laws, we have got a lot further in terms of visibility and outreach. So many people have come out and I feel like there's a whole new, younger generation that isn't so afraid to talk about being intersex anymore and who have a whole different mentality about gender. As more people openly identify as nonbinary and gender-nonconforming, that speaks to intersex people because it provides an alternative model to the binary ideas of gender that society so often tries to place on us. It creates more pride and awareness around existing along the spectrum.

Overall, though, I think the intersex movement is a lot further behind than some other LGBTQ+ movements. For me, this is because we haven't always been accepted within the wider LGBTQ+ community, maybe only for the last three or four years. Before then, it was always a discussion – 'Are we part of it or are we not part of it?' – and that discussion has slowed us down a little bit. Depending on how they identify, some intersex people feel that they don't fall under the LGBTQ+ community – for instance, if they identify as a straight female. That we have literally been changed by doctors to conform to 'cis female' or 'cis male' can also make us believe that this community isn't for us.

Yet we all go through discrimination and I feel like together we're stronger. A lot of the problems the intersex community have are actually related to issues for the trans community – like not having access to hormones or surgery, particularly as children. The trans community are asking for surgeries they desperately need while the intersex community is forced into surgeries without even knowing why this is happening or if it's what they want. We are all punished by the same heteronormative approach to keeping the population in line with rigid ideas about gender and sexuality. We are all told to hide or change what is natural.

'So are you a man or a woman?'

'Oh, but you're so lucky you don't have a period.'

'What do your genitals look like?'

These are just some of the things that I have heard from people I've met inside and outside of the medical profession. So, it's not just surgeries that need to change when it comes to intersex rights, it's the way in which the medical lens is applied to intersex people from the moment we are born – how people look at us like we are human experiments, bunny rabbits. A lot of our traumatic experiences are not just due to surgery but the way we are treated, specifically by doctors. I remember visits to the doctor's office that should not have been the way they were, where I was touched for no reason without my parents' consent. If we're healthy we don't need to be going through this every time we go to the doctor.

As long as intersex is seen as a mistake, an error, we will just be encouraged to carry on being secretive about who we are. My trips to the doctor's office always made me feel like there was something wrong with me – 'You have to take this pill to be normal' or 'We're going to change your hormones, then you'll be great' – when my body was perfectly healthy the way I was born. Being intersex is different, yes, but it's not a problem. Yet constantly being told that you have a problem is terrible for your mental health. In the intersex community, I hear a lot about the trauma of medical interventions as well as the PTSD that can follow. We've been humiliated, we've had our most private parts examined and been judged for them, we've been made fun of by health professionals in front of their colleagues: 'Did you hear her clit was a centimetre bigger?' These experiences are occurring repeatedly, and the psychological damage they cause lasts a lifetime.

The medical community has to step it up. Prominent organisations like the United Nations and the World Health Organization have called forced intersex surgeries a form of torture, but right now Malta, Chile and (partially) Germany are the only countries that don't allow these surgeries on children before they are old enough to give consent themselves. Beyond that, we also need to hear more stories of intersex people who didn't have surgeries and are fine, to help show parents that these surgeries aren't necessary. There are not many intersex people in the public eye – but I know they are out there. We need more visibility. And finally, we need the rest of the LGBTQ+ community to help make a change. Uplift the voices of intersex activists fighting to end these surgeries, support intersex groups, and show up for us at protests. Be an ally.

'Let us take up a common mission that no queer young person be left without housing.'

Carl Siciliano is the founder of the Ali Forney Center (AFC), the world's largest organisation dedicated to homeless LGBTQ+ youth. Located in New York City, AFC provides emergency and long-term housing, drop-in services, medical and mental health treatment, and vocational and educational services.

Breaking Through: Centering the Needs of Homeless LGBTQ+ Youth

CARL SICILIANO

It was 28 June, 1969; a typical hot, muggy New York City summer night. A group of gay and transgender homeless teens were hanging out in Sheridan Square when they noticed a commotion across the street. Police had raided the Stonewall Inn and were arresting some of the bar's patrons for not wearing gender-conforming clothing, forcing them into a police van. Such raids were common, but tonight several of those being arrested began to fight back.

A crowd gathered, and some began to resist, shouting and throwing garbage at the cops. The police grew nervous and retreated into the Stonewall Inn, barricading themselves behind the bar's wooden door. Suddenly, one of the teens, known only as 'Miss New Orleans', uprooted a parking meter from the sidewalk. Hoisting the meter into a vertical position, she was joined by several other street queens, using it as a battering ram to demolish the door. Some recall Miss New Orleans's act of ferocity as the pivotal moment when resistance became a full-fledged riot.

Having dedicated my life to working with homeless LGBTQ+ young people, it is tremendously inspiring to realize the extent to which Miss New Orleans, Marsha P.

Johnson, Sylvia Rivera, Danny Garvin, Zazu Nova and many other homeless queer youths were at the very center of the uprising that gave birth to our modern struggle for queer liberation and equality. But I am also deeply saddened at how, in the decades that followed, homeless youths were exiled from our LGBTQ+ movement's concern, like they were exiled from their parents' homes.

I began my work in New York City in 1994, twenty-five years after the Stonewall uprising. I discovered a dreadful situation where the overwhelming majority of NYC's homeless LGBTQ+ youth could find no shelters where their lives were not endangered by homophobic and transphobic violence and abuse. Consequently, most felt they had no choice but to struggle to survive in the streets, often resorting to sex work. They were incredibly vulnerable; many young people I knew became addicted to drugs, contracted HIV, and were criminalized by racist policing.

Tragically, many were killed in the streets – one of whom was Ali Forney, a courageous, fiercely compassionate young Black genderfluid person. Their murder led to the founding of the Ali Forney Center, which has since grown to become the world's largest organization dedicated to homeless LGBTQ+ youth.

It seems to me that protecting teens who are driven from their homes because of their sexual orientations and gender identities should be a core responsibility of our LGBTQ+ community. Can there be a crueler, more pervasive form of homophobia, biphobia and transphobia than hundreds of thousands of young people being rejected by their families and driven into destitution in the streets? In the US, numerous studies show that LGBTQ+ youths make up a staggering 40% of the nation's total homeless youth population, despite LGBTQ+ youth comprising merely 5% of the overall youth population; they furthermore estimate that over 200,000 LGBTQ+ youths are currently experiencing homelessness.[1]

This epidemic is an international phenomenon, with studies in the UK, Canada and Australia demonstrating similarly disproportionate rates of LGBTQ+ youth homelessness.[2] In the UK, for example, it has been estimated that LGBTQ+ people make up 24% of the homeless youth population, and that one in four trans people have experienced homelessness.[3]

Tragically, our response to this epidemic of homelessness has been infinitesimal in comparison to the need. In the US there are fewer than 600 shelter beds dedicated to homeless LGBTQ+ youths, while there are fewer than 6,000 beds for an overall homeless youth population conservatively estimated to number more than a million.[4] Given the international scope of this humanitarian crisis, there is an urgent need for further research into LGBTQ+ youth homelessness across the world, perhaps conducted by the United Nations.

What has caused this woefully inadequate response to so grave a crisis within our community? Historically the LGBTQ+ movement has not been especially responsive to issues of poverty. I suspect this has partly been the consequence of our leading advocacy organizations not having steady access to government support, thereby being reliant on major donors, most of whom are wealthy white cisgender men who do not usually have much personal experience of destitution. These donors often have outsized roles in the governing boards of the organizations and play a major role in setting the advocacy priorities. In recent years there has been a far greater effort to view the work through an intersectional lens and to bring greater racial and gender diversity to leadership. However, it must be frankly acknowledged that the decades where racial and economic diversity were not prioritized resulted in a radical devaluation of the needs of the most impoverished and oppressed members of the LGBTQ+ community.

Another barrier has been the corrosive effects of the predominant homophobic narratives used against us in the first decades after Stonewall – namely those making appalling efforts to stigmatize and vilify LGBTQ+ people as pedophiles. I'll never forget what was happening when I first came to New York City to serve the homeless back in the mid-eighties. At the time I was a pious young Italian Catholic, struggling to figure out how to reconcile my spiritual beliefs with my queerness. In the months before a law protecting LGBTQ+ people from discrimination in employment and housing was passed in New York City, it had a powerful opponent in the local Catholic arch-bishop, Cardinal John O'Connor. He held a press confer-ence on the steps of Saint Patrick's Cathedral in which he threatened to shut down every Catholic school and orphanage if he was compelled to hire gay men. In such an environment, many LGBTQ+ adults feared that any attention paid to teens could be misinterpreted as sexual, and the needs of our youths went unrecognized.

And even our own narratives set up barriers. The most urgent objective for the early movement for queer libera-tion to achieve any power was to persuade us to come out of the closet. Early on a narrative was crafted which portrayed the act of coming out as the key to enter a promised land of joy and freedom. We would finally discard the shackles of shame and fear, and at last discover fulfilling, rewarding lives. Yet the plight of homeless queer teens, discarded by parents and reduced to desperation in the streets, embodied the very fears so many of us harbored. There was no space for the bleak realities of their lives in our uplifting narratives, and we chose not to see them.

While recent years have seen more awareness of the plight of homeless LGBTQ+ youth, there continues to be a woeful disconnect between the size and scope of the crisis and the extent of our collective response. However, there are several ways in which the LGBTQ+ community and our allies can begin to improve in this area.

First, we need to support organizations that provide housing to them, either through our donations and/or our volunteering. In the UK, there is the Outside Project, a shelter and community center for LGBTQ+ people; in the US, the Ali Forney Center website has a list of America-wide homeless LGBTQ+ youth-serving organizations. At the Ali Forney Center, volunteers provide invaluable support, cooking meals, sharing job skills, assisting with support groups, even making long-term commitments to be supportive to our youths when they move on from our programs. These efforts go far in fostering a true sense of community, both for our young people and for our volunteers.

Second, we can become advocates for them, urging politicians to allocate funds to housing initiatives as well as urging our LGBTQ+ advocacy organizations to prioritize homeless LGBTQ+ youths in their agendas. Especially important is encouraging these kinds of organizations to include the voices of homeless youths themselves; I have observed that homeless youth are quite effective in their passionate insistence that more housing needs to be created.

Finally, we need to develop strategies to address the singular role of religious hostility in creating a climate where parents reject their LGBTQ+ children. More than 90% of the youths who have come to the Ali Forney Center for help have indicated that their parents' religious beliefs were the primary reason they were exiled from their homes. If we are to protect youths from being thrown to the streets, then we must foster partnerships with religious groups aimed at helping parents to love and accept their LGBTQ+ children.

More than fifty years have passed since Miss New Orleans and the other homeless queer youths broke open the door to the Stonewall Inn. The time is long past for our LGBTQ+ movement to center the protection of her many descendants still struggling to survive. Let us take up a common mission that no queer young person be left without housing.

1 'LGBTQ youth experiencing homelessness', Homelessness Policy Research Institute, 19 August 2019, https://socialinnovation.usc.edu/wp-content/uploads/2019/08/LGBTQ-Youth-Lit-Review-Final.pdf

2 'Why are so many young LGBT people in Britain homeless?', *Big Issue*, 26 July 2017, https://www.bigissue.com/latest/many-young-lgbt-people-britain-homeless/; 'LGBTQ2 youth homelessness', Homeless Hub, https://www.homelesshub.ca/about-homelessness/population-specific/lesbian-gay-bisexual-transgender-transsexual-queer; Shannon Molloy, 'Shameful statistic staining Australia: Young LGBTI people twice as likely to be homeless', News.com.au, 27 February 2020, https://www.news.com.au/national/shameful-statistic-staining-australia-young-lgbti-people-twice-as-likely-to-be-homeless/news-story/36a798f2491cdf9c2abc07737925d881

3 Samir Jeraj, 'Homelessness charities say "high volume" of LGBT youth at risk during pandemic', *New Statesman*, 22 April 2020, https://www.newstatesman.com/spotlight/coronavirus/2020/04/homelessness-charities-say-high-volume-lgbt-youth-risk-during-pandemic; 'LGBT youth homelessness', Albert Kennedy Trust, 2015, https://www.akt.org.uk/Handlers/Download.ashx?IDMF=c0f29272-512a-45e8-9f9b-0b76e477baf1

4 https://www.ncsl.org/research/human-services/homeless-and-runaway-youth.aspx#:~:text=Each%20year%2C%20an%20estimated%204.2,ages%2013%2D25%20experience%20homelessness

'Let's start to care a little more about the elders in our community. Because at some point that's all of us.'

Juno Roche is a writer and campaigner from south London. They previously founded Trans Workers UK and the Trans Teachers Network. Juno educates around trans rights and HIV awareness and they have published three books: *Queer Sex*, *Trans Power*, and *Gender Explorers*. They are currently writing a memoir.

As We Grow Older

JUNO ROCHE

A few years ago, I took an impulsive leap into the unknown. I've always dreamed about having a view, a room with a view, a beautiful view. It's silly and romantic I know, but I've spent nearly all of my life in London gazing out over pencil-thin gardens attached to rows of single-Lego-brick houses. It had become stifling. By some bizarre turn of fate (a key worker mortgage and many lodgers walking around in novelty boxer shorts) I'd managed to both buy a house and hang on to it, despite my precarious freelance income. In what others described as a reckless move I decided to sell up and follow my dream. Within a year I'd left London and bought a 200-year old village house in the mountains of Andalucía, in the middle of nowhere.

I'd never been in the middle of nowhere before, I'd never stepped foot in Spain before, and I'd never been further than a tube ride away from my beautiful queer community. But from the first day I knew it was right because every morning I get to look out and breathe in the beauty of the mountains. For a working-class queer living with HIV, it felt like heaven. It felt like the space I'd never had, internally or externally: a vast wide-open space in which I could forget my lifelong city anxieties, as if they'd never existed.

I wanted to be like Julia Roberts playing Liz Gilbert in *Eat, Pray, Love*. I would travel, I would enjoy my room with a view, and perhaps I would even find a lover I could melt into. I needed to find a different meaning to my life.

Last year I hit the impossibly high age of fifty-five – impossible because I was diagnosed with HIV approximately twenty-seven years ago and was told I'd be dead before I was thirty – and I started to feel scared of ageing here alone in my dream.

For someone living long-term with HIV, thinking about ageing is a new concept. I worry what my life might be like if I'm alone and in need of care or support. Will my transness and my HIV be respected by carers, by the people that might need to come into my home, into my personal space? People that don't know me but people that may need to be intimate with me? If I needed residential or supportive residential care would my identity be celebrated, would queer and trans high days and holidays be honoured or even known about? I've heard urban rumours of trans folk not being respected, their hormones discontinued and their correct pronouns ignored. I read recently that some carers have been found trying to pray the LGBTQ+ away in some of their clients. A kind of enforced biblical detransition. Perhaps my lifelong sense of my queerness, my gender and my sexuality might just end up on a narrow, dusty shelf next to the books I'd written many years before, ignored now and meaningless. Or what might happen if I develop dementia?

While thinking about this, I went in search of others' experiences. I discovered an old letter to the *Daily Mail* in which a gay man who lived in a supported care environment said, 'how could I be happy in a "home" where all there is to do is talk to the other inmates, if they're all straight and don't talk to me? I'm not going back into the closet again.'[1] Elsewhere, a sixty-eight-year-old lesbian said that after harassment in her home town she moved into sheltered accommodation in London but felt that it was 'like having a split personality'. She went on to say: 'I couldn't really tell them anything about myself. I could talk about the past and my children, but I couldn't say anything about the real me. It was almost like speaking a different language.'[2]

Older LGBTQ+ people are often single, often childless (although this is changing) and according to data far more likely than straight older people to be isolated and lonely.[3] Why don't we see safety and comfort in this later part of our lives as being as imperative as spaces in which we can laugh, fuck and dance away our twenties and thirties?

In today's world the needs of white cis heterosexuals are always planned for from the centre and often met – almost all spaces feel welcoming and there are 'safer' resting places which don't rely on a narrow band of cafes, pubs and night-clubs squashed into a single street or a small part of town. There isn't a reliance on a youthful night-time culture to feel both seen and understood, whereas our comforting queer ghettos fulfil exactly this purpose. But what happens when you can't reach that place, or no longer feel welcome there? It's strange how we as LGBTQ+ folk neglect our elders' needs when ageing is pretty much unavoidable.

It's only when you start to age that you realise how age makes you invisible, and how invisible, marginalised people find it harder to connect with the people like them who are also becoming invisible. Our nuanced queer support network starts to crumble as we age and drift away from our week-in-week-out hubs. I'm wondering how I can future-proof my queerness so that it stays intact as I grow older, whatever happens to my body's capabilities. Where can I be with others like me and talk about being us and laugh about the lives we led? I want a commune or at least a queer housing option.

Spaces like this would mean that we could not just feel safer but be around people who understand us and share our memories. I remember punk; I saw Crass, Bauhaus, X-Ray Spex and Annie Anxiety in the late seventies, and I remember the very early days of the AIDS pandemic. I remember exactly where I was when I first heard the words 'gay plague' and somehow, deep down, I knew that it would affect me. I was eating a Welsh drop scone and I wanted to cry. Good memories, queer-tinged memories, poignant memories and memories that still fill me with horror. I can't share my life or my thoughts with someone who wasn't there, I just don't want to. On one hand I fear ageing but on another I adore the process of collective memories that build up as an internal library. Those memories make me, me.

Moving to the mountains was my choice and it's easy to see why I might feel alone here, but when I speak to queer friends around my age and older they express the same thoughts, even if they live in cities across the UK. They talk about starting to feel isolated. In some way when that happens and we don't get to share our intimate thoughts or the brilliance of our queer memories it's like our queer souls start to disappear. On a personal note, I never get to talk about my HIV and how it impacts my life with anyone outside of my queer group. While times may have changed, many people still see HIV as AIDS and as a moral death sentence.

As queer people, we experience the world from a completely different angle – we're often raised to deny our truths and we face discrimination, stigma and rejection from the get-go. Only we can truly understand the joy we experience when we find others like us. It's bliss. Queers get queers and support other queers; it's not perfect but it's what we have: each other and our community.

*

As the concept of ageing becomes a reality for me I've become obsessed with the idea of creating queer co-housing. When I was in my early twenties I was part of a group who, as a response to Section 28, set up and ran a housing cooperative in east London for the LGBTQ+ community. After Section 28 was introduced a growing number of young people were thrown out of their family homes when their parents discovered they were LGBTQ+. We were given housing stock by the local council that we agreed to maintain and improve, which helped the housing department with their what-to-do-with-the-17-year-old-homeless-queer-who-doesn't-have-enough-points-to-be-high-up-in-the-list-but-is-in-real-need dilemma.

We grew exponentially in number and eventually started to trade many of our short-life properties for permanent council housing. Young LGBTQ+ folk would never have stood a chance of getting housed without our project. Creating safe housing is concrete activism. Safe LGBTQ+ housing is a community in which you can just be yourself.

I type into Google 'shared LGBTQ+ housing schemes' to see if anything like this exists today and found lots of adverts for rooms in queer house shares (tick, more queer houses please), but most of the rooms cost over £1,000 per month and most ads defined their ideal housemate as being 'like-minded', 'professional' and 'in their twenties'. Hard to see where a fifty-six-year-old or a sixty-seven-year-old or an isolated retired seventy-two-year-old might fit into that seemingly idyllic queer scenario. One ad for a beautiful room said: 'I have friends right up to fifty so age is not a problem.' I chuckled as I realised that at fifty-six I'd already be off the cliff.

Wouldn't it be great to develop the opportunity for queer and LGBTQ+ intergenerational housing which encourages socialising and the support to enable the continuation of our lifestyles and identities? (I'm talking 28 Barbary Lane, from Armistead Maupin's *Tales of the City*, here.) In 1995, Polari carried out a small but ground-breaking piece of research called 'As we grow older' – they found that 91% of the lesbians and 75% of the gay men they surveyed agreed with me, saying they wanted queer-specific accommodation.[4] In 2020, LGBTQ+ organisations Tonic, Stonewall Housing and Opening Doors London conducted a survey of 600-plus older LGBTQ+ Londoners. Over half of respondents wanted LGBTQ+-specific housing with care, a quarter wanted LGBTQ+-accredited housing with care (so mainstream housing where staff are trained on LGBTQ+ inclusivity) and only 1% said they would want general provision.[5] Overall, there was agreement on the need for greater safety and choice.

As of 2021, LGBTQ+-inclusive retirement initiatives exist in the UK but are extremely scarce. Anchor Hanover, England's largest provider of specialist housing and care for older people, has a strong LGBTQ+ tenants group. In Manchester, a new scheme – still in the planning stage – will deliver more than 100 apartments for people aged 55 and over. In 2014, Tonic Housing was established as a not-for-profit community interest company and is now a housing association, set up to provide LGBTQ+-affirming housing with care. Tonic's CEO, Anna Kear, works with a small team and the integral support and scrutiny of a 'Community Panel'. In March 2021, Tonic announced they will be opening the UK's first LGBTQ+ retirement commu-nity in London, after which it can then look to provide affordable and social housing. All staff in the scheme are being trained to provide respectful and informed care and, Anna told me, have been 'incredibly engaged and positive'.

There is another significant organisation up and running: Alternative Care Services, the UK's first independent LGBTQ+ domiciliary care provider. Ramses Underhill-Smith founded it after watching a friend in New York who was living with HIV receive appalling homecare and then endure rejection by carers who refused to work with someone with HIV. When I spoke with Ramses, he said: 'It was heartbreaking seeing people I know, who've lived happy, comfortable and proud lives, having to go back into the closet to get dignified care and support in later life.'

He went on to say that 'as younger people we never really understand the vulnerabilities that happen as we age. If you can't express those vulnerabilities openly to someone who you can trust it becomes harder and harder to just be yourself.' All of Alternative Care Services' staff undertake extensive training, and Ramses is planning to open small-unit residential care homes specifically for the LGBTQ+ community as soon as possible.

For Ruby Rose, an eighty-one-year-old trans woman who works with Age UK, the issue is that when you need care, you need 'total holistic care'. It must not be given begrudgingly or with a lack of understanding about the identity of the person – or worse still, in an atmosphere tinged with homophobia or transphobia, she emphasised. If the person receiving poor care isn't robust or confident they will undoubtedly suffer, and being confident is tough as we age, as loneliness and perhaps health conditions erode our sense of self. We need to be nurtured as we grow older – we need our lives to be meaningful and worthy of celebration, not denial.

Of course, LGBTQ+ elderly care won't be for everyone. I talked with one older trans woman who said that after transitioning she saw herself as a woman like any other woman, so why shouldn't she be part of the wider whole? I really get that, but often, even if that's how we experience ourselves, the world can treat us very differently. We sometimes pass, blend or become absorbed into cis hetero society because we iron out our queer edges, but if, like me, you take hormones and HIV medications every day then you're outed by your daily bread. We cannot rely on feeling safe as we age by hiding ourselves, we deserve much more than that. Besides, I haven't lived a radical queer life to have others ignore who I am in my later years, even if my dream has led me to try and emulate Julia Roberts in *Eat, Pray, Love*. I am rewriting the script – and I want a queerer version.

We will all get older and we may lose our confidence, our ability to move, to remember, to be well, and that might make us vulnerable in a world that we know is cruel far too often. Let's make plans for that and support the initiatives to build and to deliver LGBTQ+-specific services – housing, day centres, domiciliary care, breaks away and befriending groups. Let's start to care a little more about the elders in our community. Because at some point that's all of us. You, you, you, and me.

---

1 'I'd hate to be the only gay in the care home', *Daily Mail*, 3 August 2012, https://www.pressreader.com/uk/daily-mail/20120803/282660389559153

2 Gene Robertson, 'Out of the shadows', *Inside Housing*, 24 February 2012, https://www.insidehousing.co.uk/insight/insight/out-of-the-shadows4-30647

3 'Lesbian, gay and bisexual people in later life (2011)', Stonewall, January 2015, https://www.stonewall.org.uk/resources/lesbian-gay-and-bisexual-people-later-life-2011

4 Ruth Hubbard and John Rossington, 'As we grow older', Polari, November 1995, https://lgbtsand.files.wordpress.com/2013/07/as_we_grow_older.pdf

5 'Building safe choices 2020', Tonic, Stonewall Housing and Opening Doors London, 29 September 2020, https://static1.squarespace.com/static/5a620d960abd04e6cae4477f/t/5f6e01d8b8d1734bd4a0dece/1601044961828/BSC+2020+Report.pdf

BEYOND THE BINARY

'The world doesn't always embrace individuality or difference, but with fashion we can open up possibilities.'

A fashion designer with a curatorial approach to fashion-making and brand-building, **Jonathan Anderson** has earned both critical acclaim and commercial success with the collections he designs for his eponymous label, JW Anderson, and as the creative director of LOEWE. In 2017, he curated an exhibition with the title *Disobedient Bodies* at the Hepworth Wakefield gallery.

Disobedient Bodies

JONATHAN ANDERSON

When I look back on the history of clothing, I've always been obsessed with people who dressed defiantly, especially queer people. The old cliché of liking Oscar Wilde aside, I find his way of dressing to be incredibly romantic, and when you look at womenswear, I have long admired a British painter from the 1920s called Gluck. She would have likely been classified as a lesbian in her day, but today we might think of her differently. She wore men's suits and would go to Savile Row to have them fitted, squared off perfectly. The writer Fran Lebowitz is another hero of mine. She has very staunch beliefs in the power of outsiderness and, with her oversized pinstripe suit jackets or tuxedos, I think the way that she dresses reflects that.

Queer people have always broken the rules when it comes to fashion, or rather, have used fashion to break the rules of society. Fashion can be a way to experiment with character or to work out your identity and I believe that clothes can have a protective role on a more emotional level. Clothing choices can sometimes pose a risk, but clothes also allow you to put a guard up, or you can wear them as a weapon. Clothing is sometimes about signalling association – like an association with a subculture, or a certain pack of people – but it can be a marker of individuality, too. A way to conform or to rebel. I collect queer photography, and looking at images of queer people at liberation rallies in the sixties or seventies, you can see that those people are dressing with a political message. Clothing is full of paradoxes, but ultimately it can empower us – and in a world that has historically taken power away from queer people, that can be vital.

For me, clothing has been all of these things at different moments. Growing up in Northern Ireland, experimenting with clothes helped me to discover who I was. I used to go to TK Maxx and buy whatever was on sale that no one else wanted, like a pair of orange trousers, a big pink fleece or a fluorescent jacket. Something excited me about dressing like that against the grey landscape I existed in. It was a disaster in the playground of course, but even if I was bullied it didn't matter because I knew I was on my own voyage, and I was lucky in that my family was incredibly liberal. My dad was a rugby player and my mum a teacher and they brought us up in an unusual environment for Northern Ireland during the Troubles: we were not raised Protestant or Catholic, and we were taught not to see differences or to worry too much about being different. The way that I dressed obviously made people question me but I think that maybe I *wanted* to be questioned, I wanted to be forced to get to know myself better through confrontation.

My penchant for dressing outlandishly continued when I first moved to London. I used to wear all kinds of things – there was a new look every day. I remember working at Prada and coming to work in pyjamas, which, I think, was again about standing out. Then at some point my approach to clothes started to change; I found that the more I worked in the industry, the more I would wake up in the morning and be unable to make a decision about what to wear because I was focused on coming up with another collection. Over time, I started to just wear a pair of jeans and a sweater, which is what you'll likely find me in today. I wouldn't say I dress this way now because I have chosen it – it's more to do with my work than who I am. I've certainly never thought: Oh, I need to look more masculine. Still, we all do it to some extent: get up in the morning, brush our teeth, get dressed, look in the mirror and think about who we are – or who we *feel* like – that day. Some people have days when they feel more feminine, other days more masculine. Clothing can help us articulate that.

In a world that often expects certain things for certain people when it comes to clothes – where society wants men, say, to wear some things, and women to wear others – I sometimes question why I do menswear and womenswear shows. But for me it's not about classifying people, it's about using these categories as ideas – ideas to borrow from. When I did menswear collections that put men in bustiers and tank dresses, it was about asking people to think about what makes something 'male' or 'female' to begin with. I like operating across menswear and womenswear in that sense because I like to have parameters to fight against – something to subvert or question, not because I believe that zips or buttons should be in a specific direction for men and another for women. I'm also very into this idea of the shared wardrobe – I've always been obsessed with the white shirt on Robert Mapplethorpe as one thing and on Patti Smith as a completely different thing, though it's the same garment. You can have many meanings to a certain piece and items can be twisted in so many ways. A painter paints a moment and a fashion designer sends a moment down a catwalk. It's not to say 'you must do this'; it's a proposition to people, and they can choose what they take from the proposition. I hope that this is how fashion can help people – by expanding our ideas around choice and freedom of expression.

In the media today, fashion has in some ways become public enemy number one. We're rightly in a time where we are examining fashion as capitalistic, which it is – it's expensive. I work in luxury – it's aspirational, but, for most people, unattainable. Even though fashion houses these days cast more queer people in their campaigns and on catwalks, many global brands still consider sales first. Some brands are hesitant to become more inclusive because if they are selling in Saudi Arabia, Russia and China, for example, there might be a concern that LGBTQ+ representation could alienate some buyers. I remember doing an advertising campaign for LOEWE about six years ago that had two men kissing in it, and it became clear that we may only be able to feature it in stores, not on posters and billboards in the streets. In the end, the campaign was restricted to Europe. Ultimately, fashion is a market-driven business, and as an individual working within that, you come up against certain barriers.

Despite these barriers, I believe that we can use fashion to educate about queer history, raise money for queer causes, and offer more information that might help queer people. With both my brands I've collaborated with P.P.O.W. Gallery to use art by David Wojnarowicz, an incredible gay artist, to raise awareness about his work and his struggle and raise funds for Visual AIDS. I also believe that fashion must get to a point where we don't have to talk about what gender anyone is, where we just see the beauty in people. The people in fashion are incredibly liberal and the industry is made up of misfits who love creativity – the work should reflect that, championing many, many different ideas about what can be beautiful. More diverse representation in fashion can influence the mainstream – it has the power to break down boundaries around how we dress, and to send out the message that there are no rules.

The world doesn't always embrace individuality or difference, but with fashion we can open up possibilities. Fashion is about visual identity – when you meet someone, it confronts you. It's a kind of storytelling that is so important, specifically within queer culture: it's a way to project confidence, it helps you to find your people. Being able to dress how you want is about having your own identity, walking out into the big, bad world and saying: 'This is who I am.'

'We have a lot of work to do before society reflects the myriad ways that people experience their genders. We need to take a long hard look at the structures we've built – from sports to physical spaces to legal framework – and bring them up to date.'

Amelia Abraham is a journalist, editor and author from London. She's the author of *Queer Intentions: A (Personal) Journey Through LGBTQ+ Culture*, and is the editor of this collection. In 2018 she did a TEDx Talk called 'Why feminists should support transgender rights' and often speaks at events about LGBTQ+ rights and queer culture.

If It's Broke, Fix It

AMELIA ABRAHAM

From the age of seven years old, I was obsessed with football. My life revolved around practising kick-ups in the garden, playing *Euro 2000* on my PlayStation, and watching *Bend It Like Beckham* on loop (a classic lesbian origin story). My parents allowed me to be as much of a tomboy as I wanted, but when I was ten, and becoming increasingly naughty, they sent me to a new school – a convent school. Suddenly, everything was gendered. Girls were required to wear skirts, not trousers, and we had to do 'needlework club' under the watch of a terrifyingly strict older nun. The greatest horror came during the first PE lesson, when it was revealed that girls had to play netball and boys had to play football. Eventually, after much campaigning with the football coach, I managed to have this rule overturned, but the message to my younger self was clear: you can't do what you love, because of your gender.

OK, so me not being allowed to play football with the boys when I was ten is hardly a gross injustice in the grand scheme of things, but it is one of my earliest memories of being put in a prescriptive gender category. I was reminded of it recently, when a friend asked me to write a story for her magazine, about the inclusion of trans and intersex people in sports. At the time, I knew of a few trans sports stars, like American triathlon competitor Chris Mosier and mixed martial arts fighter Fallon Fox. I also knew that sports is a world with very little LGBTQ+ visibility, and that the topic of trans and intersex people competing in elite sports is shrouded in controversy. Beyond that, I understood woefully little about the subject. I'm embarrassed to say that I'd always slightly avoided the conversation about trans and intersex inclusion in sports – partly because I knew how complicated it was and partly because – dreams of 'bending it like Beckham' now long forgotten – I rarely understand what's going on in sports anyway.

In the end, I spent six weeks on the article. The subject was as vast and technical as I'd guessed. There are many differing opinions, from scientists' to ethicists' to sportspeople's, but here's the top line: at club or recreational level, trans and intersex people can generally play for the gendered team that they identify with (although whether they are accepted is a different story), or they can choose to play in mixed gender teams. At the elite level however, many sports are divided into men and women's categories, and to determine which you can compete in, there are tests involved. In the past, Olympic athletes have gone through invasive genital inspections and DNA-testing to determine their gender. Today, testosterone seems to be the deal-breaker. In World Athletics and International Olympics Committee (IOC) guidelines, athletes' testosterone has to fall within a certain limit if they want to compete in the women's categories – this limit is wider for trans women, who must also have been medically transitioning on hormones for at least one year. For trans men on testosterone competing in men's teams, there is no limit.

These rules have been put in place with the aim of encouraging fairness but don't always achieve their goal. On the one hand, some trans and intersex people cannot compete in the Olympic category of their identified gender because their testosterone is not at the required level. On the other, some sportspeople – particularly cis female sportspeople – complain that trans women who *do* get to compete have an unfair advantage, not just because the testosterone remit is broader than for cis women, but because, generally speaking, people who are assigned male at birth tend to have a bigger muscle mass or lung capacity, potentially enhancing performance. While this is true, many trans sportspeople report that taking transition hormones decreases their sporting ability, and studies have found that hormone therapy reduces muscle mass and drops oxygen consumption.[1] One recent study, however, found that trans women who had been taking hormones for two years were faster than cis women. Overall, scientists cannot seem to agree on whether trans women on hormones have an advantage or a disadvantage over cis women (one reason why the IOC delayed plans to lower the testosterone limit for trans women ahead of the 2020 Olympics). And so, the debate rages on, with trans athletes caught in the crossfire. When asked whether the transgender New Zealand weightlifter Laurel Hubbard should be allowed to compete in the Olympics, for example, cisgender Australian weightlifter Deborah Acason commented: 'I feel that if it's not even, why are we doing the sport?'

In pursuit of 'fairness', some organisations and institutions have banned, or tried to ban, transgender women from competing. Sporting body Fair Play For Women have said that they do not believe that trans women should be allowed to compete in female only sports at all. In early 2020, three cisgender female high-school athletes in Connecticut launched a legal case against two transgender classmates, on the alleged basis that their competing has deprived cisgender girls of track titles and scholarship opportunities.[2] Similarly, in March 2020, an Idaho state law declared that girls or women's teams in schools, colleges and universities will not be open to transgender students who identify as female. The law has been challenged by civil rights groups as a breach of Title IX, the 1972 US law that bars sex discrimination in education, and in August 2020, a federal judge blocked the ban.[3] In October 2020, World Rugby banned trans women from competing in contact rugby, claiming that it puts cis women at risk of injury (a broad assumption about the physicality of all trans women). Then, during 2021, the situation escalated severely in the US. Reports have found that eighty bills were proposed with the aim of preventing young transgender people from playing in school sports teams consistent with their gender identity. While writing this essay, Mississippi, Arkansas and Tennessee passed bills to implement state-wide bans on female trans athletes.[4]

Feeling concerned by these stories, I went looking for examples of trans and intersex people who have fought to compete in their sport by taking on the system (another reason the article took so long: I got a little obsessed). I discovered Renée Richards – an amazing American tennis player who fought to compete in the 1976 US Open after transitioning. Richards took a case against the United States Tennis Association's genetic screening process all the way up to the US Supreme Court, and won, allowing her to compete. I also read about Mara Gómez, the Argentinian footballer who, in December 2020, became the first transgender woman to play professional league football for a women's team, despite enduring criticism on social media that her inclusion is unfair.[5] 'On the field, you can have speed and strength, but that doesn't help you if you don't know how to play football,' she has said in response. 'I always hold up the example of Messi … He measures 1.6 meters (5 foot, 7 inches) and is the best player in the world.'

Most famous, perhaps, is the case of South African middle-distance runner and Olympic gold medallist Caster Semenya. A female athlete with naturally high levels of testosterone, she was subjected to intrusive gender testing, which she has spoken out against. Eventually, governing body World Athletics (formerly known as the IAAF) ruled that her level of testosterone gives her an unfair advantage over other women, and it was decided that she has to take hormone suppressants to reduce the amount of testosterone in her body if she wants to compete. She contested this ruling but in September 2020 lost the appeal.[6] In February 2021, Semenya announced that she is taking the case to the European Court of Human Rights. Her lawyer said the challenge is 'for all women' (experts note that the scrutiny Semenya has experienced particularly affects women of colour, women in the global south and intersex women).

It's easy to picture the effects of all of this discrimination and policing. A trans kid with a passion for sport might see the stories above and believe that biology is destiny, or that they are not welcome in sports at all. Research from Stonewall suggests that this is true, finding that while one in eight LGBTQ+ people avoid going to the gym or participating in sports groups because of fear of discrimination and harassment, this rises to two in five for trans people specifically.[7] Intersex people are also likely to be put off – they might see stories like Caster Semenya's and feel discouraged from a career as an athlete. And what about nonbinary people? Sports divided into male and female teams offer no place for people who identify as neither. As Robbie de Santos, director of sport at Stonewall, put it to me: 'Sport is an exceptionally powerful tool for social change and for making people feel a sense of community and belonging, but by organising competitions by gender, we create obstacles to nonbinary people's ability to access sports, and the life-changing impact it can have.'

While I do not identify as trans, intersex or nonbinary myself, reading all of the above, I felt the familiar sense of frustration – for all of those times I've felt excluded for being a woman, or genderfluid, or for being queer. When I finished writing the story, I also felt extremely *guilty* – guilty for avoiding the topic of trans and intersex inclusion in sports because it had felt too complicated. That was precisely why there was no solution to this problem, why no one has worked out a better system for the one that we have – which is clearly broken.

This brokenness does not just apply to sports, although sports is a very good example. It applies to various parts of our society. Research is showing that in certain countries more people than ever before are identifying outside of the gender binary (although this is not a new concept – there are countless examples of cultures who did not think of gender as binary until colonisers imposed the idea). This is especially true among younger generations. The Pew Research Center, for example, found in one American study from 2019 that 41% of Gen Z (defined as anyone born in 1997 and beyond) surveyed identified as neutral on the spectrum of masculinity and femininity.[8] They have also found that one in five American adults say they know someone who goes by a gender-neutral pronoun.[9] Even beyond these studies, we know that there are now many people who do not identify as cis male or female, so why is the world not set up to reflect this reality?

Try to go one day, let alone a week without encountering the gender binary and you'll be hard-pressed to succeed. Public toilets, mandatory prefixes on forms, 'male' and 'female' clothing sections – they all ask us to choose a gender. When we interact with people on transport or in shops, they tend to make assumptions about our gender and let us know exactly what those assumptions are, by calling us 'sir' or 'madam' or else assuming our pronouns. So much of our lives is constructed around the idea that there are only two ways to experience your gender; we split everything into binary categories and ask people to choose one (usually the one assigned at birth) or else be left out. As a consequence, gender-variant people's ability to partake and succeed in the world is inhibited by a system that excludes them, or sets them up to fail. Nonbinary people in some of the essays in this book offer examples, explaining how misgendering makes them feel like they're 'not real', and that, worse yet, exclusionary attitudes from society can perpetuate violence.

On this, Lauren Lubin, a nonbinary runner, documentary maker and campaigner for nonbinary inclusion in sport makes a point that I found interesting. Lauren said that they love running because, in a world that says 'no' to them at every turn, they can 'just put their sneakers on and go' without anyone stopping them.[10] For Lauren, sport offers the potential to escape social structures that can be exhausting, oppressive. If the disjunction between a strictly binary approach to gender and people's experiences of living outside of this binary has a negative impact on people's lives, we are doing something wrong. The system is broken, and it is up to us to fix it.

The positive news is, small shifts towards greater inclusivity for trans, intersex and nonbinary people in sports are starting to be made. On a grassroots level, there has been a blossoming of initiatives to better include LGBTQ+ people. Among these are more training and awareness around gender-neutral pronouns and a push for the introduction of more gender-neutral changing rooms. Raising awareness and platforming LGBTQ+ sports role models is also vital, which Stonewall are focusing on by asking LGBTQ+ sports ambassadors to give talks to young sportspeople. But there is still more work that can be done, says Robbie de Santos. 'While attitudes are improving, we know that lesbian, gay, bi and trans communities still feel unwelcome in sporting environments, often starting from a young age.'

When it comes to elite sports, campaigners are challenging existing models and starting conversations about more inclusive versions. In her TEDx Talk, trans Ultimate Frisbee player Jenna Weiner asks us to question our fundamental assumptions about why certain people are naturally better at sports than others. Campaigners like her point out the logical failings of arguments that exclude trans women from sports. For example, that if size and strength are the basis of the argument for making things 'even', then what about the massive discrepancies that already exist between cis competitors? That in sports which are skill-led with physical strength or speed being slightly less important – such as skateboarding, golf and fencing (which are all gendered at Olympic level) – it makes very little sense to have gendered categories as the deciding factor in judging your ability to take part.

Weiner calls for sports that are less binary, and for more mixed teams. Others suggest we need to do away with gendered categories altogether, since – as long as they exist – intersex and other people with naturally higher hormone levels will be policed and nonbinary people must pick a gendered category that does not apply to them. Plus, using testosterone as the bar in sports enforces a culture where trans women who want to play elite sports feel they *have* to medically transition with hormones in order to qualify, or else not compete at all. Some experts have suggested that we could categorise by height or weight.[11] It would be great to see these kinds of ideas from white papers turn into more real-world experiments or trials sooner rather than later, since discrimination is currently so rife. More research is also needed, given that the narrative around trans women in sport having an undue advantage is lacking in robust evidence, and doing a disservice to athletes. De Santos from Stonewall agrees: 'There is still a lot of prejudice across the sporting world, particularly for trans and intersex athletes, whose bodies are constantly scrutinised and monitored in the public eye,' he summarises. 'Suggesting that strength is the only component of sporting success undermines the complex mix of teamwork, talent, tactics, strength and agility which athletes know make up real sporting success.'

Beyond sports, in other areas of society, we are gradually seeing the emergence of more options when it comes to gender, too. Despite the derision of right-wing and conservative pundits (think Piers Morgan) over the last five years, British schools have been introducing gender-neutral uniforms, while many public institutions now have gender-neutral toilets. In Sweden, gender-neutral schools have had positive effects on children: research has found that their pupils are less likely to gender stereotype or gender segregate, while other research has shown that gender neutral textbooks have led to more mixed gender applications to typically gendered courses. This would suggest that less policing around gender is also a positive step in diminishing sexism.

The next frontier is a widespread implementation of third gender categories. Countries such as Argentina, Australia, Canada, Denmark, the Netherlands, Germany, Malta, New Zealand, Pakistan, India and Nepal now have gender-neutral third category options for passports.[12] In November 2020, Belgium joined in – deciding to offer an 'X' option. It is shocking to me that today, when so many people do not identify as male or female, this is not more widespread. Campaigners are still fighting for these options to be introduced in the UK, as well as America and many other countries, but arguments over how this could pose a threat to security or lead to increased fraud are often brought forward in response.[13] Without this change, nonbinary people do not have legal recognition – and so cannot, for example, register at the doctors or get married as their lived gender. Notably, the option of identifying as nonbinary was also excluded from the UK's 2021 census. This undermines nonbinary people's right to participate in society and to have their existence recognised.

These steps are hugely important but they are just the beginning. We have a lot of work to do before society reflects the myriad ways that people experience their genders. We need to take a long hard look at the structures we've built – from sports to physical spaces to legal framework – and bring them up to date. Understanding that current systems are broken and need to evolve is not about doing away with the categories of male and female altogether, but acknowledging that there is a whole spectrum of expression in between these poles and around them. This might be messy or 'complicated' work, but it is urgent work too. It is a matter of basic inclusion, and one that brings the world in line with the realities of the people living in it. Beyond that, it's also a chance to celebrate trans, intersex and nonbinary people's infinite talents.

1 Katherine Kornei, 'This scientist is racing to discover how gender transitions alter athletic performance – including her own', *Science*, 25 July 2018; Sean Ingle, 'Trans women retain 12% edge in tests two years after transitioning, study finds', *Guardian*, 7 December 2020, https://www.theguardian.com/sport/2020/dec/07/study-suggests-ioc-adjustment-period-for-trans-women-may-be-too-short

2 'Teen runners sue to block trans athletes from girls' sports', *Guardian*, 13 February 2020, https://www.theguardian.com/us-news/2020/feb/13/transgender-athletes-girls-sports-high-school

3 Madeline Holcombe and Andy Rose, 'Federal judge says Idaho cannot ban transgender athletes from women's sports teams', CNN, 18 August 2020, https://edition.cnn.com/2020/08/18/us/idaho-transgender-athletes-ban-blocked/index.html

4 https://eu.usatoday.com/story/news/2022/01/20/2022-anti-trans-legislation/6571819001/

5 Francisco Navas, '"Now it's the girls' dream": Mara Gómez on becoming Argentina's first trans footballer', *Guardian*, 11 December 2020, https://www.theguardian.com/football/2020/dec/11/mara-gomez-argentina-trans-football

6 Paul MacInnes, 'Caster Semenya blocked from competing at world championships', *Guardian*, 30 July 2019, https://www.theguardian.com/sport/2019/jul/30/caster-semenya-blocked-defending-800-metres-title-athletics-world-championships

7 'LGBT in Britain: hate crime and discrimination', Stonewall, 2017

8 http://2030.vice.com/identity

9 A. W. Geiger and Nikki Graf, 'About one-in-five U.S. adults know someone who goes by a gender-neutral pronoun', Pew Research Center, 5 September 2019, https://www.pewresearch.org/fact-tank/2019/09/05/gender-neutral-pronouns/

10 Video interview available on PBS at https://www.pbssocal.org/programs/first-person/first-person-we-run-non-binary-inclusion-sports/

11 Andria Bianchi, 'Something's got to give: reconsidering the justification for a gender divide in sport', *Philosophies* 4.23, pp. 1–13, May 2019, https://www.mdpi.com/2409-9287/4/2/23/pdf

12 'Gender X passports', ENEI, 23 March 2020, https://www.enei.org.uk/resources/news/gender-x-passports/

13 Owen Bowcott, 'High court backs UK's refusal to issue gender-neutral passports', *Guardian*, 22 June 2018, https://www.theguardian.com/world/2018/jun/22/high-court-backs-uk-refusal-to-issue-gender-neutral-passports

'When I share my pronouns it is an invitation to have a more authentic and intimate relationship with me. It's an invitation to be a part of a more inclusive world together.'

Bobbi Salvör Menuez is an actor and transdisciplinary maker. Recent acting credits include working on *Euphoria*, *Adam*, *I Love Dick* and forthcoming experimental features from Daniel Askill and Kuba Czekaj. They are one-third of Spiral Theory Test Kitchen, with which they make queer food-based art. They live on Lenape land (aka Brooklyn) with their partner, two cats and pet snake.

Pronouns as Portal Magic

BOBBI SALVÖR MENUEZ

Pronouns are far from being every tool that we need to build a new world, but like a spell, they can summon the opening for that world to feel more possible, maybe even available to us right now in this moment.

In 2018 I was staying with a partner in LA on and off. Near their house was a modest and often empty canyon. My hair was still long to my waist, and I was in a time of withdrawal from several things, from work, from New York, from the majority of what had previously shaped my life. Many mornings I wandered into the canyon alone and told the canyon about myself, speaking myself into being, in a new form. It was to the canyon I told my chosen name first. With so few folks using they/them pronouns for me back then, it was the canyon whose space made this new language feel most accessible to me. I would lie in the shade of a small tree, tucked away in the grass and in my feelings, thinking, The trees will never misgender me, the grass will never misgender me, the sky will never misgender me. The natural world felt like my first and most steadfast ally, in the tender process of one of my many coming outs.

It was in the canyon – this held place – that I felt able to safely germinate the seeds of new language, to foster my own belief in my name and pronouns as true for me. Small roots started to grow; I slowly integrated these words

more and more with those close to me. Before I was ready
to hear others speak my name aloud, I would spell the
letters out to them, 'B–O–B–B–I', sometimes holding back
tears. Slowly I invited those who I felt safest with to venture
into the new space of calling me this name, as it became
more and more my own. And like an incantation, there
was a distinct magic to hearing my new name and pronouns
in their voices and to feel myself believed as real. It opened
a portal for me into being more present or, rather, into a
more liveable world.

Sometimes I wonder how much more liveable this world
could become for all of us if everyone really understood
that trans people have legitimate genders. Or if we all
opened ourselves to not assuming the genders of those we
meet anew? Untangling inherited transphobic assumptions,
regardless of your gender and relationship to it, takes time.
Asking people their pronouns, using them, and then sharing
your own brings this intention into a place of action, where
we can speak ourselves into recognizing others' realities.

In P. J. Hogan's cinematic depiction of *Peter Pan*, when
Pan finds Tinker Bell dead he cries slumped over her and
slowly starts to murmur over and over, 'I do believe in
fairies. I do, I do.' In one way apology, in one way invo-
cation. The repetition builds as Wendy and the Lost Boys
(now hostages, bound in rope on Hook's ship) join in,
and in a montage showing all other characters in the film,
even the children's father – mid-business presentation –
declaring to his co-workers with great gusto, 'I do believe
in fairies! I do, I do!' This collective affirmation revives
Tinker Bell. Just like this, being spoken into being can
truly be life-reviving and life-saving for us as gender-
variant people, too.

When we are asked to start using they/them or other
pronouns – whether for ourselves or someone else – we must

confront the vulnerability of being in a space of newness. This feeling of newness can lead to a kind of performance anxiety, with fear around messing up, or embarrassing yourself, or hurting someone's feelings. (Spoiler alert: Trans people mess up other people's pronouns too.) This fear can be amplified if you see yourself as an open and accepting person with inclusive politics, as misgendering could threaten your self-perception. Deeper fears can arise that 'if I misgender someone, it makes me bad' or 'others will think/know I am a bad person'. The process of retraining ourselves in ways we use language will inevitably take different amounts of time for each of us, so accepting discomfort as part of that process is important in moving forward.

Regardless of where someone is in their personal relationship to gender, I try to maintain the belief that everyone has the capacity to understand and relate to the desire to be seen as real – and with that belief, connection across our differences feels more possible. This is not to say that being misgendered is not exhausting and violent. I don't share my pronouns with everyone. Sometimes I don't have the energy to be put in the teaching position that often comes with bringing up non-dominant pronouns. Despite efforts to shift my body, my presentation and my modes of gender expression, I am misgendered almost every day. That consensus-based reality tells me that I am not what I feel I am, it makes me feel like an imposter, and can be truly maddening. I often fantasize about committing to a more binary masculine expression, imagining that this would solve the problem of being 'she'd all the time, but I know that it is not straightforward to 'pass' and that it wouldn't truly solve the issue of being unseen.

On International Transgender Day of Visibility, March 2020, a friend of mine, Matthias, posted an image of himself taken in the mirror, with his phone covering one nipple while he holds a small trans flag over his other nipple. The beginning of his caption reads:

> I have been on hormones for four years and still don't pass as a man 90% of the time. In trying to ascribe a sensation to this, I think of the exercise I give my students in ballet class. While in arabesque I pull on their front arms, in opposition to the leg extended behind them. It's a position about yearning. A constant pull of the limbs away from one another, reaching for what's just beyond your grasp ... [I]n being lucky enough to know so many resilient souls, I have to insist now more than ever: the urgency with which we render ourselves palatable as subjects to the powers that be, impelled toward some intact feeling, can never really liberate us.

Reading this, I feel a kind of affirmation that there is power in not having to arrive at a final gender – despite the immense pressure I feel and receive to arrive at something more convenient, something more binary.

It is my trans and gender-variant siblings, kin and community who offer this affirmation to me often just in their being, and in the inherent resilience that comes with their existing through and against these 'powers that be'. I remember at a friend's recent memorial I was struck by the tone of the gathering. While still full of immense grief, there was a swelling sense of even greater gratitude – gratitude that we got to have this shining being, so authentic and full, with us as long as we did, even if that only meant twenty-seven years. Nico Gogan, rest in power – not only did you make me feel real and seen as your friend in our shared visioning of new worlds, but I saw how you did that for so many just in the visibility of your transness and your world-conjuring online. Nico celebrated himself and those close to him, showing us that trans bodies are not only beautiful amidst all their variability, but that they are deserving of immense self-love and celebration. From a world that tells me I am unnatural and undesirable for my variance and transness, Nico built worlds that said otherwise. And so to me, he remains a guiding light and true portal master.

When I share my pronouns it is an invitation to have a more authentic and intimate relationship with me. It's an invitation to be a part of a more inclusive world together. I'm still learning and unlearning when it comes to gender, and I'd like others to join me in that, too. I recall the revelatory moment a few years ago when, in a circle of people sharing our pronouns, someone explained sincerely, 'I don't really know what my pronouns are right now.' Right there, I learned something profound about why we ask for pronouns – it's maybe less about getting pronouns 'right' instead of 'wrong', and more that the question allows unassumed answers to arise and, simply, the opening up of a space. When we make this space, it creates an opportunity for all of us to re-examine how our use of language affects the way we think, and to reconsider the assumptions we make about people in general. While it might start with not assuming gender, it goes far, far beyond that.

I believe that this is part of how some of us are summoning a new world – but when will the rest of the world catch up with this more inclusive and liveable one we are building? One where we can be spoken into being? I am impatient for that time because lives, lives that I deeply love, depend on it. We depend on it to feel real or seen and at times to keep surviving.

In an astrological reading given by my friend Tourma-line, I am opened to the idea that 'when you let go of timing, everything becomes possible'. And so I have patience for growth at its own pace, and I'm emboldened by the promise that this better world is not only coming, but that it's already here in some way. Just because no fruiting bodies reveal themselves on the forest floor, it does not deny that the mycelium of mushrooms underground may make up the largest and perhaps most essential organism in the ecosystem of that whole forest. Similarly, there are more of us who unravel the gender binary than you may realize and we are more essential to our shared ecosystem than our treatment suggests. If we can believe in each other, notice the mushrooms and fairies along our paths, and conjure the portal magic of pronouns, we can make this world and all of our interwoven lives so much more free.

'I see that all our infighting comes down to this: we simply cannot agree on what exactly is the truth of sexuality and gender.'

Kate Bornstein is an American author, playwright, performance artist, actress and gender theorist. She/they have been writing award-winning books on the subject of nonbinary gender for over thirty years, including *Gender Outlaw*, *My New Gender Workbook*, and a memoir, *A Queer and Pleasant Danger*.

When It Comes to Sex and Gender, You're Right

KATE BORNSTEIN

Divisiveness is rampant – it always has been. As a global civilization, we have always divided along the lines of politics, nationality, race, class, age, religion and so on. Splintering along lines of sexuality and gender is nothing new: the war between the sexes, straight versus queer, cisgender versus transgender. But boy oh boy, is it all coming to a head these days, or what? This is especially and I think sadly true of infighting within the sprawling, loosely knit communities and identities that comprise LGBTQ+.

I'm seventy-two years old, and I have been analyzing gender every single day since I was four. I've seen and still see gay men at odds with lesbians, drag queens at odds with trans women, and monogamists at odds with poly-amorists. I've seen nonbinary folks at odds with gender-queer. As I'm writing this, a group of lesbians, gays and bisexuals in England have broken off from Stonewall, that nation's oldest and most inclusive LGBTQ+ civil rights group. The splintering Ls, Gs and Bs claim they have nothing in common with those Ts.

> In every one of the above cases, the language
> almost everyone feels justified in using about

their perceived foes is often harsh, mocking,
and cruel. We praise others for their accom-
plishments in the field of hate speech. We like
and retweet the particularly nasty bits. And
the more we do that, the deeper a wedge we
drive between people who by all rights should
be part of a loving family.

Continued and escalating infighting amongst factions of
LGBTQ+ people will only result in the inability and unwill-
ingness to come together when we really need to unite in
some big emergency that affects us all – the prospects of
which are becoming more likely with each passing day.
From my vantage point as an elder in our subculture, I see
that all our infighting comes down to this: we simply cannot
agree on what exactly is the truth of sexuality and gender.

Truth

About seven years ago, I went to a talk by the Dalai Lama
in New York at the Beacon Theater with 2,700 other
people. The title of this particular talk was 'Profound
wisdom and vast compassion: Tsongkhapa's "Essence of
True Eloquence"'. Tibetan Buddhism teaches that eloquence
is defined as *the telling of a truth in such a way that it
eases suffering*. In order to tell a truth in a way that eases
suffering, you need a lot of wisdom; you need a lot of
compassion.

Buddhists acknowledge myriad truths, but for the
purpose of teaching eloquence, they break truth down into
two basic categories, a conscious binary, if you will:

There's definitive truth and there's arguable truth.

Definitive truths. There's not too many of them. They're always simply stated.

Everyone dies.

Can't argue with that. That's a definitive truth.

Nobody knows what the exact moment of their death is going to be.

Another definitive truth. Can't argue that one either.

There is a limitless number of arguable truths. They're usually more complicated to say:

> Pizza is the very best food on the planet. It is. That's the truth of it. It can be sweet, it can be savory. You can get any kind of topping you want. It's usually available anywhere. And if it isn't, you can go to your freezer where you've probably kept some. You can always customize it. It's always good to eat. And so, pizza is the best food on the planet. And that's the truth. Arguably.

Everyone subscribes to the arguable truth of gender that most eases their suffering and gives them a shot at some happiness. And why not? I do. You do. It's fine. Sitting there, listening to the Dalai Lama talk about this stuff, I realized that the infighting amongst LGBTQ+ people came down to clashing truths about sexuality and gender. In fact, there were so many truths about sexuality and gender that it became obvious to me that all of those truths are arguable.

And I wondered, is there a definitive truth of gender, a definitive truth about sexuality, that everyone would have to agree with no matter how grudgingly? Well, I found one. I found a definitive truth of gender. The most simple way to state this definitive truth of gender is:

Gender is relative.

The academic way of stating this definitive truth of gender is:

Gender is relative to context and point of view.

Here's how that works: gender is different depending on where we are, when we are there, and who if anyone is keeping us company. Six or seven hundred years ago, village women were little better than property of their God-fearing husbands. Change the time, place and company, and you've essentially changed the basis of gender.

The trouble starts when people believe that their arguable truth of sexuality and gender – their identity – is the definitive truth. Say I believe that a trans woman is a woman, and someone else says no they are not. We both dig in to our truth of gender without giving an inch. And that somehow gives each of us the right to hurt, punish and laugh at the other. But we are digging in our heels about an arguable truth. Well, what's arguable about the truth you believe?

Truth of Identity

Two of the most personal arguable truths we've got and hold on to are our gender identity and sexual identity. These arguable truths, these identities, we believe they tell us who we are. But the fact is, we are so much more than that. 'I am a man', 'I am a woman', or 'I am nonbinary' is stating only a part of who we are. And that makes our statements of identity arguable.

> Gender identity is an arguable truth.

> All identities are arguable truths.

> Why? Because you are not an identity. You are a sentient being who is using an identity in order to better navigate the world at large.

> But that's hard to grasp, so we opt for the easier statement: I am this or that identity.

When we proclaim our gender or sexual identity, we like to believe that we have accomplished a personal goal. We go so far as to say *this is the real me,* or *this is my authentic self.* But no, not really. Look at the word *identity.* To identify as something, we are saying *something over there is just like me.* Gender identity assumes that some complete, detailed, discrete identity exists in the world. If that were the case, then everyone would agree on what's a man and what's a woman. But nope, neither of those identities are complete or detailed, and neither *man* nor *woman* are discrete, independent identities in that both are tied to the defining person's point of view. We tend to identify with the version of *man* or *woman* that most pleases us, and most makes life easier for us. And we don't give up that identity once we've settled on it.

> So, in fact, gender identity means something from outside yourself has become fixed inside you.

Gender identity reflects only your past long-ings.

If your gender identity were truly in the present, it would have to adapt to all the shifts and changes in your ideas, opinions, and all the new stuff you learn about gender as you grow older. In other words, your gender would be relative to context and point of view.

But living with constant change and the possibility of more and more constant change is really hard to do. So we get in the habit of thinking of gender as some identity that never needs to change. Gender becomes an unconscious habit, the embodiment of some past desire. And this is what we fight about. This is what we defend and protect. Naturally, we look for and find other people who think the same way. This is the basis of us versus them, me versus you, one or the other.

The more we understand that sexuality and gender, like everything else, are subject to change, the more accepting we become of other people's viewpoints. When we can embrace nuance and subtlety in the arguable truths of sexuality and gender, we begin to see beyond the binary.

So Now What?

As a global civilization, we are gradually moving away from coarse binaries – more and more people have begun to consider subtler possibilities. If we truly wish to dismantle the bickering, the infighting, and the us-versus-them-ism in the complex LGBTQ+ community we need to acknowledge the validity of multiple arguable truths of gender and sexuality.

So yes, everyone subscribes to the arguable truth of gender that most eases their suffering and gives them a shot at some happiness. And that's just fine, that's as it should be. But no one has the right to enforce their arguable truth onto anyone else. That's bullying, and there's too much bullying going on in our own ranks.

So what's the alternative?

> Get in mind a person who is opposed to the very idea of your sexuality or gender identity.
>
> Now imagine that person saying this to you:
>
> 'I want you to teach me how your truth of gender eases your suffering, and gives you a shot at some happiness.'
>
> How would that make you feel if they said that to you?

That's how a conversation begins between people who've got conflicting views on sex and gender. Once a conversation is opened like that, there's the possibility of compromise, cooperation, and coalition – three modes of social behavior that are only possible in a setting that acknowledges the coexistence of multiple arguable truths. Our challenge would be to work together to devise and agree upon some arguable truths of gender and sexuality that ease more suffering than they cause.

And while we're hammering that out, we measure out the resources of our activism based on shared values – and we set priorities based on triage of suffering: Who among us is most at risk? From where I'm standing, that's at-risk youth. You may see someone else from where you're standing.

I hope this gives you a jumping-off point for making some peace among our family of lesbians, gay men, bisexuals, trans people, queers, intersex, asexuals, BDSMers and all the rest of us who embrace a sexuality and gender identity that falls outside the cultural mandates for cisgender heterosexuality. Come together now. Please. So we'll all be there for each other when the time calls for it.

'If we could fast-forward again to a trans-positive, a trans-majority future – then I wonder what possibilities we could all achieve without surveillance?'

Travis Alabanza is writer, theatre-maker and performer. Their recent play *Burgerz* toured internationally to critical acclaim, received the Total Theatre Award for an Emerging Artist and was voted one of the top shows of the year by *Guardian* readers. Their work has appeared and been referenced in numerous publications, such as *Dazed*, the *Guardian*, the *Independent*, *Metro* and *Vogue*.

'Everyone's Trans, Now What?'

TRAVIS ALABANZA

And as he said 'f*ggot', I could swear
I was hearing 'I m*ss you'.
As he swung the punch, I could swear
it was nearly a hug.
He said he could not believe how I left
the house looking like that.
And I wonder if instead he just wished
that he could.

Violence and intimacy being side by side is not a new discovery. Unfortunately, we know too well that often those that hurt us are those closest to us, as if with closeness comes something uncontrollable. As if to stay in control we must be far apart. In British culture everything works as long as we pretend everything is fine. We keep a distance from strangers in order to ensure none of us ever get close enough to realise we could be more than just fine. So, when someone is close to us, there is a danger in the rarity. As if the sink can finally overflow. As if the bridge can snap. As if we know we can offload our anger, our pain, our past, our fears, our frustrations onto someone because we have held everything in for so long with everyone else. As if that makes it OK.

The first person that called me a faggot to my face was called Justin* when I was fourteen years old and decided to wear a skirt at school. Six years later I saw Justin at a festival and he was wearing a skirt and glitter with all the boys as they danced to an EDM beat that had not changed for four hours.

When I was sixteen, during a forced family Easter break together, a cousin* of mine asked why I had painted my nails when I was a boy (side note: it was pretty obvious I wasn't). That night I went through some old family photos, desperate to find the photo of when we as cousins were a younger age, with painted nails and messy faces.

Just last year a group of businessmen during rush hour on the tube started laughing hysterically at me while pointing at my heels. I asked them what their problem was, and they said they 'just liked my heels', and I said, 'Thanks for being so honest,' before walking away.

I once had sex with a man who called me degrading names while we slept together. Afterwards, he asked if he could try on my heels. I wish I hadn't let him. Both call me those names and try on my heels. The shoe has not fit the same since.

We know too many trans women (and those like me who do not identify as either, but due to gender expression will experience similar violence) are often harmed after or before or during intimacy or sexual advances. Just before or after the kiss. As if to come too close to the sun will always send us into flames. As if some things are too illuminating to hold close.

I do not mean for this to be a list of horrors. I hope you know there is no self-pity creeping within the gaps of my keyboard as I write this, I do not deal with a currency I have no use for. What I am describing pushes beyond what they will simply call 'transphobia'. Something that feels so much more complicated than a phobia, something that feels much deeper than a fear, a thing that feels far more intimate than a hate crime. A thing that we lose when we simply say they are afraid of us, or that they hate us, or that they do not understand us. Of course, I believe all of that is there, bubbling on the surface with real and harmful consequences, but I believe what is underneath is something far scarier for men, and others that harm us, than a lack of understanding or fear. I believe that rather, and often, it is a desire, an intimacy, a closer proximity.

To think of transphobia as just a fear is to distance yourself from something that you know *too* well, it is to say that gender is this neat thing which we who are trans just happen to fall outside of. Rather than a thing that is incredibly messy that some of you just avoid looking into. Maybe you 'fear' us because we hold a mirror to a possibility, and the reflection is too strong to look at. What if 'fear' is rather a word you are using for mourning. As if we say 'cis' and 'trans' because we are too afraid to use the words 'hiding' and 'honest'. What if, say, in fact, and stay with me now: we were not the minority, we were not the outsiders, we were not the small few, but instead – you were us too. What if, in fact: everyone was trans.

Yes, OK, let us go with that. We know I am trans, we know others are trans, you may already be trans reading this, but what if in this imagination the cisgender is too. Or to be more specific, that there was a possibility the cisgender could be. Or to be clearer, that in the world I am trying to imagine the words 'trans' and 'cis' have become redundant because all of us have understood the instability of our own gender. That we have all leaned into the trans politics before us and realised that there was something underneath it pointing to our own discomfort.

That your prior agitation with us was actually an agitation
with your own forced understanding of gender. I am not
suggesting that we all experience this agitation at the same
level; I know for me and many others the dysphoria we
feel is not comparable to a nagging under the skin, more
a constant pulling at your teeth, but I believe so much of
violence from cisgender people stems from a lack of acceptance that there is even a nag underneath their skin too.
As if you know nothing more stable than your gender and
the sight of someone else's change ruptures the insecurity
in yours.

So, if everyone is trans.
I decide to take a deep breath.
To release some tension from my shoulders.

What could we learn from this moment?
What could we learn from a trans-majority future?

I think we would learn about autonomy and consent. We
would learn that a future in which we assume everyone
is on a spectrum or journey or complication with their
gender is one where we decide that everyone deserves to
tell us who they are. For there to be autonomy in that
declaration.

It seems simple, yet a trans person living in our present
knows how dangerous the path to autonomy is. A trans-
majority future sees the act of telling someone who they
are at birth and making it their responsibility to fight to
convince us otherwise as the first act of violence. It knows
that for many, even those who have not yet told us, this
will cause a lifetime of pain. This pain may not be something we all feel or notice, but that does not mean it is
not causing pain. A future in which trans is seen as the

majority realises that allowing ourselves to decide who we are teaches us very valuable lessons about our body and consent. It makes us realise that to place transness in false opposition with cisgender feminism is to not understand that both teach us about consent. That both teach us about ownership over our own body. That a future in which the possibility of a trans majority is understood is one that allows all of us to not allow someone else to gender us, to damn us, to tell us who we are.

So much of the sentiment around anti-trans rhetoric in the present day is actually just a surveillance of bodies. It is saying this person cannot be what they say they are because of [insert a physical attribute]. I think about my mother telling me stories of her and other women growing out their armpit hair in a time long before I was born. How she grouped together with other women to grow out things they were told to get rid of, boldly stating that by doing this it doesn't make them less of a woman. That they can grow this hair and wear this suit and still be seen as a woman.

Fast-forward to today and suddenly we are in the middle of a time where we are policing borders around genders, stating that Adam's apples, or hair, or things as temporary as body parts, are the things that determine our gender. And I pause. Knowing that if these are the things that prove a gender, then gender must be such a fragile thing. If we could fast-forward again to a trans-positive, a trans-majority future – then I wonder what possibilities we could all achieve without surveillance? What all our bodies and outfits and feelings towards them may look like if we learned that surveillance helped no one. What I mean to say is that a future where everyone is assumed trans until proven otherwise allows all of us to breathe lighter. If body parts are not the prerequisite to prove a gender, then if they are ever to leave us, we just mourn their departure – not what they could mean for our personhood as well. Maybe we would find out who really wants to wear the skirt, and who does not, who really wants to shave, and who does not, who really wants to sit legs crossed, and who does not.

Suddenly, I feel I am getting to know you all far better, because gender is not the first person I meet.

It is so hard to think about futures without feeling silly. As if imagination and dreaming are things we are encouraged to do only until we grow up. As if to be realistic is to always be weighed down. As if we mock any idea of a future that we do not know now. I am sure if we held the idea of everyone being trans to the light, you could find cracks, but instead I wonder what imagining the future allows us to bring into the present. Less surveillance around our bodies, consent around who we are, a loosening of shoulders, and ultimately a safer society for trans people (and therefore, ultimately, you as well). How so much of phobia is built around distance, which actually marks our desire to be closer. How if your solidarity for trans people is built around distancing yourselves from us, then is it really an honest solidarity at all?

I go back to thinking about Justin, who called me a faggot for wearing a skirt at fourteen years old, and I think about seeing him in a skirt years later at that festival. I think about what my abuse would look like if men were told they did not need to be afraid of my freedom but could try it on themselves. If the women who stopped us from entering bathrooms did not see us as the danger, rather see the systems that placed us both in opposition as the danger. If the men in suits during rush hour who laughed at my heels instead interrogated why they felt trapped in the suits themselves.

I want to say everyone is trans. And say that with some of my tongue in my cheek, and the other part maybe believing it. Either way, I know if it makes people think more deeply for a moment about what their fear of us is covering up, then maybe such a statement feels worth it.

* Details have been changed.

COMMUNITY AND ORGANISING

'This is the beauty and the potential of LGBTQ+ solidarity – we pave the way for future generations.'

Born in 1968 in Remscheid, Germany, **Wolfgang Tillmans** is regarded as one of the most influential artists working within photography today. Since the early 1990s his work has epitomised a new kind of subjectivity in photography and expanded conventional ways of approaching the medium. Tillmans has been the recipient of numerous awards, including the Turner Prize and the Hasselblad Foundation International Award in Photography. He has had prominent solo exhibitions at numerous international institutions and his work is held in museum collections worldwide.

A Better Connection

WOLFGANG TILLMANS

Every new generation that grows up can't necessarily
understand how it was before –
how the current normal was achieved.
It is normal for each person to assume that
where they're at has always been that way.
To look at the struggle, to even be aware of the struggle
of previous generations, is work, is labour.
No one tells you that.
It's a quagmire.
We just want to be able to love the way we love and
be left alone, be left in peace. At the same time, the
way we are poses a huge challenge perceived as a
provocation to society.
But I don't mean to provoke.
But the very difference and fluidity of gender and of
sexual orientation is unsettling to many people with a
heteronormative mindset.
But they should feel nothing about it. They 'should' just
accept that some people are not heterosexual, that some
people love differently.
How to bridge this gap:
the personal feeling of wanting to just live one's life
without having to be an activist?
and the obvious need for continued and continuous
activism to protect the advances that have been gained
by previous generations?

We need self-respect.

We need a way to deal with abuse received before we even knew it.

Because the thing is, others felt we were different before we even knew it ourselves.

We couldn't put a name to it, but the sense of difference was already there.

Without the mirror of history, we will always be lagging behind.

This is the beauty and the potential of LGBTQ+ solidarity – we pave the way for future generations.

We can't let go of our responsibility if we want to hold on to the advances achieved so far.

And we need to pass them on.

We are truly global. We exist everywhere, and our experience of being 'found out' as different is something we share.

We know love knows no borders. We know we are born equal though we are perceived as different. It's easy to enjoy the personal freedom offered in open societies and forget about the misfortunes suffered by many siblings in other parts of the world.

We need to teach self-respect.

We need to learn how to respect ourselves.

We need to unlearn disrespect for ourselves.

Self-hatred keeps us from growing.

Smalltown Boy by *Bronski Beat*.

Difference has to be learned again and again every year and by each generation.

Difference is not wrong.

Difference is nature.

Difference is our responsibility for the future of society at large.

Our role is central not peripheral.
The luck to be born gay forced me to see the world
differently from an early age.
Smalltown Boy by *Bronski Beat*.
The feeling of not fitting in.
The fear of not fitting in.
The fear of male violence.
The fetishisation of male stereotypes from butch to
femme to violent.
Camp strategies and entertainment allowing us to make
fun of the system that holds us captive.
Mimicry and wanting to be 'normal'.
The fear of the body. The fear of one's own body.
This is (one of) the biggest underlying problems in
our world.
It is the cause of so much denial, resulting in violence.
We lack a counterweight to all the prevailing quests for
a perfect body. Gym culture not for health but for
fitting in and being liked.
Bettering the body.
The resounding demand, as a command, for a better
body emanates all around.
Dissenting voices are hard to hear.
Who builds confidence without building muscles?
It is urgent to counter this cannon.
Where do you turn when lonely, when not fitting in?
And the ongoing loss of alternative meeting places in
an urban landscape that is only serving commercial
optimisation. Politicians and local authorities have been
deaf and haven't realised that something truly
valuable is being lost.
*un*social media.
Am I just nostalgic for the playful subversion offered by
BUTT magazine? Were there really more places in the

past where you didn't need to conform? Or numb out feelings of inadequacy by getting drunk?

Gay places can be dark. Male privilege and misogyny and masc to fem male prejudice is prevalent.
Stop the copying of the heteronormative mainstream in our own communities.
Your Body is Yours.
We should talk more about sexuality and not stop talking about it. We are in a strangely prudish time: sex is pushed at us in advertising all the time, but free sexuality is increasingly suppressed. The world is totally sexualised, but only for marketing purposes. Free sexuality, free of charge, and free of control is seen as dangerous. I think one has to treat sexuality with honesty and acknowledge its importance. As attitudes shift gradually and therefore happen unnoticed, it is important to remember that the techno, acid house and general dance culture of the late 1980s and early 1990s was actually a political project. It was derided by some as hedonistic and inherently non-political, but the annual Love Parades in Berlin, which had hundreds of thousands of people from socially diverse backgrounds, who would party together in a polysexual way, were in themselves political statements. The act of experiencing your body playfully and without fear speaks to an irrational side in us, which is not irresponsible.
Clubbing, enjoying yourself, experimenting with your body, exploring unusual social interaction, exploring audio adventures – pose no harm – consciously experiencing the body in a nonviolent or non-competitive way. But as capitalism has progressed as the only way, the only model in the past thirty years, it has suppressed these islands of irrationality and freedom. Not because

of a central manifesto, but because people enjoying themselves for free or almost free, in inner city spaces, does not follow capitalist logic. This lopsided and apparently unstoppable reorganisation of urban and media spaces has pushed out nightlife and music and the freedom to think things differently.

I hope people have a sense of what is lost and will push back. I have a feeling that young people today have an awakened sense of what the 1980s and 1990s might have been. And while they certainly were not all golden and fabulous, they gave expression to a longing for a sense of community and purpose that went beyond the self.

'History requires us to honor those who came before by learning their stories, seeking out the past however we can, and making the truth available to others.'

Matthew Riemer is the co-creator of Instagram's @lgbt_history and co-author of *We Are Everywhere: Protest, Power, and Pride in the History of Queer Liberation*, a critically acclaimed look at the radical origins of the queer liberation movement.

Ceaseless Struggles, Infinite Possibilities: Finding Liberation in Queer History

MATTHEW RIEMER

In March of 1968, James Baldwin appeared before a subcommittee of the US House of Representatives to endorse a bill establishing a national commission on Black history and culture. Lending his considerable authority to the proposed legislation, Baldwin also offered a stinging critique of the American facade and the historical myths on which it stands. Teaching Black history, he said, required teaching the country's truths, and that would require white America to be honest with itself, an unlikely scenario given that 'the Black experience indicates something about the total American history which frightens Americans.' In essence, Baldwin explained, the truth 'attacks the American identity'.

'If we are going to build a multiracial society,' the brilliant queer writer told the all-white, all-male congressional panel, 'then one has got to accept that I have learned a lot from you, and a lot of it is bitter, but you have a lot to learn from me, and a lot of that will be bitter. That bitterness is our only hope ... What we are involved with here is an attempt to have ourselves.'[1]

Any sincere struggle for freedom and collective liberation – that is, any 'attempt to have ourselves' – begins or ends with an understanding of history. When marginalized people connect with, learn from, and build upon the efforts and struggles of those who came before, we inch ever closer to a new and better world. At the same time, those denied their history – separated from their *truth* – struggle even to see themselves as worthy of liberation. Thus, radical educator Paulo Freire explains, when marginalized people are denied the opportunity to imagine their freedom, they are uniquely vulnerable to the powerful lie known as 'fitting in'.[2] As a result, the oppressed often dream of little more than gaining access to the very institutions that terrorize us. When we long to join the status quo, we yearn to be part of a system that depends upon our destruction.

This process – being denied our history by those seeking to limit our future – is a fundamental part of queer oppression. Despite the work of teachers, activists, artists, academics, griots and witnesses of all stripes, too few queer people have any real sense of our community's radical past nor how that history inexorably links us to the ceaseless struggle against oppression in every form. To the extent it's ever made accessible, queer history is often sterilized, manipulated and forced to conform to our oppressors' false memories and fatal visions. We are robbed of ourselves and our rightful claim to liberation, left instead with empty dreams of 'fitting in' and an insidious faith in 'equality'. Names, events and struggles are plucked from the infinite past and used as fodder for those focused on the finite aims of the present: LGBTQ+ people have *always* been in your military, they say, so let us serve openly; we've *always* gotten married, so let us do so with the state's approval. The fullness of our collective history is whittled down to talking points, used in service of the lie that, if we just get *this* or win *that*, if the courts allow us to do *x* or a despot stops killing us for *y*, then 'equality' is at hand.

Queer people – all oppressed people – deserve far more than this. We deserve ourselves, our freedom. And we deserve – we *need* – our history.

In late 2015, my partner Leighton and I attended a celebration of the life of Frank Kameny, a founding parent of the gay liberation movement who is perhaps best known for coining, in 1968, the phrase 'Gay Is Good' (inspired, as Kameny often noted, by the 'Black Is Beautiful' campaign). At the time, my knowledge of gay history consisted of little more than a few inaccurate and disconnected ideas about the homophile movement of the mid-twentieth century, Stonewall, Harvey Milk, AIDS and marriage. So, as speaker after speaker remembered some aspect of Kameny's decades-long career, I felt overwhelmed by a language at once familiar and far away. I was confronted by my history, isolated by my ignorance, and furious at the forces keeping me from myself.

Almost as soon as we left the event, Leighton and I started absorbing the past, seeking out photographs, ephemera, periodicals and other primary materials as our points of entry. It's difficult to describe the joy and rage that consumed us as we connected with ancestors who'd made our lives possible; as each photo and story we came across led to exponentially more photos and stories, we grew more confident, more complete, and infinitely queerer. We grew conscious of how deeply intertwined are the struggles for queer liberation, Black freedom, economic justice, prison and police abolition, disability justice, women's liberation, immigrant justice, binary destruction, body positivity and countless others. These overlaps and connections – the intersections of oppression – are the foundations of freedom, for only in solidarity will the marginalized defeat the machines of power.

We had no idea what we were doing when we started @lgbt_history in early 2016; our goal was, and still is, to connect, learn and empower. And, while there has always been a great deal of joy in the work, I'm driven, more than anything, by rage. I've found, as Baldwin famously said, 'that precisely at the point when you begin to develop a conscience, you must find yourself at war with society'.[3]

Though it's not a war we started, it's war nonetheless, and only those armed with their history have any chance of survival. Because society needs you to believe that the status quo is the limit of what's possible, history is taught as a disconnected series of events organized by a few extraordinary people. If you're not extraordinary, the false logic goes, you have no role in our collective destiny. In truth, though, history is a continuum, a dimension in which time collapses and struggles collide such that everything we do – and all that which we choose not to do – matters. Once inside the continuum, history requires us to honor those who came before by learning their stories, seeking out the past however we can, and making the truth available to others. (That means doing whatever you can to engage with *your* history: visit queer archives, go to queerhistory.com, connect with queer elders in meaningful ways, avoid simple summaries of complex realities, demand queer curricula.) Then, armed with our ancestors' energy, we can organize the present to build a liberated future, one in which the most marginalized among us lead, teach and live rather than merely survive.

We honor Frank Kameny, for example, when we understand the connections between 'Black Is Beautiful' and 'Gay Is Good', but we make history *ours* when we unapologetically proclaim that 'Black Queer Lives Matter'. To learn about the street kids, trans folks and people of color who fought on the front lines at Compton's Cafeteria and Stonewall requires those of us who've gained the most from their bravery to fight on the front lines for the street kids, trans folks and people of color who are still violently denied basic decency. To learn about Sylvia Rivera holding accountable those gays and lesbians who shunned gender warriors, sex workers and incarcerated queers means holding accountable those who continue to do the same. To study the Black, queer brilliance of James Baldwin, Angela Davis, Barbara Smith or Audre Lorde is to embark on a ceaseless struggle against bigotry in every form, requiring those with the most privilege to divest themselves of any power acquired from playing the oppressors' game.

'Each one of us is here because somebody before us did something to make it possible,' Lorde taught.[4] It is within that history of possibility – that continuum of struggle – that our liberation resides.

Learn the queer past, internalize queer power, project queer possibilities.

¡A luta continua![5]

---

1 Statement of James Baldwin, in *Hearing Before the Select Subcommittee on Labor of the Committee on Education and Labor. House of Representatives Ninetieth Congress, Second Session on H.R. 12962: A Bill for the Establishment of a Commission on Negro History and Culture* (Washington, DC: US Government Printing Office, 1968)

2 Paolo Freire, *Pedagogy of the Oppressed* (New York City: Continuum Publishing Company, 1993)

3 James Baldwin, 'A Talk to Teachers', *James Baldwin: Collected Essays* (New York City: Library of America, 1998), p. 685

4 Audre Lorde, 'Learning from the 60s', *Sister Outsider: Essays and Speeches by Audre Lorde* (Berkeley: Crossing Press, 2007), p. 117

5 'The struggle continues!'

'Everyone's story is different; everyone's story is valid. But allyship is the greatest gift you can give somebody. It can improve their quality of life and perhaps even save it.'

Riyadh Khalaf is best known for fronting the groundbreaking BBC docuseries *Queer Britain*. He rose to prominence covering LGBTQ+ topics on his YouTube channel and is the author of the bestselling book *Yay! You're Gay! Now What?*

Allyship Starts at Home

RIYADH KHALAF

I grew up in a mixed home with an Iraqi Muslim father and an Irish Catholic mother. It was bacon and cabbage one night, falafel and hummus the next and I loved it. My parents were incredible beacons of love and support throughout my childhood. Even still, I experienced the all-too-common shackles of shame and fear about telling them I was gay. Looking back, I think my young mind wanted to prepare for the worst outcome: the possibility of a parentless life or at least one where they didn't love me anymore.

When I told my mother I was gay she was wonderful, instantly throwing her arms around me and letting me know that nothing I could ever do or say would compromise her love for me. She was upset, but not over my sexuality. She hated that I had been struggling with this secret on my own for so long, but one becomes a master at hiding who they truly are in the years prior to coming out. I, for example, somehow managed to hide my sexuality in spite of obsessions such as Nigella Lawson, *The Sound of Music* and Eurovision.

Mum and I had a shared anxiety about the reaction my dad might have on hearing the news. He's a sensitive and deeply caring man who would appear the model father and likely to readily accept his son, no matter what. But we were acutely aware that some cultural and familial issues could lead to a negative response and we had no idea just how bad it could be. This unknown was terrifying to us.

We badly wanted to keep our picture-perfect family life going, so we decided to hold the secret from him. But then nine months later, after an explosive argument, breaking point came. I tried to say the words 'I'm gay' for what must have been ten minutes but nothing would come out. Finally, I hastily scribbled the dreaded words on a piece of paper and slid it across the table to my father. On hearing the news, he said: 'It'll be okay, we'll fix this.'

Not exactly what you want to hear after spending four years learning to accept and finally love your shiny new identity. I didn't need anything about me to be fixed, I needed it to be embraced, cherished, protected. I was impatient and expected an immediate showering of love. That wasn't a realistic expectation. He needed time.

Dad's mood began to spiral downward in the weeks following my coming out. It became so bad that he had a breakdown. The man I once saw as a best friend and loving father couldn't bring himself to look at me. I was afraid of being rejected by him for good, or even made homeless. In retrospect I know these things would never have happened, but this is how I, as a young queer person, dealt with trauma in order to survive. As painful as it was, by presuming the worst I was able to rehearse that eventuality in my head to prepare for it and protect myself. These exhausting mental acrobatics were all happening while juggling the standard teen stresses of exams, a rapidly changing body, and bullying from classmates. Put simply, it was a pretty shit time.

After a while my mother decided to give my dad an ultimatum. She simply and sharply put the reality of the situation to him: 'This family is the four of us and nobody else's opinion matters. Who will be by your bedside telling you that they love you when you are about to die? It will be your two boys. Don't throw that away.' This was a wake-up call for my dad, bringing empathy and understanding into the situation, and making him realise that he needed us just as much as we needed him. From what I could tell, he suddenly saw the bigger picture, and I believe now – with hindsight – that he had little issue with me being gay, but that he was instead more worried about prejudice from others, or that they would somehow see him as a 'failed father'.

My dad's transformation (that's what I call it anyway) was a slow and conscious process that took effort from all of us. When I say effort, I mean in terms of having difficult and honest conversations, exposing him to queer culture, involving him in a narrative of equality campaigning, (sensitively) joking about each other's attractions to men and women, and eventually physically bringing him into queer spaces. He appeared at the other side of his confusion as a Pride-marchin', drag-queen-befriendin', boyfriend-acceptin' wonderful ally of a father.

His allyship, and other people's, has been vital in my development into a confident young gay man. Without it, I doubt I would be alive today, let alone happy and content with how my life has turned out so far. Over time, my expectation of what an ally should be has evolved beyond recognition. During my closeted years when I was a pimple-faced gay teen, an ally was merely anyone who didn't call me a 'faggot'. Well, at least not to my face. After coming out my understanding of allyship shifted to a family member or friend who still said they loved me. A decade on and my ally 'scorecard' is tougher than ever. To be worthy of the coveted title you must be vocal in your support of queer rights, you must shut down everyday micro-aggressions aimed at queer folk, you must do all you can to uplift your LGBTQ+ family members, friends or work colleagues, and where possible, educate those around you about the struggles of our marginalised community. Not much to ask really, is it? As you can tell, I am not in the game of being someone's GBF (Gay Best Friend) and that being enough to classify allyhood.

Of course, being this kind of a support in someone's life isn't something that can happen overnight. It takes a willingness to change prejudices cemented in us from growing up in a society that is inherently homophobic, biphobic and transphobic. It's not always your fault that you might have problematic thoughts, it's what you do about them that matters. Can you put yourself in the shoes of a queer person to truly feel what life must be like for them, then think about how much it differs from yours and, as a result, respond with the actions needed to make their life better?

Allyship isn't just for straight and cis people though, but for all of us, regardless of gender identity or sexuality. We have a crisis in intersectional queer allyship within the community that needs to be addressed too. White gay men who find themselves at the top of the LGBTQ+ privilege hierarchy have a duty of allyship to their trans, bisexual and gender-nonconforming siblings that's often left unfulfilled. This has to change. It's also important that we as queer people make space for allies – fifteen-year-old me desperately needed someone to tell me I wasn't sick, crazy, broken or unlovable. But back then I didn't realise that opening the door to that 'one accepting person' was partly my job too. Those people were all around me in the form of teachers, friends, aunties, uncles and even strangers, but without me giving them a licence to speak to me about my sexuality, they were too polite or afraid to broach the subject. Seeking help and giving it can sometimes be a two-way exchange.

Everyone's story is different; everyone's story is valid. But allyship is the greatest gift you can give somebody. It can improve their quality of life and perhaps even save it. There's every likelihood that it will enlighten you in the process too. Everyone's a winner. So, here are some key messages to think about when trying to be an ally to a queer friend or family member – all of which were important for my father.

They knew long before you did. When someone comes out to you please know that this isn't new to them. They've likely toiled over this aspect of themselves for years. If you feel sad, angry or confused, that is normal. The best thing to do is step away and ask for time to process the information before speaking too soon. Saying anything charged in this moment will likely hurt one or both of you, and it may take a long time to recover from it.

They are still them. My dad struggled with the idea that I had changed in a fundamental way and that I was all of a sudden a stranger to him. That is frightening but, thankfully, not true. A person's sexuality or gender identity does not define them. What does, however, is what they believe in, how they treat others, their passions and dreams, and the memories that you share together. Use things you both loved in the past like favourite movies or activities to reconnect after they've come out. This will bring the comfort of familiarity back into your relationship and hopefully nurture constructive conversation. Humour is your friend, too – after coming out to my dad, the first time I noticed a glimmer of light in him after weeks of darkness was when he made a joke about something on TV to break the ice. It worked. For a while, we flung jokes back and forth making friendly jabs at each other. This had always been our language of love before I came out and we used it to rebuild our relationship afterwards. If done right and without the intention to cause pain, I think humour is a great tool.

Education, education, education. Seek out the truth, not propaganda from a religious organisation or political party. Look for information that is not swayed by external agendas about what it means to be a particular identity. Understand that the feelings and/or attractions of the person you want to be an ally for are as valid as yours in terms of sexuality or gender identity. Consume works by queer people, about queer people: there are endless documentaries, podcasts, Instagram accounts, books and speeches about queer history and the modern struggles faced by the community. While it isn't a queer person's job to forever explain and educate others about who they are, please don't take this as a 'do not ask any questions' warning. Doing the groundwork is always a good start, but discourse is also important and helpful to all involved.

Listen. Living in 'the closet' is one of the most frustrating and difficult times in a person's life – unimaginable amounts of feelings and thoughts go unheard, unspoken and suppressed. It's like having a piece of duct tape over your mouth for years. Now is their time to have the soapbox and express how they feel in an uninhibited way. It may be laboursome or feel like all they talk about is their sexuality or gender identity, but that's to be expected.

This is an exciting time for them so let them experience it and get involved by asking questions and validating what they say. It'll bring you closer. When you listen, also be sure to take them at their word – if someone tells you they are bisexual, for example, that is their truth, it is not 'a phase'. Likewise, if someone says they're questioning their sexuality, don't try to bring them to any conclusions – they'll reach their own, eventually, and it might be that there isn't one.

Create space. Imagine you believe someone in your life may be queer and closeted. You can make it easier for them to reach out to you by displaying your unwavering support both verbally and in how you behave around them day to day. Simply tell them you are there for them (in general terms), you appreciate their friendship, you will never judge them and that you know you can count on them too. Be clever with your timing and wording as to not spook them into thinking you're making a premature ambush to 'out' them. That is their information to tell in their own time. Additionally, be respectful in your comments about other people's identities around them and, when appropriate, actively show your positive feelings for the community at large. These signals will get through and could be just what they need to hear.

Cut them some slack. Try to be understanding if they have a short fuse or hot temper. They likely default to this in times of stress, and it's a by-product of having to endlessly defend themselves and their identity over the years. They may be battling shame or combatting stigma in other places where they have come out. They will need buckets of encouragement to outweigh feelings of worthlessness, including in work, hobbies or in their expression of their hopes for the future. Celebrate their achievements in a loud way – they will appreciate being seen and lifted up during these times of success.

Remember, this is not about you. But it does involve you. Time and time again I hear from young queer people about a parent who makes their coming-out experience all about them. If you're taking someone's coming out personally then take yourself away to decompress and unpack the news, processing it alone or with someone else. Remember, too, not to be offended if someone doesn't come out to you before anyone else. It's often the people who mean the most to them that they want to tell last. I had several 'coming out guinea pigs' who were people on the periphery of my life. They were less important to me than family but vital in my coming-out journey in terms of practice, confidence building and motivation to carry on declaring who I am.

Be present for key moments. Give yourself time, but when you're ready, the biggest sign of love and support for your queer friend or family member is asking them if you can join them as they go to one of their community's safe spaces or events. Having my parents join me for marriage equality protests, at a drag show and in Pride parades are some of my most cherished memories and I know it's the same for them. Making the effort to do something or go somewhere out of your comfort zone is a wonderful gesture and you'll likely have a great time, too. But if the queer person in your life says they'd prefer to go alone or without you, don't take it personally. These spaces are sacred to many queer people and they may not be ready to bring you along just yet.

Be outwardly vocal in your support. It's one thing to tell someone you love them and will support them unconditionally, but it's another to fight their corner when they aren't even there. This can be done in many ways, from the kinds of causes you post about on social media, the charities you support, the news you actively make a point of understanding, the opportunities you turn down because you know a queer person would be better suited for them, and the bigotry you call out in day-to-day life. Allyship isn't about showing off to a queer person by virtue signalling, it's about getting into a habit of only expecting and accepting for them as you would for yourself – more, even!

Spread the love and learning around. When you hear a hurtful or damaging opinion that contradicts what you now know to be true, take time and patience to share the facts with that person from your perspective. You after all are someone who knows a queer person and what affects their life positively or negatively. Fighting fire with fire can often lead us nowhere so I encourage you to use empathy, logic and a gentle touch where possible. You may be challenging ideologies that someone has held for a lifetime, so it can take time to win them over.

Language is important. Getting a gender pronoun wrong, inadvertently calling someone by their deadname (their former name) rather than their chosen name, or introducing your son's boyfriend as his 'friend' are common mistakes in the early days. Apologise, use the correct word and move on. Language that is connected to identity or relationships are only words, yes, but they are also verbal validations which are cherished by queer people who for so long couldn't be fully themselves. Also, please don't

say the words 'gay', 'bi' or 'trans' in hushed tones when
in public. Say them with ease!

Support unconditionally. Finally, make your love undeni-
able and unconditional. There is no roadmap for this, only
you and the individual that you're an ally to can know
how deep your bond truly is. After years of uncertainty
about the fragility of their relationships, now is the time
for them to breathe easy, knowing that you've got their
back and aren't going anywhere.

'Queer people need a space not only to gather and find community, but a space where you may feel safe either to come exactly as you are or where you can look forward to showing up as you really see yourself.'

madison moore is a cultural critic, DJ and assistant professor of queer studies at Virginia Commonwealth University in Richmond, Virginia. madison is the author of *Fabulous: The Rise of the Beautiful Eccentric*, which was published by Yale University Press in 2018.

San Francisco

MADISON MOORE

Growing up closeted in Ferguson, Missouri, a deep *deep* red state in the Midwest, I always dreamed about bigger cities like New York, Chicago and San Francisco because TV shows and movies told me that's where all the queens go. I'd already spent time in Chicago and New York, and loved them, but San Francisco really excited me because I knew it was supposed to be this big, gay, rainbow-coated oasis. On one level, I was so ready to pack my bags, put Sylvester on my headphones and pump to the West Coast in search of queer space and community. On another, I was too closeted to express much interest in visiting and exploring the city because I thought my folks would realize I was gay and then chop me from the category.

The summer I turned nineteen/reached peak twinkdom was the summer I finally made it to San Francisco, and it was really the first time I felt free as a Black queer person. Technically I was enrolled in an eight-week beginners French immersion course at UC Berkeley to help me meet a language requirement at my home university, but the tea is that I was actually on a mission kissing rainbows, making out with absolutely any boy with a pulse, bleaching my hair blonde, wearing that seashell necklace all gays wore in 2002, storming the streets in ridiculous looks, and pretending to be French to get into 21+ gay clubs. At the time, all the big gay clubs were largely 21+ at the weekend

which means that the 18+ parties were on random week-
nights like Tuesday or Wednesday, and getting back to
Berkeley from San Francisco at 1 a.m. when you had an
8 a.m. class was a nightmare. To slide into the 21+ nights
I would speak in English in a very thick, very fake French
accent, telling the bouncer I was just visiting, I don't have
my passport, please let me in. Sometimes, getting a whiff
of the underage desperation on my breath, they would
wave me through.

Carrying!

I don't remember too many details about these clubs, such
as what they looked like or the outfits I wore, sadly, but
I won't forget how I felt in them at the time. Girl, I thought
I was absolutely it. I remember thinking there's something
so special about walking up to the club in one of your
favorite outfits, your best Judys in tow, feeling glamorous,
like you own 51% of this company and the drinks are on
him tonight. This is not to say that clubs are perfect utopias
without problems – they most certainly are not. But for
an eager, bright-eyed twink from Missouri, those clubs
were the first time I really felt OK with my queerness. The
effort I put in going to them was proof that I was actively
challenging the conservative world view that brought me
up. These spaces cemented my interest in and ongoing love
for queer nightlife and the queer dance floor as a cathartic
zone of expression, fun and release, but also as a vital
space of politics, community and imagination.

Then as now, the club represents a space to be fabulous,
a theme I explore in my book *Fabulous: The Rise of the
Beautiful Eccentric*, a love letter to queer creativity and
aesthetic genius. This is not the kind of fabulousness that's
focused on designer labels, expensive jewelry and Holly-
wood glamour, which only ever positions white women as

glamorous. For me, fabulousness is not about fancy clothes, diamonds or high-street labels. It's an aesthetic strategy people forced to the margins use to embrace ourselves in wildly imaginative ways, primarily because society keeps telling us we do not deserve to be embraced. Society says we don't deserve rights or visibility or love or companionship or help or sex or freedom or money or a job or protection or safety or romance or peace of mind. But the joke's on them because we turn the pain and struggle we are forced to deal with into stunning aesthetics, LQQKs and visual effects, relying not on money or expensive labels but on our own imagination. Style is a political gesture because for queer and trans people the aesthetic is a politic. We use aesthetics to stretch out, expand and take up space at the same time as we are regularly denied space, access and safety. This embrace of style puts people doing fabulousness at even further risk of harm, danger and marginalization. But there comes a moment when you are so fed up with all the systems and structures that are trying to annihilate you that you take the risk of fabulousness anyway.

These performances of fabulousness take place on the street, on public transport, on campus, in class, at the workplace and on Zoom, especially as queer nightlife experiences moved online during the coronavirus pandemic in 2020, opening the door to digital raves and digital drag shows. There are also conversations happening about how online parties are more accessible for people with different lifestyles or needs, such as queer people who live in rural areas, or queer people living with disabilities for whom clubs are still dismally inaccessible. Whether virtual or face to face, gestures of fabulousness are important because they allow you to bring a little piece of queerness to whatever space you find yourself in. Most staged performances of fabulousness take place in the little nooks and crannies of society for three main reasons: because queer people fight for space as we often don't own the building or the land where our performances and social worlds take place; because our creative genius is often not welcome in more mainstream, capital-V venues or institutions until those in charge see commercial profit potential; and finally because queer livelihoods thrive in places where it's actually OK to get really messy, far from the logics of surveillance, commercialization and police found elsewhere. If it wasn't messy, did you really have fun?

Queer artists, creatives and misfits have invented so many spaces to be fabulous, all in the name of queer livelihood. Queer people need a space not only to gather and find community, but a space where you may feel safe either to come exactly as you are or where you can look forward to showing up as you really see yourself. When I think back on my journey to the Bay Area during my blonde ambition phase/gay summer of 2002, and what I was seeking by traveling so far away from home, I'm reminded of the cultural critic Jack Halberstam whose book *In a Queer Time and Place: Transgender Bodies, Subcultural Lives* urges us to think hard about queer livelihood as a pushing-back against the structures of heterosexuality we are all born into. Halberstam wants us to reach for wilder, alternative pastures and practices that open us up to living otherwise – if we can just detach ourselves from the heterosexual matrix.[1] A French class in the Bay Area was a nodal point both in my queer journey and in my work as a writer, and over the past eighteen years I've been committed to the classroom and the nightclub as necessary queer space in hope that future generations of queer creatives, misfits and troublemakers will be inspired to foster their own community-building and world-making practices.

For the record, the clubs I went to that summer weren't my first gay clubs, but to me they were the most symbolic because they were in San Francisco, a place with such an important queer history. In a book called *Wide-Open Town: A History of Queer San Francisco to 1965*, the historian Nan Boyd tells a layered story about the city's rise as something of an oasis for queer and transgender communities and the role bars and clubs played in the grassroots activism that led to gay civil rights in that city. The book is fascinating, with alarming details of the strategies, tools and tactics such as entrapment that the police would often use to terrorize suspected gay spaces. *Wide Open Town* plays a key role in a seminar on Queer Nightlife I teach in the Department of Gender, Sexuality and Women's Studies at Virginia Commonwealth University, and every semester my students are absolutely shocked to learn that not long ago gay bars were not legal, hence the back-alley entrances, red lights and blacked-out windows you might still see today. They're surprised that not long ago an undercover cop might flirt with you, get you all hot and flowing, and then arrest you for being gay. Girl, the nerve! And they learn that not long ago, gay clubs often had racial quotas to limit the number of Black people inside.

Wide Open Town always moves my students to reflect on the contemporary struggles they feel around the battle for queer space: access to affordable space at all, which because of urban neoliberalism is becoming increasingly impossible in most cities; rampant transmisogyny on the part of staff at the venue, especially when these claim to be 'safe spaces' but then do no work to ensure that this is so; and a violent police presence matched with an enduring, rampant, unchecked anti-Blackness.

Unfortunately, today many queer spaces are at risk of closure. In May 2020, the Stud, which at fifty years was the longest-running gay bar in San Francisco, closed its doors due to a lack of revenue spurred by the coronavirus pandemic. A 2018 article from the *Advocate* also tells a dark story. '62 Dead (or Dying) Gay Bars in the United States', a photo essay of small bars and mega clubs in cities around the country that have closed, illustrates the sprawling breadth and depth of the kinds of gay spaces that have folded, many of them after several decades in operation. Though the article focuses only on US gay club closures, the problem extends beyond the US. A 2017 study conducted by the Urban Lab at University College London details how since 2006 the number of queer venues in London had fallen from 125 to 53, nearly a 60% loss.[2] Indeed, over the last decade dozens of news outlets from the *Guardian* to the *New York Times* have been sounding the alarm about the death of queer spaces. 'Why are so many gay bars closing?', a 2016 article from the queer-centric blog *Queerty* wondered. 'Turn the showers off. Splash is closing', a *New York Times* headline from 2013 said in a story about the demise of Splash, a popular New York bar that ran from 1991 to 2013 near Union Square. It was known for cute gogo boys who danced in sealed showers on the dance floor.

Gay-bar closings are not an easy thing to shrug off. If a straight bar closes, that straight person can walk twenty feet to the next bar, roll in and know they can talk to people, maybe flirt and not be harassed. But when a queer space closes, to say nothing of a Black queer space, a world closes along with it. A world of secrets, alternative histories, gossip. And that means there are fewer and fewer spaces for queer people to congregate, meet new friends, socialize and learn how to lean into their queerness, the same way I was able to during my summer in the Bay Area. The reason I wanted to go there so desperately was to figure myself out and to unlearn what my family taught me about gay people. Without queer coffee shops, queer book stores, queer game rooms, queer community centers, queer dance floors like those I found in the Bay, where do we go to learn?

Gentrification always forces queer communities out of the neighborhoods and geographies we have built, but because the maintenance of space in urban areas is so astronomically expensive, truly unaffordable except for government and big corporations, we need to rethink what the queer spaces of the future will look like. With the decline in queer spaces, will people start using their homes even more for queer socializing and community engagement? Will people turn their apartments into saloons where drag shows, poetry slams and reading groups take place? You're already paying the rent, so why not? Or are the queer spaces of the future temporary, popping up from place to place, here and there, flashing up for extended but brief periods of time? Do these new spaces embrace a membership model, where the community can 'buy' a share in the building on a pay-what-you-can-afford subscription model? Does the city donate a building to a local LGBTQ+ charity tax-free, who then turns it into a queer community center that has a club room, a queer coffee shop and a queer book store? Or does the queer space of the future live partially online, not least because it is much more affordable, permanent and accessible from anywhere?

I hope not entirely. What I love most about the physicality of the queer club is how messy it is at the end of a good night. The floor is caked in sweat, glitter, crushed cans, debris and other ephemera from the pleasures of the night. That is a queer pleasure that refuses to be orderly, and disorderly queer pleasure is where all the fun lies.

It's helpful to think of queer spaces, particularly those that are more below the radar, as fugitive spaces – fugitive because the people who frequent them are often closeted to others or themselves and they are often in flight from social norms that work tirelessly to persecute their non-normative lifestyles. The unfortunate side effect of this dynamic is that as queer spaces close or get co-opted by hen parties, tourists and the brunch set (all of whom, in my experience, tend to treat the queer space like a zoo), they are forced to start over again someplace even more discrete, even more remote. In some ways this keeps the culture on its toes, and in others it absolutely forecloses histories, stories and communities.

For all these reasons, we need to work to save queer spaces. We can do this by not only frequenting venues we like as often as possible but also by lobbying our local councils to save spaces that look like they may be in danger. If you already run a venue but don't own the building it may be worthwhile to make a plan to purchase this space, maybe even engaging your community as part of this protective effort. What if patrons could 'subscribe' to the club, money that could go towards ensuring the space stays open? We should also continue to open queer worlds in our own communities, which might start as small as using your home as a salon. Your queer space doesn't necessarily need to fit fifty or a hundred people. Even ten is a community. Or you might go in with a few friends to try to find a cheap garage, studio or basement you can use to hold your larger gatherings. This do-it-yourself model may be the most effective because you're not necessarily waiting for permission or permits, which are roadblocks and take ages. You can invite ten people to your place right now, hold a drag show and the experience would be much more raw, messy and fabulous than a night in more commercial Soho.

At the end of the day, queer world-making is about community. It's about bringing people together and working to imagine and build a better world through space, music, dance, fashion, dialogue and pleasure. Sometimes that coming-together doubles as a kind of escape hatch that queer and trans people go through as a way to find ourselves and reject the negative impressions we have been taught about queer and trans livelihoods. It's the reason I was so desperate to get to San Francisco, an invaluable experience for a Midwestern teen determined to find his truth in queer community. The outside world may suck, and it will always try to suppress queer articulations of fabulousness and creativity. But in queer community you can build restorative futures and WORK (*snap!*) towards something truly fabulous.

---

1 Jack Halberstam, *In a Queer Time and Place: Transgender Bodies, Subcultural Lives* (New York City: NYU Press, 2005)

2 Ben Campkin and Laura Marshall, 'LGBTQ+ cultural infrastructure in London: night venues 2006–2017', UCL Urban Laboratory, 2017, https://www.ucl.ac.uk/urban-lab/sites/urban-lab/files/executive-summary-lgbtq-cultural-infrastructure-in-london-night-venues.pdf

'A lot of what we do requires money. This is why we cannot be afraid to talk about money. We cannot be afraid to ask LGBTQ+ people in countries with more of it to help those of us with less of it.'

Leticia Opio is a Ugandan trans woman. She founded Queer Youth Uganda in 2006. She was instrumental in putting pressure on the Ugandan parliament to reverse their Anti-Homosexuality Act of 2014, sometimes known as the 'Kill the Gays bill'. Today QYU is a nationwide programme that educates, sponsors and defends young marginalised LGBTQ+ community members. Same-sex sexual activity is still illegal in Uganda, with penalties of imprisonment.

Global Grassroots Funding

LETICIA OPIO

I developed the idea of Queer Youth Uganda after my family rejected me. I was a university student when one day my eldest brother, who was working in Kampala and paying my fees, called me into the living room and asked if I had a girlfriend. When I said no, he asked if I was gay, and I said: 'Yes, of course, I am!' I had been waiting for this moment. A friend had advised me not to tell anyone that I was attracted to men unless they asked, and this was an opportunity to finally tell someone who I was. My brother gave me two weeks to decide if I really wanted to be gay; if I did, he would stop paying my fees and I would be kicked out of home. I had to make a quick decision. Two weeks felt like two years – so I said, 'Darling, I think two weeks is too long. I am gay and I cannot change.' (I say 'gay' because in those days in Uganda most of us did not know the word 'trans', even though, at this time I knew inside that I was a woman, not a man.)

I called a friend and I went to live with them for a while. After I moved in, I realised that I was for the first time truly happy. I had been forced to drop out of school, but I was now living in an environment where I was accepted: the friend was gay, and as we shared our experiences, I understood that I'd basically been living in a prison before, because I couldn't be myself. If I had stayed with my family, they probably would have tried to make me get married, so I made the right choice to live my own life. But I worried about others like me. I thought about how there must be so many people out there going through the same things, but who are less fortunate. People sleeping on the streets after being rejected, people dying of HIV/ AIDS, people who could no longer go to school or to work because of homophobia. When I had these thoughts, I wanted to make a difference.

The original idea was to create a social platform. I do not mean social media – this was the early 2000s, we didn't even have computers or phones. By 'social platform' I mean a real-life place where queer people from all over Uganda could gather and learn from one another. The only place like it that we had back then was called Mammamia, a cafe in Kampala that we treated like a gay bar, as it was owned by a gay diplomat who worked for the Italian embassy. I found out about it from newspapers and then heard people talking about it. Those who went there would go across the street to Sheraton Gardens to cruise, sell themselves in order to survive, or to have a look around. The cafe was a place to hook up with people or to gossip, but it was one of the only places we could be free.

Around that time, I was dating an expat who worked for a big corporation. He had a very large compound. (Remember, I was a young, beautiful girl who was new in the city, and who doesn't want to keep up with what's new?!) I told him about my dream to help other LGBTQ+ people and he said that I could use the compound if I wanted to have friends to sit and share their experiences, so I invited some people from Mammamia to come along. I had expected around fifteen people but I was shocked and thrilled when over fifty came. That alone assured me that I was doing the right thing. We talked about the various things that we were going through, and discussed identity – whether we were a trans woman or a gay man or bisexual or intersex. In the days afterwards, whenever people from the gathering saw me, they would tell me how much they'd loved it and had enjoyed meeting people with similar stories. There was nothing like it at the time and we realised we needed to keep coming together.

A lot of young LGBTQ+ people were dying of HIV/AIDS in Uganda then because they couldn't go for medical check-ups or access the medicine that they needed. The services required money, which we didn't have because being queer meant we couldn't get jobs. We were all street kids or sex workers. If you went to a clinic for a test as a male they would always ask you to come with your girlfriend, but in our cases, we didn't have girlfriends and we couldn't come in with our men. Besides, when you have no money – and when there is homophobia all around you as everyone is very traditional – you can't even think about trying to seek medical treatment as you have more immediate concerns. All of this played against us.

After thinking about this, I asked a doctor from an international hospital who I knew to come to one of our meetings and talk us through HIV/AIDS awareness: the modes of prevention, proper care in case you're ill, and also about other STIs. It went so well that, a few weeks later, I asked an acquaintance from Amnesty International to kindly give us the basic knowledge on the human rights aspect of being LGBTQ+, as we had no idea that our rights existed. He gave some tips on who to call if you were unsafe, and what to say and not say if you were put in police custody. He even gave us the number of a lawyer who we could contact if anyone was arrested. Soon, other people volunteered to help with counselling and guidance for those who felt traumatised from attacks or helpless due to poverty. Our casual meetings were gradually evolving into an educational network.

However, there was only so far we could go without any money. When a friend offered an introduction to a potential donor – a programme officer from the development aid organisation Hivos in the Netherlands – the six of us who organised the meetings knew that we had the opportunity to make a real difference. Before the donor arrived in Uganda, I spoke to my friends, the late LGBTQ+ rights activist David Kato and Victor Juliet Mukasa, another amazing activist, and they said we needed to come up with a name. We chose 'Queer Youth Uganda'.

Soon, we had met with the people from Hivos, set a budget and received their grant. We took time to develop a strategic plan, a mission statement, overall goals, and used some of the money to gather information on LGBTQ+ people's needs so that we could work out how best to help. We also began funding healthcare and food as well as emergency housing for LGBTQ+ Ugandans in danger.

We started with four members of QYU but now we have around 600, countrywide. That's a lot. The area of operation has also increased. We began in Kampala but then opened branches in Jinja, Mbarara and Masaka, moving from operating in six districts to twenty-three. That makes QYU the biggest LGBTQ+ operation in Uganda. We have a proper structure, sixteen employees, and we create employment opportunities for members who cannot find jobs.

It has not always been easy: I have been attacked many times for the work that I do. In 2008 newspapers started to publish pictures of gay people in Kampala, including myself, outing us. Many people I know had to hide in the name of fear, and disassociate themselves from their queer communities or gay bars. Fundamentalist preachers started holding large conferences spreading hate about LGBTQ+ people. When hate crime happens, there can be nowhere to turn because we have been blackmailed by the police many times. In 2014, the Uganda Anti-Homosexuality Act, 2014 was reversed, but even today many Ugandans still act like the law is in place – queer people are still beaten and excluded from homes and schools. Some MPs in our country are still pushing for the death sentence for homosexuality. We are a long way from safety and liberation, but I believe Queer Youth Uganda has made a big difference.

Our donors have changed over the years. Since 2010 we have been funded by the Fund For Global Human Rights as well as private donations. Without this money none of our work expanding LGBTQ+ rights in Uganda would have been possible. We wouldn't have been able to rent safe houses, create jobs and implement new programmes. A lot of what we do requires money. This is why we cannot be afraid to talk about money. We cannot be afraid to ask LGBTQ+ people in countries with more of it to help those of us with less of it. And for those without money we need you to think about what other resources you have to offer – like those friends who, when we started, gave us their time or knowledge.

I would encourage as many as possible to keep finding and supporting organisations like ours, especially because our voices are still not heard everywhere on the planet. We have few platforms where we can express our issues, and I know this also means that people in the UK, US and beyond don't have enough information from us about our projects. People see us getting arrested and I think they're surprised that we keep operating – but even if there are anti-LGBTQ+ laws in a country, we can work underground. We exist, and we are already doing it.

'Intersectionality calls us to pay attention to the violence in order to end it, and at the same time to recognise the human on the receiving end of that violence so we may raise them up.'

Phyll Opoku-Gyimah, widely known as Lady Phyll, is the co-founder and executive director of UK Black Pride, Europe's largest celebration for LGBTQ+ people of colour. She is the executive director of international LGBTQ+ human rights charity Kaleidoscope Trust, and writes and speaks regularly on race, gender, intersectionality and human rights.

I Am My Grandmother's Daughter

PHYLL OPOKU-GYIMAH

When I think of my grandmother, I see a church. It's not a big church, but it's hers. She was a woman of such unshakeable faith, and the church stands as testament to her determination. The path to the church was, at the best of times, one that led towards a community united in faith and purpose; at the worst of times, the path was strewn with obstacles so obstinate and frequent, many would have thrown their hands up and quit. Not my grandmother. She was motivated by more than a love for God and the blessings she attributed to her persistence and his benevolence; she knew her community needed a space that was more than a place of worship, but of communion – a place support groups could meet, food could be served to those without it, and children could learn what they weren't being taught in school. She built a space that was needed because she was called to, and she let nothing get in her way.

When I think of my grandmother, I think of all the things I learned watching her. There were lessons, attitudes and beliefs that passed through my mother first, and those I absorbed chasing after the tails of my grandmother's hurrying coat. She was a worker, a grafter and a leader who was pragmatic, passionate and assertive. There were few men who didn't quiet when she addressed a room, and even fewer with the gall to challenge her in public or private. There was authority in her hips and power in her shoulders, and yet she remained tender and vulnerable – and mine. She had that rare ability to be many things for many people simultaneously, and I remember admiring how she was always so busy but available to me. My questions, my wonder, my teenage dramas, my hopes, dreams and concerns all seemed to land so softly in her ears. And out of her mouth came the hard-earned wisdom, advice and admonishments of a woman who fought for herself and for others.

Of enduring impact was her refusal to speak English to me and her other grandchildren. She knew how to speak English, but was adamant that we hear her in the tongue she was raised with. Like many, she seemed to remain steadfast in her distrust of white people and colonial influences, and was angry at the myriad ways our countries and tribes had been so ravaged by Western imperialism. Of course, she never said any of this out loud. It was in her eyes and her silences, and her refusal to pass on to her family the repressive tongue of the English; we would learn it elsewhere, but not through her. When Queen Elizabeth offered me an MBE in 2016, I rejected it not only because of the UK's toxic colonial legacy around the world, but because I could hear my grandmother's voice in my head: *Yempe dea yede ama yen no* ('We do not accept what is given to us by them'). She didn't accept their language, and she wouldn't have accepted their 'honour'.

I think often about the many times she must have bitten her tongue in frustration as she butted up against the egos of men, the other women she must have called upon to exorcise self-doubt, and the tears she must have cried quietly after the house was cloaked in the dark of midnight. I call upon her spirit when I reach my own impasses, when the weight of the world bears down on my shoulders and when I'm not sure I'm going in the right direction. Like she did, I feel compelled to do the work I do, though it doesn't mean I bounce into the day lightly. She reminds me, in legacy and spirit, that she didn't do her work for those that didn't need it, and she didn't explain herself to those who couldn't see the necessity of her work. Her ministry was her people, other women and children. She was focused, intentional and unwavering in vision. She put the onus on others to either catch up or stay back, pitch in or be quiet. UK Black Pride was built with that energy.

As I continue to nurture and expand upon the legacy she and many grand, determined and powerful Black African women left to me and the women of my generation, I think about the language we have to explain our lives that she didn't. She perhaps wouldn't have taken too easily to changes in pronouns and gender identity, though she would have tried, and while she may not have understood sexuality outside of its (alleged) biblical and reproductive imperative, I know she would have supported my work in fighting alongside LGBTQ+ people around the world for our rights, freedom and happiness. She would have understood intersectionality, even if she didn't have it to hand as a unifying theory to rally herself and her troops.

When Professor Kimberlé Crenshaw coined 'intersectionality', she did so to find a language to explain the ways overlapping societal and systemic oppressions (sexism, racism, misogyny) compound in and on Black women. In any case, I imagine intersectionality would have become for my grandmother what it has become for many of us: another reality to be denied by others, another useful tool to explain our lived experiences and to point to what's wrong with society that is then disparaged, disbelieved and denied by those whose interests are counter to freedom.

But what I know of intersectionality is undergirded by the example my grandmother set. Those of us who wear our Black skin with pride and who live proudly and defiantly as women understand that intersectionality is not just a word that opens our lived experiences up to theoretical and legal analysis, nor just a framework for organising that helps catch those who might fall between the cracks of thinly assembled liberation movements. No, we know that intersectionality is about our relationship to each other. Seen or hidden, speaking or silenced, Black women are the connective tissue between local initiatives for church-building and liberation movements around the world, between chosen and biological families. We are life. It is our (often unchosen) place as those who keep everything moving that allows such abject violence, such sweeping erasure against us. But in the darkness, life is birthed, movements are founded and worlds are changed. We knew intersectionality long before it had a name. My grandmother lived it, too.

It is with the blueprint she drew for me that I work to create a world that is better for LGBTQ+ people. For each of us – and future generations – to live in the world we deserve, I'm creating spaces by us and for us that celebrate us, and these spaces should be common, should be thriving, should be everywhere. I'm leading organisations that are helping to change the way people interact with, support and stand in solidarity with grassroots activists and community organisers. I'm in constant conversation with my trans and gender-nonconforming siblings, my Black brothers and younger people to understand how my thinking, activism and outreach continues to include the most marginalised, the most in danger. And like my grandmother and those I admire, I'm leading by example. But the key, in this particular moment, is much the same as it has been since long before my grandmother: we must prioritise and uplift all who live and move through the world as Black women. We must organise around dismantling the systems and structures that continue to make such quotidian and extreme violence possible.

We know now that intersectionality helps make clear the many ways in which the bodies and lives of Black women are devalued across the world, by systems, structures and societies that have rendered us expendable; but intersectionality can *also* be a lens through which we see, acknowledge and appreciate the divinity of Black women. Here, in this space of profound erasure, she still shines and loves and fights. She is in danger and luminous; forgotten but never silent; disregarded and making culture-shifting contributions to the lives of all who orbit near her. Intersectionality calls us to pay attention to the violence in order to end it, and at the same time to recognise the human on the receiving end of that violence so we may raise them up. To use intersectionality devoid of the Black women at the centre of it is the erasure that intersectionality seeks to redress; it is her very life, her heartbeat, hopes and dreams that we're called to fight for.

I learned from my grandmother that we African Black women share between us and among us an innate understanding of each other's life. It's through this, under cover of theory, we do the life-giving work of supporting each other meaningfully and saying: 'Sister, daughter, lover, fighter, mother, warrior woman, I see you.'

'The queer movement is only as strong as the movers it consists of and the direction it is moving in ... We really move forward when we show up for each other.'

Adam Eli is a New York-based community organiser whose work focuses on international issues and the importance of queer history. His first book, *The New Queer Conscience*, was published in 2020.

Doing Better

ADAM ELI

Knowing we need to do better and actually doing better are two very different things. One of my core beliefs is that queer people care about each other and that they, along with their allies, want to help and show up for each other – they just don't always know how. As activists, changemakers, organizers it is our job to create tangible ways for people to contribute and then spread the word far and wide. But that can be difficult in a community as diverse as ours.

Queer people come from every walk of life and therefore have different experiences of the world and of being queer. Denying that certain queer people have advantages or privileges that others do not is disrespectful, detrimental and, frankly, a waste of time. Not everyone's stories and struggles are the same. However, a queer person can always relate to another queer person on at least a basic level because all queer people were born into a predominantly straight world.

I believe that because queer people are able to identify with each other in this way, we have an obligation to stand up for each other. This idea acts as the basis for our movement but also creates some of our biggest struggles. Movement work, or the direct-action organizing that fuels change, is inherently disorganized – that's why we call it 'organizing', that's why we say after a protest 'great organizing'. The aim is to create a coalition of different people from different backgrounds who have different opinions but face and care about the same issues. An organizer's job is to take the energy, power, resources, abilities and passion of a crowd and bring it together into an effort that is communicable and can drive change.

This is difficult enough, but now factor in systems built to exclude us and the trauma we all have as a result, then factor in a lack of healthcare, the rise of nationalism and so on. It is sort of a miracle we get anything done at all. But, of course, we do. We persevere, and we have seen, time and time again, that when we *are* able to come together despite all of these differences and challenges – and come together in a way that takes responsibility for those people in our community who need our love, care and attention the most – that's when progress happens.

At the end of June 2019, I found myself reflecting on a queer movement that, I feel, had partially lost itself. Of course, June is Pride month around the world, but June 2019 in particular was destined to make queer history. That weekend, the world and I watched in awe as millions of people descended upon New York City to simultaneously celebrate the 50th anniversary of the Stonewall riots and WorldPride, an international culmination of Pride events that travels to a different city each year.

Estimates show that as many as 5 million queer people came for the weekend, and I would imagine that locals, visitors and digital onlookers were not disappointed with the show that was put on. From Billy Porter's multiple outfit changes to a performance by Madonna and a 19,000-seat opening ceremony at Barclays Center, New York City really showed up and turned it out. I live an exact eight-minute walk from the Stonewall Inn, giving me a front row seat to everything.

Pride is vital because it allows us to celebrate how far we have come and commit to the work that is left to be done; however, from this vantage point I could also see that underneath the branded floats, body glitter and celebrity appearances was a more nuanced and complicated truth. Institutions like NPR, the Met and Google were taking up huge amounts of space and flouting their ability to celebrate this monumental moment, and there were so many fashion collaborations, branded parties and signature cocktails I literally couldn't keep track. A gay dating app even invited me to a male-only dinner party at a fancy hotel the same night as the three-year marker of the Pulse Orlando shooting. Meanwhile, the NYC Heritage of Pride, the group that works with the city to put on Pride, was planning the biggest parade ever (parade, not march). The parade was planned in deep collaboration with the police and its route had little input from the queer community.[1]

Outside of all of this, there was the violence and serious discrimination that queer people were experiencing. That year, during Pride month alone, four trans women of color (that we know of) were killed in America.[2] Another, Layleen Polanco Xtravaganza, died from an epileptic seizure in solitary confinement on Rikers Island – hardly ten miles away from Stonewall – twenty days before the 'celebrations'. It was later discovered that staff had not checked on her regularly, and New York City has now paid a multimillion-dollar settlement to her family.[3]

This disconnect confirmed something I had been feeling for a while: that Pride was becoming less about the people it was actually supposed to be for. But I was not the only one to feel this way – a group of activists created an alternative march: the Queer Liberation March.

This march was a rejection of corporate pride, aimed to center marginalized Black, brown and trans voices, and refused any police involvement. The tone of the march was, after two and a half years of the Trump administration, angry and riled up. An estimated 45,000 joined us to follow the original 1970 Pride route from Stonewall to Central Park. The Queer Liberation March took over the great lawn, with queers spilling out everywhere and giving political speeches from a massive stage. It was beautiful and by any and every account it was a *triumph*. Larry Kramer spoke, and Miss Major opened the event with a recording saying: 'If you need your own thing – create it. I'm with you. Hooray, hallelujah, enjoy.'

For me, the Queer Liberation March felt like the only meaningful part of that entire month. At its core, it was about taking responsibility for one another, and bringing the most overlooked and targeted in our community to the front so that their voices were heard. It was about actively considering what made queer people from all walks of life feel included.

When we look back at history, it will show that Stonewall 50 was celebrated amidst a blitz of corporate fanfare at the same time as there was a dramatic rollback of queer rights around the world. Stonewall 50 was also a strong reminder that the queer community has more allies than ever before – but that it's still in dire danger. It indicated that there's disagreement about what 'Pride' actually means, and a big gap between perceived progress from the outside and what was really happening for queer people and their safety. Like most of the queer organizers, journalists and drag queens I knew, by the end of the month I was confused, tired and a complete and utter wreck. I went back to my parents' home for a break.

Being in those surroundings allowed me to reflect. During my upbringing, many of our family decisions, moralities and beliefs were based in Jewish history. In times of crisis we called on the strength, knowledge, success and failures of our Jewish ancestors to understand the present. Based on our shared histories of state-sanctioned oppression, ability to survive at all odds, and a serious penchant for narratives with a strong female lead (see: musical theater and Barbra Streisand), I figured it wasn't such a big leap from Jewish problem-solving to queer problem-solving, which is how I ended up looking to the past in my search for how we could make Pride 2020 better than Pride 2019.

Reading about past Pride events, I turned my eye to New York City 1994, and the celebrations of Stonewall 25. Both anniversaries were seen and treated as major landmarks in the queer rights movement and both earned the title of largest LGBTQ+ event in history when they happened. Both events focused on the global community and were influenced heavily by queer people from around the world. Most importantly, however, the discourse surrounding both events kept referring to an internal schism during the Pride planning stages, which ultimately resulted in separate protest marches. What had happened in 2019, I realized, had happened before.

In 1994, the organizers had made it clear that they had a particular vision for their parade. Brian Griffin, aka Harmonie Moore Must Die, who was an activist in the AIDS advocacy group ACT UP and Women's Health Action and Mobilization (WHAM) remembers: 'The committee for Stonewall 25 had actually asked – and it still seems quite unbelievable – that they didn't want anyone to show up in leather or drag.'[4] He continued: 'It still, 25 years later, blows my mind. They wanted to normalize the image of gay America for a mass audience. They wanted to present a palatable image of gay men and women, men and women who were *normal*.' In reaction to the announcement, plans for a separate event called the Spirit of Stonewall March were drawn up. Additionally, the first New York City Drag March took place the Friday before Pride, where drag queens and the leather community marched defiantly away from the main parade.

Twenty-six years later, if all of this sounds ridiculous, it should. The New York City Drag March is now a permanent fixture of Pride Weekend and drag queens and displays of kink are vital aspects of any pride celebration. I realized, looking back, that making these efforts to include all members of the LGBTQ+ movement, and to protest a Pride that didn't feel inclusive, paved the way for much of what we have today. Finding out about 1994 left me feeling hopeful and inspired, but it also left me with the question: Why does the more inclusive march always have to be the alternative? When will it become the main event?

In September 2019, the Queer Liberation March team began planning for Pride 2020. Those plans, along with much more, were instantly shoved aside in March 2020 when – BOOM – the entire world shut down due to COVID-19. Then, on 25 May, George Floyd was killed by the police. Like many others, I watched as protests against systematic racism and police brutality erupted in every state in America, and as thousands of people attended protests in Paris, London, Berlin and across the world. With official NYC Pride events cancelled, queer people took to the streets to support Black lives and Black queer lives, and there were at least four big rallies at the Stonewall Inn itself.

Day after day, week after week, queer people from all over carried signs with the names of Black trans people who had been killed. Going to take part in these heavily charged, intensely political spaces, I saw the folks I expected to see – the activist-leaning crowd and the folks who marched in the Queer Liberation March the previous year – but I also met other queers, many of whom had never campaigned like this before. With much of the world in lockdown, being at these protests, especially at the beginning, felt inherently radical (although of course we wore masks). Every day more and more people joined.

On 14 June, our action reached its peak at a march called Brooklyn Liberation to honor Black trans lives. The organizers asked the attendees to wear all white and meet outside the Brooklyn Museum. There were six speakers and they spoke from a balcony above the museum's entrance. Organizer and writer Raquel Willis led the crowd in a call-back chant which became the day's rallying cry: 'I believe in my power. I believe in your power. I believe in our power. I believe in Black trans power.' The march was, without question, a movement-making moment. I had never seen anything like it before, none of us had. In 2019, Melania Brown had addressed a protest of 600–700 people to demand justice for her sister Layleen Polanco Xtravaganza. Now, exactly a year later, she was addressing a crowd of 15,000.

Later that month, on what would have been the official day of NYC Pride, there was only one event taking place: the Queer Liberation March for Black Lives. The day was extraordinary. The message from 2020's Queer Liberation March and the protests of the past month guided the day: our most marginalized community members come first. No longer was this the alternative or a counter protest – it had become the main event.

*

Reflecting on the Brooklyn Museum rally, Raquel Willis told the *New York Times* that the event 'felt like we had arrived in a new era,' with a 'new, grander version' of queer and trans people of color's embracing of community.[5] The number of attendees suggested the same. While there is not really a rubric or measuring stick for how a social rights movement progresses, and the queer movement like any movement is subject to the tides of history, this was undoubtedly a turning point.

This essay is not about the failings of corporate pride – it is about checking in with your gut. The queer movement is only as strong as the movers it consists of and the direction it is moving in. The queer community may never totally agree on what Pride should look like, because we are – as we know – all different. But as activists, organizers and changemakers, what matters is that we stand by our principles and do our best to create moments where progress can be fueled. To create a movement so bright and so loving that folks can't help but flock to us. Stonewall 25, Stonewall 50 and the Brooklyn Liberation march for Black trans lives all, in my opinion, show that though the movement is always evolving, we really move forward when we show up for each other. They prove that we can always find new ways to do better.

When lost, I ask myself and the parts of the queer movement I am engaging in the following questions to get back on track: Are we centering our most marginalized communities? Are we leveraging the privileges some of us now have to benefit the whole? Is this space diverse on racial, class and gender lines? Are we accepting people as they identify, without judgment? If the answer to any of those questions is 'no' it is safe to say that we have veered off course.

Things don't *always* get better for queer people, but we can.

---

1 'NYPD shares security plan, parade route for 2019 New York City pride march', NBC New York, 25 June 2019, https://www.nbcnewyork.com/news/local/nypd-shares-security-plan-parade-route-for-2019-new-york-city-pride-march/1638507/

2 'Violence against the transgender community in 2019', Human Rights Campaign, https://www.hrc.org/resources/violence-against-the-transgender-community-in-2019

3 Mihir Zaveri, 'N.Y.C. to pay $5.9 million in death of transgender woman at Rikers', *New York Times*, 31 August 2020, https://www.nytimes.com/2020/08/31/nyregion/layleen-polanco-settlement-rikers-transgender.html

4 Rose Dommu, 'Hundreds of drag queens fill the NYC streets every year for this "drag march"', *Huffington Post*, 25 June 2018, https://www.huffpost.com/entry/nyc-drag-march_n_5b2fb345e4b0040e274410a0

5 Anushka Patil, 'How a march for Black trans lives became a huge event', *New York Times*, 15 June 2020, https://www.nytimes.com/2020/06/15/nyregion/brooklyn-black-trans-parade.html

Resources

UK NATIONWIDE ORGANISATIONS

African Rainbow Family
Support, community and campaigning.
www.africanrainbowfamily.org

All About Trans
A project that positively changes how the media understands and portrays trans people.
www.allabouttrans.org.uk

Bi Pride UK
Community and support for bisexual people.
www.biprideuk.org

BlackOut UK
Information, events and networking run by and for Black queer men.
www.blkoutuk.com

Deaf Rainbow UK
Information and campaigning for the deaf LGBTQ+ community.
www.deaflgbtiqa.org.uk

Galop
Advice and support for LGBTQ+ people who have experienced hate crime, domestic abuse or sexual violence.
www.galop.org.uk

Gendered Intelligence
Aims to increase understandings of gender diversity and improve trans people's quality of life.
www.genderedintelligence.co.uk

Imaan
Supporting the LGBTQ+ Muslim community.
www.imaan.org.uk

Just Like Us
Campaigning and support for LGBTQ+ young people.
www.justlikeus.org

Mermaids
Support for transgender, nonbinary and gender-diverse children, young people and their families.
www.mermaidsuk.org.uk

MindOut
Mental health service run by and for LGBTQ+ people.
www.mindout.org.uk

Opening Doors
Activities, events, support and information for LGBTQ+ people over 50.
www.openingdoorslondon.org.uk

Regard
Advice and campaigning for LGBTQ+ disabled people.
www.regard.org.uk

Stonewall
Campaigning and lobbying group.
www.stonewall.org.uk

Switchboard
Support and information.
www.switchboard.lgbt

Terrence Higgins Trust
Campaigns about and provides services relating to HIV and sexual health.
www.tht.org.uk

UK Black Pride
Europe's largest celebration for LGBTQ+ people of African, Asian, Caribbean, Middle Eastern and Latin American descent.
www.ukblackpride.org.uk

UKLGIG
Supports LGBTQ+ people through the asylum and immigration system.
www.uklgig.org.uk

UK REGIONAL ORGANISATIONS

AKT
Support for LGBTQ+ young people facing or experiencing homelessness, with offices in London, Bristol, Manchester and Newcastle.
www.akt.org.uk

Birmingham LGBT Centre
www.blgbt.org

Brighton & Hove LGBT Switchboard
www.switchboard.org.uk

LGBT Cymru Helpline
www.lgbtcymru.org.uk

Leicester LGBT Centre
www.leicesterlgbtcentre.org

Positive East, East London
HIV-related care and services, including testing, workshops, benefit advice and information on employment law.
www.positiveeast.org.uk

SASH, West London
Support on sexual health, relationships and mental health.
www.sashlondon.org

The Outside Project, London
LGBTQ+ crisis/homeless shelter and community support group.
www.lgbtiqoutside.org

LGBT Foundation, Manchester
www.lgbt.foundation

The Proud Trust, Manchester
Support for LGBTQ+ young people, with youth groups across the UK.
www.theproudtrust.org

Cara-Friend, Northern Ireland
www.cara-friend.org.uk

The Rainbow Project, Northern Ireland
www.rainbow-project.org

LGBT Youth Scotland
www.lgbtyouth.org.uk

INTERNATIONAL ORGANISATIONS

ILGA
Worldwide federation of LGBTQ+ rights organisations.
www.ilga.org

InterACT
Advocates for the human rights of children born with intersex traits.
www.interactadvocates.org

Kaleidoscope Trust
Supports LGBTQ+ activists around the world.
www.kaleidoscopetrust.com

Lambda Legal
Campaigns for the full recognition of LGBTQ+ civil rights.
www.lambdalegal.org

OutRight Action International
Campaigns for the human rights of LGBTQ+ people worldwide.
www.outrightinternational.org

Acknowledgements

Thanks first and foremost to Alex Russell for being so smart, attentive and understanding as an editor. To Emma Paterson, the greatest agent. Thanks to my early readers ... Lucy for your love and support, and honest and helpful feedback. To Alix and Jee for a Zoom meeting filled with not just useful but transformative advice. To Alice for your excellent notes and eye for detail. Thanks to Adam Eli, for making so many introductions and suggestions. And thanks to Fiontán Moran for the introduction to Wolfgang. Thank you to Mau and Matthew for translating on Pabllo and Holland. A huge thanks to all of the agents, PRs and managers who were instrumental in making this book a reality. Finally, thanks to the contributors for sharing their personal stories in the interest of opening up a conversation, and for putting up with endless emails and nagging from me. I urge everyone reading this book to further explore the contributors' work, buy their books and follow them online.